"Harold Talbott's uncanny childhood fasc. become a pioneer among Western Tibetan Buddhist practitioners. He was instrumental in one of the most inspiring encounters between Christianity and Buddhism, that of Thomas Merton with the 14th Dalai Lama and with the great hermit Chatral Rinpoche. . . . His memoir stands as a moving and precious testimony about a lifetime of dedication to the spiritual quest."

— **Matthieu Ricard**, Buddhist monk and co-author of
*The Monk and the Philosopher: East Meets West in a Father-
Son Dialogue*, and other international best-sellers

"Of Harold's many qualities, for me two stand out: an interest in religious matters that blossomed into a love of truth; second, his great kindness and humanity. . . . Harold had a journey of his own to make—into the heart of Tibetan Buddhism, his spiritual home. Harold's gentle, humorous, insightful generosity has left many in his debt. For me he was truly an opener of the Way. He helped me also on my way into the presence of Tibetan masters—a pilgrimage like Harold's, from which there has been no return. That gift was inestimable, utterly beyond repayment."

— **Wulstan Fletcher**, translator and scholar of Tibetan Buddhist texts

"Harold Talbott is a gentleman, and a great, devoted practitioner of the Nyingmapa tradition of Tibetan Buddhism. For more than fifty years, Harold has nurtured the Nyingma teachings in America, and this is the highest, best good fortune."

— **John Giorno**, poet, performance artist,
founder of Giorno Poetry Systems

TENDREL

a memoir of

NEW YORK

and the

BUDDHIST HIMALAYAS

HAROLD TALBOTT

BUDDHAYANA FOUNDATION

MARION, MASSACHUSETTS

Published by
Buddhayana Foundation, Inc.
204 Spring Street
Marion, MA 02738

Hardcover ISBN: 978-1-7335812-0-2
Paperback ISBN: 978-1-7335812-1-9

Book design by Peter Holm, Sterling Hill Productions

Dedicated to
TULKU THONDUP
and
MICHAEL BALDWIN

CONTENTS

ACKNOWLEDGMENTS

My thanks to Michael Baldwin for sponsoring this book and to my teacher, Tulku Thondup; to Ian Baldwin for magnificent editing and Carola Lott for helping me with the writing of this book and her splendid editing. Thanks to Madeline Cooke for her work and encouragement; to Rebecca Baldwin for making this book possible; to Willie Cunningham for the photographs; and to Sandy Edgell for help all along the way of the book's writing and production. With Special thanks to Peter Holm of Sterling Hill Productions for designing and overseeing the production of this book.

PREFACE

Harold Talbott was born into a highly respected old family from New York and Pennsylvania, in the land of freedom and opportunity—America. He has fulfilled his unique lifelong mission of serving spiritual causes selflessly.

Harold has been instrumental in preserving Tibetan Buddhism abroad at a crucial time in its life and in welcoming it into the culture of American society. He has been a great patron of Buddhadharma and a beloved friend to many Tibetan Buddhists and Buddhist communities, both in India and in the West. All the publications that Harold and I have produced in English are the fruits of his unstinting support and erudite editing.

Harold's amazing spiritual journey was inspired and guided by great religious luminaries of Christianity in the West and Buddhism in the East. In the 1960s, he studied Catholicism with the theologians and writers Dom Aelred Graham and Father Thomas Merton. He enjoyed the rare opportunity of ten hour-long sessions of private teachings from H. H. the Dalai Lama. He studied for years under Lama Gyurda-la, the great Dzogchen master whose father had attained *ja-lü*, or the rainbow body, by merging his conceptual mind into the enlightened nature and fully dissolving his mortal body into wisdom light at his passing in 1953.

His memoir, alive with fascinating anecdotes and illustrations, reads like an enthralling novel. But at the same time, it is highly informative, full of historical treasures and revelations of the true religious wisdom that Harold had been seeking all his life. I believe that readers will enjoy and benefit from this historical and valuable memoir.

—Tulku Thondup Rinpoche

PART ONE

Swanning About

CHAPTER ONE

The Talbotts and the Thayers

Although my ancestors were rather distinguished, I was always out of step with the rest of my family. Instead, I preferred to go my own way, which may explain how, from my beginnings in the sophisticated world of New York and Europe, I ended up as a student of Tibetan Buddhist lamas in both India and America. And to show you how far afield I strayed, I will begin by describing my parents and grandparents.

My father's people, the Talbotts, migrated from Virginia to Cincinnati, Ohio, where my grandfather Harry Elstner Talbott was born in 1860. Like many men of his day, he was an entrepreneur and a leading figure in a number of the industries that were just then coming into being—railroads, engineering, and finally airplanes. A graduate of the engineering division of the University of Cincinnati, he was first involved with several railroad companies, including the Northern Pacific Railroad and later the Chesapeake and Ohio.

In 1887 he married Katherine Houk, one of the three children of George Washington Houk and his wife, Eliza, whom my father called Gramps and Yannie. A lawyer, Gramps was involved with politics and in the 1850s was a member of the Ohio House of Representatives. He was a delegate to the Democratic National Convention in 1860, when he supported Stephen A. Douglas, and again in 1876. Beginning in 1890, he served for two terms as a member of Congress in Washington, DC, where he died during his second term.

In 1892 my grandparents moved to Dayton, Ohio, where Grandfather opened a contracting engineers' office and soon built up a substantial business. They lived at Runnymede, the large house Katherine's parents had built on the crest of a hill south of the city in the suburb of Oakwood.

In 1899, Grandfather was responsible for constructing the Michipicoten Branch of the Algoma Central Railroad to bring iron ore south from the Helen Mine to Sault Ste. Marie in Michigan's Chippewa County on the Canada-US border—a colossal undertaking that few believed could succeed. However, in the dead of winter, living in a rough shack with his crew of twelve hundred men, Grandfather built one hundred miles of track through wild rough country in the scheduled time. It was said that "Mr. Talbott endeared himself to the workers who loved 'the Chief,' as they called him, for his comradeship and genial nature."

In 1911 my grandfather became involved in the pulp and paper industry, founding and becoming president of the Lake Superior Paper Company. Before long he had large interests in a number of paper companies and at the same time was a dominant figure in Dayton's business world; he was president of the City National Bank and the City Trust and Savings Bank of Dayton. In 1913, after a disastrous flood in Dayton, he was put in charge of cleaning up the wreckage. In recognition of his work, the governor gave him the honorary title of colonel.

In April 1917, Grandfather established the Dayton-Wright Airplane Company, along with my father and two Dayton businessmen, Edward A. Deeds and Charles F. Kettering. By 1918 my father had joined the company, which employed twelve thousand people and turned out hundreds of fighter planes for the US government during the First World War—more wartime aircraft than any other US plant. In addition to four hundred training planes, the plant also built the two-seat fighter, the DeHaviland-4, later modified to the DeHaviland-9. In 1923, General Motors Corporation purchased the company, and it was later sold to Consolidated Aircraft.

During these early days, my grandmother was busy raising her nine children and managing Runnymede. She was a devout Christian Scientist and a friend and supporter of the founder, Mary Baker Eddy. After my grandfather died in 1921 and my grandmother's children were grown, she became, as befitted the widow of one of Dayton's most prominent businessmen, a generous benefactor of local causes. She helped found and was the first president of the Dayton Garden Club but was perhaps better known for her involvement with music.

She was one of the organizers of the Dayton Symphony Association as well as a staunch supporter of the Dayton Civic Orchestra, often making up any deficits to guarantee its continued existence. Most importantly, however, my grandmother was known for her association with the Westminster Choir, an organization that was not merely a choir but also a demanding school that required the students to practice four hours every day for three entire years. Herself a talented musician, Grandmother usually accompanied the group of fifty singers on their tours when they performed before enthusiastic audiences of thousands in major American cities, including New York, Boston, Philadelphia, Washington, Buffalo, and twice in Pittsburgh.

In 1927 my grandmother built the Playhouse at Runnymede. This glass-topped structure was used primarily for community events, including graduations, dances, and meetings, as well as for Talbott family entertainments. In addition to the ballroom and stage, there were indoor tennis and squash courts as well as a sixty-foot-long music room with a pipe organ. In the summer, the wide lawn also served as a place for concerts.

In 1929 my grandmother accompanied the Westminster Choir on its grand tour of Europe. Immediately before the choir sailed on the *Leviathan*, after performing at Carnegie Hall, they were given an official send-off led by the mayor of New York, Jimmy Walker. In Europe they performed at the Royal Albert Hall in London before going on to Manchester, Liverpool, and Leeds. In Paris they sang at the Opera House; in Vienna they performed at a reception given by the American ambassador; while in Berlin they received twelve encores.

After my grandmother's death, the Runnymede Playhouse was put to a decidedly nonmusical use. In 1943, Dr. Charles Allen Thomas, who had married my father's sister Margaret, arranged for the government to use the playhouse for a secret scientific project. Nearly ninety people worked at what was known as Unit IV. Oral histories state that big trucks rolled in and out, and floodlights and heavy-duty power lines were strung around the property. Guardhouses were constructed, and a barbed-wire-topped fence surrounded the grounds. To conceal this suspicious activity, Secretary of War Henry L. Stimson stated that the playhouse was being used as a film laboratory for the Army Signal Corps. From April 1943 to August 1944, Manhattan Project scientists raced to find an initiator, code-named Urchin, for the atomic bomb that was being designed at Los Alamos. More than fifty tons of radioactive bismuth was processed at the playhouse between 1943 and 1945. Thomas had promised the Oakwood City Council that after the war he would return the Runnymede Playhouse as he had found it. However, by then the building had become so contaminated with radioactivity that it was dismantled in 1950 and buried in Oak Ridge, Tennessee.

My mother's family, the Thayers, came to America from England in the eighteenth century. In addition to everything they might need for life in the new country, they brought their horses along on the ship, which allowed them to hunt foxes as they traveled down the Eastern Seaboard until they finally settled near Haverford, Pennsylvania.

My grandmother, Marian Longstreth Morris, was a descendant of Robert Morris, one of the Pennsylvania signers of the Declaration of Independence. The Morrises were Quakers who lived at Dundale estate, their farm at Villanova, Pennsylvania, where my grandmother grew up. In 1892, Marian Morris married my grandfather John Borland Thayer, who was a celebrated athlete. Captain of the lacrosse team at the University of Pennsylvania, he was internationally known as a first-class cricket player. When he was only fourteen, he played his first match for the Merion Cricket Club and continued playing for the club until he died. For cricket aficionados, Thayer was a part of the Philadelphian side that visited England in 1884.

My grandparents lived at Redwood, a large white Craftsman-and Tudor-style house, in Haverford, where their four children were born: John Borland, known as Jack; Frederick Morris, called Teddy; my mother, Margaret; and my aunt Pauline, called Polly. My grandfather Thayer served as vice president of the Pennsylvania Railroad. When President Teddy Roosevelt launched the antitrust suits, one was against the Pennsylvania Railroad. My grandfather was asked to testify in favor of the railroad because, according to my mother—and she must have gotten it from her family—he was so innocent that he didn't realize the charges against the railroad were actually true. After he testified and it was revealed that the railroad had indeed been guilty as charged, he had a nervous collapse.

In 1912, my grandparents with their son Jack and a maid, Margaret Fleming, went to Europe for a rest cure to help my grandfather recover. Two weeks after stopping in Berlin as guests of the American Consul General, they boarded the *Titanic* as first-class passengers on her maiden voyage. After a dinner with friends in the sumptuous restaurant, they retired to their cabins and were getting ready for bed when the disaster occurred. As the lifeboats were prepared for lowering, my grandfather saw his wife and her maid safely into lifeboat 4. Like so many other gentlemen passengers, my grandfather had no intention of boarding a lifeboat and remained on the deck with his friends George and Harry Widener and Charles Duane Williams. All four went down with the ship.

My grandmother, by her own account, had a harrowing night helping to row the leaking lifeboat 4 for almost five hours before they managed to reach the *Carpathia*, which rescued them. She later wrote about the experience.

> The after part of the ship then reared in the air, with the stern upwards, until it assumed an almost vertical position. It seemed to remain stationary in this position for many seconds (perhaps twenty), then suddenly dove straight down out of sight. It was 2:20 a.m. when the *Titanic* disappeared, according to a wrist watch worn by one of the passengers in my boat.
>
> We pulled back to where the vessel had sunk and on our way picked up six men who were swimming—two of whom were drunk and gave us much trouble. Two of these men died in the boat. The boat we were in started to take in water and

we had to bail. I was standing in ice cold water up to the top of my boots all the time, and rowing continuously for nearly five hours. We took on about fifteen more people who were standing on a capsized boat. In all, our boat had by that time sixty-five or sixty-six people. There was no room to sit down in our boat, so we all stood, except some sitting along the side.

The boat I was in was picked up by the *Carpathia* at 7:00 a.m. on Monday, we having rowed three miles to her, as we could not wait for her to come up on account of our boat taking in so much water that we would not have stayed afloat much longer.

My uncle Jack and a friend were standing at the railing as the ship sank deeper into the water. The friend slid down the side of the ship and disappeared. Uncle Jack jumped feet first, and as he surfaced well clear of the ship, he felt that he was being pushed away from the ship by some force, which he believed saved his life. He swam through the icy seas and finally reached a lifeboat, which hauled him aboard. He too was saved by the *Carpathia*.

In 1940, Jack related his experiences as an attempt, perhaps, to exorcise some of the memories that still haunted him.

The ship seemed to be surrounded with a glare, and stood out of the night as though she were on fire. The water was over the base of the first funnel. The mass of people on board were surging back, always back toward the floating stern. The rumble and roar continued, with even louder distinct wrenchings and tearings of boilers and engines from their beds. Suddenly the whole superstructure of the ship appeared to split, well forward, and bow or buckle upwards. The second funnel, large enough for two automobiles to pass through abreast, seemed to be lifted off, emitting a cloud of sparks. It looked as if it would fall on top of me. It missed me by only twenty or thirty feet.

The suction of it drew me down and down. struggling and swimming, practically spent . . . and as I came up I was pushed out again and twisted around by a large wave, coming up in the midst of a great deal of small wreckage. As I pushed my hand from my head it touched the cork fender of an overturned lifeboat. I looked up and saw some men on the top and asked them to give me a hand. One of them, who was a stoker, helped me up. In a short time the bottom was covered with about twenty-five or thirty men. When I got on this I was facing the ship. Her deck was turned slightly toward us. We could see groups of the almost fifteen hundred people aboard, clinging in clusters or bunches, like swarming bees; only to fall in masses, pairs or singly, as the great part of the ship, two hundred and fifty feet of it, rose into the sky, till it reached a sixty-five or seventy degree angle. Here it seemed to pause, and just hung, for what felt like minutes. Gradually she turned her deck away from us, as though to hide from our sight the awful spectacle. I looked upwards—we were right under the three enormous propellers. For an instant, I thought they were sure to come down on top of us. Then, with the deadened noise of the bursting of her last few gallant bulkheads, she slid quietly away from us into the sea.

Another passenger reported: "After a night on the upturned boat Jack and the others were picked up by lifeboats 4 and 12; Thayer was so distracted trying to get into boat 12 that he did not notice his mother in number 4 nearby and she was so numbed by cold that she did not see him. At 8.30 a.m. boat 12 finally arrived at the *Carpathia*, where Jack was reunited with his mother. She asked him, 'Where's Daddy?' He answered, 'I don't know, Mother.'"

My grandmother returned to Redwood after her ordeal, faced with bringing up four children with nothing but a small pension from her husband. As my mother once said, "Thayers are beautiful, but they don't have any money." However, my grandmother had an extraordinary piece of good fortune. Moses Annenberg, publisher of the *Philadephia Enquirer* and father of Walter Annenberg and Edith Haupt, decided to help her with a monthly stipend. He explained, "I am Jewish, and you were the first person in Philadelphia who invited us to your house." It seems that my grandmother and the Annenbergs shared a love of music, and she would occasionally invite them for musical evenings at Redwood.

My uncle Jack graduated from the University of Pennsylvania and became a banker. Later, he returned to the university as financial vice president and treasurer. He married Lois Cassatt, niece of the painter Mary Cassatt, and they had two sons, Edward C. Thayer and John B. Thayer IV. During the Second World War, both of Uncle Jack's sons joined the services, and his son, Edward, was killed on active duty in the Pacific. It is thought that a bout of depression following his son's death led directly to my uncle's death by his own hand in 1945.

My grandmother became quite psychic after her husband died. To get in touch with his spirit, she would sit in bed with a board across her knees holding a pencil in her hand, which would move across the page in a form of automatic writing. Often what she wrote seemed as if it were coming from her husband. Probably it came from her unconscious mind, but there are lots of stories about her psychic powers.

Once, when my mother was working as a nurse in the 1916 flu epidemic in Philadelphia, she came home to find her mother in bed. From the wall next to my grandmother's bed came three very strong knocks. Recently, a friend had died of the flu, and my grandmother said, "If you are so-and-so, knock three times again." And three more knocks came. Séances and spiritualism became very popular both in this country and Europe after all the killing in the First World War.

CHAPTER TWO

Father and Mother

My father was born in Dayton, Ohio, in 1888, the eldest of nine children. After graduating from the Hill School in Pottstown, Pennsylvania, and spending a year at Yale University, he returned to Dayton to become an industrialist like his father. From 1906 to about 1913, he was president of the Platt Iron Works in Dayton. Later he was part owner of a gold mine in Canada where his father was building the railroad line near Sault Ste. Marie. When he married my mother, he gave her an extremely heavy charm bracelet made of gold from that mine.

Scarcely more than ten years after Wilbur and Orville Wright made their first flight in 1903, my father became involved with the aviation industry. In 1915 he helped build one of the first wind tunnels for aviation experiments in Dayton, and two years later he helped form the Dayton-Wright Company. My father was the new company's president, while Orville Wright, who had been born in Dayton, was given a courtesy position as a consulting engineer. My father was a passenger on Orville's last flight in 1918.

In 1925, my father moved to New York to become a director of the Chrysler Corporation. To celebrate his birthday one year, he had seven Chrysler B-70 Phaetons delivered to Runnymede, one for each of his seven sisters. There's a photograph of them all perched on the hoods of the cars. In 1933, after General Motors Corporation took a controlling interest in North American Aviation (NAA) and merged it with its General Aviation division, my father became chairman of the executive committee of NAA. He was also a director of TWA. North American held shares in the Douglas Aircraft Company, which was building planes for the military. My father prevailed on Donald Douglas to enter the commercial market by building the DC-1 and DC-2 aircraft to TWA's specifications.

My mother and her sister, Polly, grew up at Redwood in Haverford, Pennsylvania, where my grandmother had lived ever since her marriage. There's a story that suggests that possibly my mother might not have been a beautiful child, although later she became a very beautiful woman. One day her uncle, who had been in the Spanish-American War, took her on his knee and told her, using the Quaker pronoun *thee*, "Thee is just like a monkey. Thee is as ugly as Aguinaldo." (Aguinaldo was the revolutionary who led Philippine forces against the United States during the Philippine-American War.) So my mother became a confused narcissist.

I believe that my own mother thought that her mother was stupid. She often made much of the fact that when telling a joke, Gaga, as we called our Thayer grandmother, would put the punch line in the middle of the joke rather than where it belonged. Although my mother was condescending about Gaga, she loved the fact that her mother's family lived on a farm near Haverford where everything was fresh and they made their own ice cream. Never, my mother always claimed, was any ice cream as delicious.

My mother and her sister, Polly, never went to school but were educated by tutors at home. Polly was very smart; my mother, however, was not as sharp, which gave her something of a complex about being stupid—although that was by no means the case. However, she was a terrible speller, and when we used to tease her about it, she would say, "Well, Lincoln was not a good speller."

My aunt Polly had many talents, especially one for music; in fact, she was a violin prodigy. At nineteen she played Mendelssohn's Violin Concerto in E minor with the Philadelphia Orchestra under the conductor Leopold Stokowski. Because she took the last movement of the concerto much too fast for Stokowski's liking, she was never invited to play with the orchestra again. In fact, she never gave another concert because she didn't want to bother playing the violin. Instead, she wanted a very ordinary life and married a stockbroker, played fabulous golf, raised black Labradors, had huge cages of parakeets, and cared nothing about her furniture and décor. When we would go to see her, my mother would later say, "Did you see the slipcovers? She never changes them."

While she was still in her teens, my mother had a variety of jobs. After working for a time in a cheese shop, she started a business selling knitted suits on the eighteenth green of the Gulph Mills Golf Club, where she set up her racks of dresses. When the gentlemen golfers had finished their game, they would buy clothes for their wives. My mother was pretty, and she did very well. When she was in her twenties, the decorator Addison Mizner gave her a job as his assistant and took her to Spain to buy furniture for Mar-a-Lago, Marjorie Merriweather Post's house in Palm Beach, which is now owned by Donald Trump.

My mother, who had had a number of proposals from rich men, was determined to marry a man who had made his money rather than inheriting it. When Harold Vanderbilt proposed to her, she turned him down. "You didn't earn your own money," she told him. "I am going to marry a self-made man." But feelings were also important. Harrison Williams, an enormously rich man who had started from almost nothing, invited her for a drive through the Bois de Boulogne in Paris, where he proposed to her. My mother said, "No, I won't marry you, Harrison." When he asked, "Why not? I can give you a wonderful life," she replied, "Because you haven't said you love me."

Finally, a friend, Nell Cosden, invited my mother to stay for a dance she was giving. On the bed table Nell had put a photograph of a strange man. When my mother asked who he was, Nell replied, "That's Harold Talbott. You'll meet him at the party." At the party, when my father asked my mother to dance, she told him, "You've been by my bedside for the past few nights." Fairly soon after that they became engaged.

My father and mother—the Christian Scientist groom and the Quaker bride—were married in 1926 in the Church of the Redeemer in Haverford, Pennsylvania, followed by a reception at Redwood. My parents had become and would remain Episcopalians throughout their lives, becoming parishioners of St. James Church on Madison Avenue in New York. Years later the rector, the legendary Dr. Arthur Kinsolving, became my brother John's father-in-law when John married Dr. Kinsolving's daughter, Anne. As the daughter of a minister, Anne was the perfect wife for John when that he himself was ordained in

1985. My father got on very well with Gaga. She, on the other hand, failed to appreciate my Talbott grandmother, who was by all accounts a formidable woman. When someone asked Gaga why she didn't see more of my father's mother, she replied, "Because she smells."

When my parents came to live in New York, they bought a duplex overlooking the East River at 450 East 52nd Street. Sometime in the 1920s my parents also bought a beautiful Neoclassical house called the Pillars in Old Westbury, Long Island. Looking back, I always think of the Pillars as resembling a house of the Youssoupoffs in Russia before the revolution. Megalomania on my part, perhaps. The estate was, however, impressive, with fifty acres of lawns and gardens. There were greenhouses and numerous gardeners, so the house was always filled with vases of flowers. As I only saw the Pillars in my childhood, perhaps I remember it larger than it really was, but in the photograph I have, the house looks enormous.

Sundays at the Pillars my parents would have people to lunch, sometimes as many as forty. My mother would also have bridge tournaments when Al Gunther, an army officer who was a bridge expert, would arrange the duplicate tables. We were still in touch with him when he became a general.

Horses were an important part of my parents' lives: hunting, racing, and polo for my father, who was an eight-goal player—no small accomplishment as ten goals is the highest rating a player can have. Throughout the 1930s he played at Meadowbrook on Long Island, as well as in Aiken and occasionally in England and Argentina. My father was also commissioner of New York State Racing and chairman of Belmont Park. In 1943 he won the American Breeders Cup with a bay gelding named Brother Jones who was trained by Billy Miller, who lived at the Pillars and looked after the horses.

Most of all my parents shared a love of foxhunting. In the early years of their marriage, they bought a farm in Middleburg, Virginia, where they hunted mostly with the Piedmont Hunt, a foxhunting club in nearby Upperville. Dr. Archibald Cary Randolph was master, and upon his death, he was succeeded by his wife, Theo, a legendary rider who became known as the first lady of foxhunting. Scrapbooks are filled with photographs of hunts, point to points, and hunter trials, my mother the epitome of elegance, beautifully turned out in her black habit and top hat with a veil. She always rode sidesaddle, which very few women do anymore. She was a superb rider with lovely light hands—thank goodness, because she was still flying over big fences at Thanksgiving less than three months before John and I were born. She was pretty devil-may-care.

My mother's two favorite horses were a beautiful gray named The Phantom and a black horse called Black Magic. On the farm in Middleburg, everything had to be either black or white or a combination of the two. There was a set of china for the table called the End of the Day China, because it was made at the end of the day with leftovers. White and deep purple liquids were poured together and mixed just a little to create patterns of swirls, somewhat like marbleizing a cake.

When they settled in New York at the beginning of their marriage, my father served on the board of a number of companies—Dodge and Chrysler as well as the Autolite Company. He was also on the board of Lockheed Martin. Mr. Royce Martin, a friend of his, would often come to the apartment to dine with my parents. Poor Mr. Martin was dismally melancholy and sorrowful—bereft over the recent death of his wife. One night he called my mother from the Waldorf Hotel where he was staying and told her that he was about to commit suicide. As he was a great donor to the Catholic Church, my mother telephoned Cardinal Spellman and said, "Get over to the Waldorf Hotel where I am in Roy Martin's room outside the bathroom. He's locked himself in and is threatening to commit suicide." So the cardinal went over to the Waldorf and, standing by the bathroom door, said, "Roy, come out at once! Come out, Roy. You must talk to me." Roy came out.

My mother knew Cardinal Spellman because, as vice president of the New York Infirmary, she did a lot of fund-raising for them. Every year the cardinal would invite her to lunch at the rectory next to St. Patrick's Church, where he would sit across the table from my mother, flanked by a couple of monsignors. At the end of lunch, he would present her with a check for the infirmary, because she told him how many beds in the hospital that year had been apportioned to Catholics.

My father had a company of his own called Standard Cap and Seal, which among other products made the tops to Borden Dairy's milk bottles. It seems that my father was known as something of a bastard in business. He was a very tough man. Once a man who worked for him, a Mr. Holstead, came with his wife to see my parents. I noticed that he seemed very nervous in my father's presence, and I thought to myself that maybe my father was a hard man to work for.

He belonged to a number of clubs including the Links Club in New York and the River Club, across the street from our apartment. At Piping Rock, where he played polo, Jews were not accepted as members, so he founded the Creek Club, which admitted Jews so that he could play polo with his Jewish friends. He also belonged to the Deepdale Golf Club on Long Island, and in South Hampton he was a member of both the Shinnecock and the National as well as the Bathing Corporation of Southampton, also known as the Beach Club. In Washington my parents belonged to the Chevy Chase Club, where they played golf.

My father was also a founding member of the 29 Club, so called because of the twenty-nine men in New York who played poker together at a house they bought for the club across the street from the Pierre Hotel. Every Tuesday night my father would play poker there, and later after the war, when he was living in Washington as Secretary of the Air Force, he would sometimes fly up to New York to play poker at the 29 Club because he said that he needed to make money. He once told my sister Peggy, "When I go out on Tuesdays, your mother has the snakes in to dinner." He was referring to her homosexual friends like the playwright Noël Coward and Stuart Preston, the writer and art critic for the *New York Times*.

I don't know anything about my parents' private lives, but I have been told that like some businessmen in the 1920s, my father, before his marriage, had a number of actresses as girlfriends. Once, decades later when a great friend of my mother's, Edith Munson, came to stay with me in Marion, she told me about an evening at El Morocco in New York when there was a young woman at the table with my parents and other people, and my father flirted with her across the table. Later, as my mother was sitting at the mirror in the powder room, Edith said to her, "Aren't men awful." And my mother, with the powder puff in her hand, looked at her in the mirror and said, "I don't know what you're talking about." Another friend of my mother's told me that when my father had a girlfriend, my mother always made friends with her so that she could keep tabs on the situation. Nonetheless, Edith realized my mother always took everything very hard and was unable to roll with the punches. Many men thought that my mother was beautiful, but I think she was very pretty, which is not the same thing. She was immensely cordial to people and fantastically hospitable. Most of all, she never made any class distinctions with people.

My parents had two Jewish friends, the brothers Boy and Buzzie Scheftel, who once came to stay. Freddy Lonsdale, the English drawing-room comedy playwright, was also staying, and while they were all sitting on the terrace, Freddy started to inveigh against the Jews right in front of the Scheftels. My mother said, "Freddy, the butler is now going to pack your bags, and you have to go and stay in New York at the apartment because I can't have you here." And off he went. The next morning, he telephoned her from New York and said, "Well, Sarah Bernhardt!" He was allowed back.

Freddy was known for his wit not only on the stage but in his day-to-day life. Once upon entering St. James for the funeral of a celebrated collector, he asked, "Which side—Sotheby's or Christie's?" His favorite daughter, the writer Frances Donaldson, remembers him telling her: "Don't keep finishing your sentences—I'm not a bloody fool." Freddy's grandsons included the actors Edward Fox and James Fox.

Other guests of my parents included Gary Cooper and Countess Dorothy di Frasso. In the morning when the maid brought the countess her breakfast, she found Gary Cooper in bed with her. The maid, who was a good Irish Catholic, was so shocked that she went to my mother and told her what she had seen. So my mother went to Gary Cooper and said, "I'm afraid you're both going to have to leave because you've upset the servants."

My parents had many friends who were richer than they were. For example, Mrs. George Baker had a splendid house on Park Avenue that she left to the Russian Orthodox Church, who turned the ballroom into a chapel with beautiful icons and decorations. Every winter my parents would spend a week quail shooting with Edith Baker at Horseshoe, her 12,000-acre plantation in Florida, fourteen miles north of Tallahassee. The Duke and Duchess of Windsor would often stop there on their way to Palm Beach. Photographs of one of these shooting parties show a house straight out of *Gone with the Wind* or, as *Sports Illustrated* once described it, "a gleaming, pillared mansion flanked by great trees and overlooking miles of rolling land."

Lunch was brought out to the field in wagons drawn by matched pairs of mules. Servants would have set everything up ahead of time on trestle tables beneath an enormous live oak tree. Sometimes a guest would "cook" something over a fire with a servant on hand to finish the task when he got bored. Shooting would resume in the afternoon. Even today nothing can compare to the quail shooting of southern Georgia where the coveys are so large and plentiful that no one ever bothers to walk up the singles as they do everywhere else.

Vast wealth, however, is no guarantee against disaster. Edith Baker's son Grenville Kane Baker was found dead at Horseshoe in his over-turned jeep with a bullet in his head, supposedly shot by "a party or parties unknown." It is a mystery that, to this day, has never been solved, although it was rumored that he had ignored repeated warnings by some of the local men to leave one of their women alone. Almost thirty years later Grenville's older brother, George Baker, father of my child-hood friend, shot himself at the plantation.

My parents often went to Europe in the early years of their marriage. These were partly shopping trips: my father bought his clothes in London while my mother bought hers in Paris. They knew a lot of people, and if I mention them, it will sound very snobbish, but since my parents' friends were all rather grand, I have to go ahead and mention them. Besides, it gives me pleasure, and some of their stories are not without interest—although many of my friends find it quite irritating.

My mother's best friend in England was Lady Alexandra Metcalfe, the daughter of Lord Curzon, who as viceroy of India had ordered the British invasion of Tibet. She was married to Captain "Fruity" Metcalfe, who was aide-de-camp to King Edward VIII before he abdicated. Lady Metcalfe, who was known as Baba, was my sister Peggy's godmother. In later life Baba became the head of Save the Children.

Another great friend was Lady Sheila Milbank married to Prince Dmitri Alexandrovich Romanov, or Little Dmitri, as he was called, to distinguish him from his very tall cousin, the Grand Duke Dmitri, who at the time my parents knew him lived in exile in Paris. The grand duke and Prince Felix Youssoupoff were the two men who killed Rasputin. He was considered the most beautiful man in Russia before the Russian Revolution. My mother used to see him when she was in Paris, and once when he made a play for her, she said, "But I'm a married woman." And he said, "Oh, all you Americans say that." In 1919, Prince Dmitri escaped from the Crimea with his parents and grandmother, the Dowager Empress, aboard the Royal Navy ship HMS *Marlborough*. In the late 1920s he emigrated to the United States, where he worked as a stockbroker in Manhattan before returning to Europe in the early 1930s when for a brief period he managed Coco Chanel's shop at Biarritz.

Another friend in England was Eric Ward, the Earl of Dudley. When my mother would leave after staying with him, the butler would approach her with the bill for her telephone calls on a little silver tray. The earl was very stingy. Once when he stayed with her in New York, my mother had one of the telephone bills framed and hung above his bed. Some years before, Lord Dudley had behaved disrespectfully while visiting an Egyptian temple. The high priest repeatedly asked him to be quiet, but Dudley, who had had too much to drink at lunch, ignored him. Finally, the priest made a lengthy pronouncement accompanied by violent gestures, at which the guide, visibly upset, hurried the party out of the temple.

Dudley treated the episode as something of a joke until the guide made it clear that it was no laughing matter. Apparently, the priest had declared that although nothing would ever happen to Dudley himself, for years to come many members of his family would suffer violent deaths. Dudley decided that to be on the safe side he had best apologize and make amends with a generous offering to the temple, but the priest had mysteriously vanished without a trace. All efforts to find him were to no avail, and Dudley returned to England and forgot the incident. In the years to come, however, he would often be reminded of it.

The curse, for that's what everyone believed it was, usually seemed to affect Dudley's younger relatives. One little boy was riding a scooter when a puff of wind swept him up and blew him in front of a passing car, and another little girl drowned in a fountain. Another boy was killed by a sniper while doing his military service in Cyprus. He was out on a routine patrol, the accident was a fluke, and only one other British soldier was ever killed in Cyprus during those years. All of these odd deaths were blamed on what was always known as the Ward Curse.

Another of my parents' less reputable friends in England was Sir Oswald Mosley, the head of the British Fascist Party. This didn't seem to bother my parents at all. One night they went to Olympia Hall to hear Mosley speak amid all the trappings of fascist salutes and uniforms and brown shirts. A lot of communists who were there demonstrating against Mosley made so much noise that he couldn't be heard, and the event broke into a battle between Mosley's followers and the communists. My parents, dressed for the evening with my mother wearing diamonds and an ermine stole, managed to push their way through the crowd and out to the street where a green Rolls-Royce, lent to them by Mosley, was waiting for them. By the time they reached it, it had been overturned by the mob, so my parents flagged down a bobby, who drove them to a police station where someone came and drove them to the house where they were staying outside London.

Many years later when I met Mosley's son, Lord Ravensdale, I told him that my parents had been friends of his father's. He replied, "No one has ever said that to me before." Most people disliked Mosley. Even when he was at Eton, the other boys would beat him up. My mother didn't really like him either. She said that he beat his horse.

In Paris my parents also had a number of friends, including the banker Pierre David-Weill, who would send white roses to my mother's suite at the Ritz. Another bouquet of roses would come from Madame Porthault, who made all my mother's beautiful linens. A third bouquet of roses always came from the Windsors, who lived in the Bois de Boulogne in a house given them by the government of France. The duke and my mother had been friends since 1919 when he came on a tour of Canada and the United States. In Philadelphia friends of my mother's, the Makays, gave a ball for the then Prince of Wales, and they asked my mother to be his partner. During the ball, the prince got bored and said, "Let's get out of here." My mother replied, "You can go sir, but I have to stay."

Years later, Josephine Douglas, wife of Lewis Williams Douglas, the ambassador to Great Britain, took my mother to see Queen Mary. At some point during the audience, Mrs. Douglas excused herself, as had been arranged, and left my mother alone with the Duke of Windsor's mother, who was unable to see her son after he abdicated. The queen said to my mother, "Now, tell me how he is." My mother replied, "Ma'am, he is very well. I just played golf with him."

CHAPTER THREE

Early Life

My twin brother, John, and I were born February 21, 1939, at Doctors Hospital in New York, delivered by Dr. Macintosh. I was what was known as a blue baby, and after I was born, I was very ill. I had to stay at Doctors Hospital for some time, whereas John was a healthy happy baby and able to go home right away. After I had grown up, I remember Nanny telling me that my father was so worried because I was sick that he favored John, the strong healthy baby, and sort of gave up on me. This may be what cast a shadow over our relationship for the rest of our lives.

At the time my brother and I were born, my sisters, Peggy who was twelve years older than we and Polly who was two years younger than Peggy, were at the Brearley School. My father telephoned the head mistress, who happened to be the wife of Dr. MacIntosh, to ask her to tell them that twins had been born. They were allowed to leave school and go to the hospital to see their baby brothers. From that moment on, we were very close to our sisters, despite the difference in our ages. In time it seemed as if my brother and I had four mothers: Nanny, our own mother, and our two older sisters.

As the eldest, Peggy was very conscious of her seniority and held it over all of us, especially Polly, who throughout her life always felt crushed by her. Once, years later, Polly and I went to see Peggy on Fishers Island, New York, and as we left the house, Peggy said something bossy to Polly, who turned to me and said, "See, that's what she has done all of our lives."

Eleanor McLaren, whom we called Nanny, was the backbone of our young lives. She taught us the difference between right and wrong and formed us to the extent that my brother became an Episcopal minister and good pastor and I survived. She was born in Glasgow in 1888—

the same year as my father—and remembered seeing Queen Victoria's funeral ceremonies. She was still a little girl when her parents died. Her father died of gangrene because of a factory accident, and she went to live with an aunt whose brother had been killed in the First World War. To make ends meet, her aunt took in soldiers as lodgers. Every morning Nanny would have to get up early to polish their boots. At Christmas, she would be given an orange.

From Canada, Nanny came to the United States to work for Aunt Lil, my father's sister. Aunt Lil was rather hysterical, which made working for her quite unpleasant, and Nanny was looking for another job. At first my mother was reluctant to take her on as she was afraid that Nanny might carry tales about our household back to my father's family. Mummy need not have worried, although she was never sold on the Talbott family. As my brother, John, has put it, "I always thought that the Thayers were a far finer bunch, who gave much more to the nation in the way of service and civic duty than did the Talbotts. But the Talbotts were louder and tended to drown out the Thayers."

Except for Nanny, who was Scottish and Presbyterian, the other servants were Irish and Catholic. The cook, Marie Reilly, produced such wonderful food that once my father told my mother that the bills from Gristedes Market were too high. When he told her to oversee Marie Reilly's shopping, my mother said, "I didn't marry you, Harold, to do the shopping." Perhaps that's why my father once told Nanny, "I married a thoroughbred." Often when John and I were going out with Nanny, we would stop at the service entrance on the third floor so that Nanny and Esther, the laundress, could have a chat. She worked in a tiny cubicle, which John remembers as so hot in the summer that it was inconceivable anyone could work there. Agnes Dawson, my mother's maid, who came from Londonderry, was very close to the family. She had a wonderful sense of humor and, like Nanny, a great laugh. She was short and small and very Catholic. Agnes and I were great friends. After my mother died, she returned to Ireland. Sutherland, the butler, had first worked for my parents at the Pillars. When John and I were growing up, he would come in to serve when there was a party. In his green-and-black striped vest and a butler's coat, Sutherland looked just the part. There was a gun closet in the apartment, and he used to clean my father's guns.

Over the years there were three chauffeurs. Harvey, a giant of a man, had been my grandmother Talbott's chauffeur before coming to work for my father. There are photographs of him with John and me at the house at Old Westbury. The other chauffeurs were Pascal and Eddie Bigger, who was also my father's valet. When Pascal was driving us in the city, my father would spur him on and say, "No, no, no, go this way, it's faster, and get around that car!" Pascal could never seem to drive fast enough and cleverly enough to satisfy my father.

We had a number of interesting neighbors at 450 East 52nd Street, including Mary Martin, the actress and singer. Henry and Claire Booth Luce lived on three floors. Mr. and Mrs. Hertz of Hertz Rent A Car, who also lived there, were a gentle and affectionate couple, and because they were not very tall, I felt at ease with them. They were kind and generous, too. One Christmas they sent John and me a huge box containing all the Doctor Doolittle books.

Noël Coward, who had known my mother since the 1920s, had an apartment below us and often came to lunch whenever he was in New York. He was also a great friend of the Queen Mother and would make her bullshots, a cocktail made of vodka, beef bouillon, and Worcestershire sauce, which he said she enjoyed very much. One day years later my friend Charlie Cochran, who himself was a talented pianist and singer, joined us for lunch and afterward entertained us with a few songs. Noël went and stood at the top of the two steps into the living room, and in his marvelous dramatic campy way said, "You have restored my faith in the younger generation." Charlie went on to have a successful career as a cabaret singer.

When you went up and down in the elevator, you saw all sorts of well-known people. Once Greta Garbo, who lived in the penthouse, was in the elevator with John and me, and one of us said to Nanny, in front of Garbo, "Why do they say she's so beautiful?" Nanny pinched the transgressor and said, "Don't pass remarks."

My parents spent weekends at the Pillars until after the war, when they closed the house and only lived in the apartment in New York. Money, I suppose. Nanny would take John and me and other friends, including Serena Stewart, whom, as I often told people, I practically knew in utero, out to the Pillars for picnics. Our parents were friends, although I wonder if my mother might have had some reservations about Janet Stewart. Once when I asked her if she thought that Mrs. Stewart was beautiful, my mother replied, "Yes, if you like that expressionless German beauty." Janet Stewart's husband, William Rhinelander Stewart, had been a beau of my mother's. In the *San Francisco Chronicle* in the 1920s, there appeared a full-page illustrated story with drawings of my mother, who had gone to Africa on safari with the Legendres, supposedly because William Rhinelander Stewart had dropped her and married Janet Stewart instead. My mother said that it was simply gossip and there was nothing more than friendship between her and Rhinelander Stewart. Serena sent me the newspaper page, and my friend Michael Baldwin had it framed, and I have it hanging in my bathroom today. It was always said that author Kay Thompson based her character Eloise on Serena, who grew up at the Pierre Hotel in New York City, similar to her literary counterpart, who lived on the top floor of the Plaza. Serena ended up as a fashionable young woman in New York and later became a successful architect. She was also a keen sailor and once sailed around the world on her own boat.

Mrs. Canova, Serena's nurse, was a friend of Nanny's. She was a well-educated and sophisticated woman who had been married, which put her in a different league from other Scottish and English nannies. When we went to the Pillars, Mrs. Canova would bring delicious egg salad sandwiches for our picnics. We would have loved to swim in the pool, but the surface was covered with algae and moss. Lots of frogs swam in the water and hopped about the pool. Unfortunately, to my great distress for the rest of my life, John and I ran over some of them with our bicycles. Although one could say "boys will be boys," I have regretted it ever since and have said many prayers—*om mani padme hum*—out of compassion for the little frogs. Over the years I have collected frog figures. Some are humorous, and one in malachite holds down my notes on my table in memory of the frogs that we killed. It was a present from Bonnie Thurston, the head of the Thomas Merton Foundation.

According to Nanny, when my parents closed the Pillars after the war there was an unhappy atmosphere in the house. A place that had once been so full of light had become gloomy. As children we would go through the vast echoing rooms to see where our parents and sisters, "the girls" (pronounced by Nanny as "the gerrels" in her Scottish burr), had lived. There was an immense entrance hall with a double staircase. French doors opened from the living room onto a broad terrace that overlooked the swimming pool. There was a large dining room, and off it a sunny breakfast room with Buddha heads as ornaments.

In the early 1950s the Pillars burned to the ground. A fire started in the copper roof over the attic where costumes for parties were stored and spread to the rest of the house. As soon as they heard, my parents rushed down and arrived just in time to see the end of the fire. They stood almost in tears thinking of the happy days they had spent at the house in the 1920s and '30s. How ironic that things as frivolous as costumes for parties were the cause of the fire that destroyed such a splendid house.

It was a treat when my parents took John, Nanny, and me to visit Gaga, my Thayer grandmother, in Haverford, Pennsylvania. She was still living at Redwood, which had been her home ever since she married my grandfather. A circular drive led to the front door. At the back of the house a long terrace overlooked the broad lawn, which swept down to a pool. The household was very Edwardian and rather fascinating. Gaga had a charming English companion named Miss Hillie, who resembled Alice B. Toklas, only rather more mousy. She always wore a broad-brimmed turn-of-the-century hat, both indoors and out. By the time John and I were born, Gaga had done "an Emily Dickinson" and seldom left her room, where she retired for the rest of her life, a decision I found fascinating. We would climb the big staircase to visit her there. Gaga adored violets and always had them around in little vases. I think that she probably wore them, as women did back in the nineteenth century.

At the end of our visit Gaga would give us presents, usually books, each inscribed "to my darling grandchild so-and-so." In her bedroom Gaga had French windows that opened out like shutters, and instead of giving the books to us in her room, she would stand in front of an open window and throw them to us as we waited on the lawn below. In future years I used to see photographs of Colette in magazines and books, and in the French windows of her bedroom Gaga looked very much like Colette.

John and I were not yet two when the United States entered the Second World War against Germany and Japan. Mummy joined the AWVS—the American Women's Volunteer Service—and worked as a nurse. My father, as a member of the War Production Board, helped organize supplies and materiel for the European theater, which led to his friendship with Eisenhower. When he had to be in Washington, my father lived at the Mayflower Hotel.

After the war was over my father spent his days at his office, while my mother raised money for the New York Infirmary, a not-for-profit hospital established in 1853 for needy women and children. Because it was a volunteer job, she could fashion her own schedule, which allowed her to take trips either alone or with friends. This would distress my father. He once said to Nanny, "I might have to divorce Peggy for desertion." In fact, she was absent a good deal of the time. Later, when my sisters went to college, my mother served on the board of Sarah Lawrence College. In the evening my father would talk to us in his dressing room or my mother would read to us in her sitting room before they went out to dinner. On nights they entertained, we would have to come in and meet the guests. Those were ceremonial occasions we quite enjoyed, yet at the same time we felt as if we were on display.

I remember mornings when my sisters, who adored our father, would have breakfast with him in my mother's sitting room. Often he would tell them how the stocks he had bought for them were doing. As a small child listening in, I would hear the word *dividend* and think to myself, "Oh, amazing. They get on so well, and he is telling them about something called stocks." My sisters adored him, and he and John got on wonderfully as well. To me, my father was an awe-inspiring figure who always seemed to stride into a room. He had a loud rather hoarse voice and would often scold the servants. I suspect that he had quite a temper. But Nanny could handle him very well and would often intercede with him on my behalf.

One morning during one of our visits to Redwood, my brother and I were to take a shower with him. However, I was so terrified of my father that I didn't want to take a shower with him, and I made an awful scene. After that we were waiting for him at the breakfast table, and I was told that I was to sit next to my father. I couldn't bear the idea of sitting next to him, so I made another scene. Karmic terror perhaps. Fortunately, I was allowed to change my seat. Another time when I was still very small, we were staying in Southampton. One afternoon at the Beach Club, my father announced, "Now you're going to learn how to swim," and he threw me in the swimming pool. I managed to get out before having an absolute fit. John, of course, swam with no trouble, as always happened with anything athletic. We went back to the Irving House, where we were staying, and after I was put to bed, I got up and hid in the closet. When Nanny came in and saw the bed was empty, she opened the closet and found me there, cowering on the floor. She summoned my father to my room and said, "Now you see what you have done to your son."

When I was a good deal older, he tried to teach me to drive. Here he was on the board of directors of Chrysler and an automobile man, and I couldn't learn to drive because I was so terrified of him. In fact, I was so traumatized by the experience that I have never learned to drive. Underneath it all, I believe, he was a man of tender feelings, and although he may have felt sorry, I think he realized that he would never see eye to eye with one of his sons. Nonetheless, he had an enormous impact on me.

I remember that he drove incredibly fast. One time, John and I were in the car when he was stopped for speeding. When the officer asked for his license, my father told him to look at the emblem on the back of the car that proved that my father was commissioner of New York State Racing and therefore a state official. After the officer had looked at the emblem, he simply said, "Yes, Sir." My father's fast driving was the cause of the only quarrel my brother and I witnessed between my parents. Once while he was driving exceptionally fast, my mother told him that he had to slow down, which annoyed him. Finally, she demanded, "Stop the car!" He obeyed. Then she said, "Now, get out. I'm going to drive." He came around to the other side of the car and got in, and she very irritably drove the rest of the way home.

Apart from that, I never saw any clashes between them, although I'm sure there were heated exchanges in private, if only because of my mother's spending. My father once told my brother that my mother's spending was so out of control that he couldn't support her with the money he made from business, so he had to make up for it with $75,000 a year at the poker table. John asked him what happened when he lost, and he said, "Oh, I don't ever lose at poker. I can lose at bridge, but I don't lose at poker." When my father did business over the phone, he would curse a great deal and say, "God damn it!" in a loud tone of voice, which frightened me. Although we four children had a very happy childhood with our parents, I must say that much of our happiness was due to Nanny, who brought us up with so much love and patience.

Games played a big part in my parents' lives, especially bridge. My mother had a list of extra men in her address book. Some were identified as "plays bridge" and once in while "plays GOOD bridge." At one point my mother had a run of bad luck at the bridge table because of poor hands, and this irritated her very much.

My father constantly played dominos at a card table in the living room, especially with his best friend, Uncle Charlie Schwartz, as we called him. Once Aunt Polly came over from Haverford to see her sister and her family. While she and my father were playing dominos, an old friend of Aunt Polly's who had not seen her in years came into the living room. When her friend said, "Hello, Polly!" Aunt Polly looked up, said hello, and immediately looked down at the table, saying, "Your turn, Harold." When canasta became popular, my mother would have friends over to play in the afternoons. Backgammon was another favorite of my father's, and often in Southampton when we went to swim at their friends the Grieves's house, I remember my father and Uncle Charlie playing backgammon in the shade of an awning at the pool house.

When John and I were very small, we spent our summers at the Pillars. After we were three, we spent June and September with Nanny at the Irving Hotel in Southampton. Our parents came for weekends so that we could be together as a family, and they would play a lot of golf and seemed to go out to parties almost every night. In July and August, our mother took us to stay at the Deer Creek Ranch on the south fork of the Shoshone River, fifty miles from Cody, Wyoming. Because the altitude was too much for Nanny, she had a holiday with her family in New York and Canada until September, when we were happily reunited.

Deer Creek, which belonged to my parents' friend Hope Reed, was one of the most beautiful places I've ever seen. My very first memory is of playing with Tom and Barry Head during our first summer at the ranch, when John and I were three and a half. We were in a garden looking at the goldfish in a little pond, and I remember noticing how beautiful one of the Head boys was. Hope Williams Reed was a well-known comic actress of whom Noël Coward once wrote, she "had a charming speaking voice with a sort of beguiling tonelessness." She was married for six years to Dr. Bartow Reed, but later they divorced. Nonetheless, when Dr. Reed was killed in a plane crash, she inherited all his money, which allowed her to retire from acting and buy the ranch. We spent many wonderful summers at Deer Creek. My father always joined us for the week around my parents' wedding anniversary on August 11.

My sisters would write new lyrics to familiar old songs, which they and their friends would sing sitting in a circle on the floor of the lodge where we all played pool and other games. I remember our parents at a big window with their elbows propped on the sill. Mrs. Reed was there with whomever was staying at the ranch at the time. Every summer I would write a play in which I always took the female lead. One year when I based my play on *Der Rosenkavalier*, my mother allowed me to wear the incredible dress she had worn in the 1930s at an opera ball based on the court of Louis XV of France.

After the performance, when I went back to our cabin to change, I was very proud that many people came to congratulate me for my part in writing the show and my role in it. I must admit that I loved dressing up, and once in a while when I was about eight, I would put on my sisters' tutus. Nanny always made sure that I got out of these costumes before my father got home. I suppose, like many gay people, that I was attracted to physical beauty, especially boys, although I was not an especially visual person.

At Deer Creek there were usually seven or eight of us all about the same age, and we were turned loose and left to do as we pleased, providing that we were on time for meals. We spent most of our days galloping up and down the valley, visiting the neighboring ranches, many of which belonged to friends of our parents. Some of us rode in western saddles, but mostly we rode bareback, which was more fun. Often, we'd ride over to Valley Ranch, the largest dude ranch in the Shoshone River Valley. It was where the mail was picked up, and there was a store that sold Indian leather and bead goods. They also had a stagecoach called the Chuck Wagon where you could get Coca-Cola or ginger ale and cookies.

We made many friends at the ranch, some of whom have remained friends for life. Carola Lott remembers one summer when, she wrote:

> the ring leader of our little gang was Harold Talbott, who maintained control simply because he was smarter than the rest of us and had more imagination. Whatever he said, we did without question. This included sitting in the Talbotts' cabin for an hour after lunch every afternoon while Harold read to us from *The Phantom of the Opera*, and Mrs. Talbott worked on a complicated bit of needlepoint destined to become a cushion for the Cathedral in Washington. Only when Harold gave permission could we rush back to our horses. After supper, which we ate while our parents were

having drinks, we repaired to the game room for games of
Mah Jong, also organized by Harold, who taught us how to
play.

Another friend from the ranch days was Katherine Ryan, who was
known as Daffy. She was first married to Winthrop Aldrich, and after
they were divorced, she married Daniel Selznick, whose father made
Gone with the Wind. His mother was the daughter of Louis B. Mayer.
Then there was Tony Mortimer and his sister Ba, whom I always loved
as a child. She later married Carter Burden, and we'd sometimes go to
the opera together.

Deer Creek had a big influence on my life in a few unexpected ways.
Hawk Eye, the neighboring ranch, belonged to my godmother, Loretta
Howard, who would often come over to Deer Creek for dinner. She
was a fervent Catholic whose house in New York was filled with her
remarkable collection of Neapolitan crèche figures, which she left to
the Metropolitan Museum, where they can be seen every December on
the enormous Christmas tree. Monsignor Dockery of the New York
diocese, who spent the summer months at Hawkeye, would celebrate
Mass every Sunday in Loretta's private chapel. I would be allowed to
attend the service, but although I longed to take Communion, it was not
permitted as I had not yet been confirmed. My father, who happened to
be present at one of Loretta's Sunday Masses, remarked when the bell
rang before Communion, "It's the good humor man." Freddy Lonsdale,
the English playwright whom I mentioned before, once said, "Loretta
has made more atheists than anyone I know."

One day at the ranch when I was eight or nine, I found *The
Autobiography of a Yogi* by Paramahansa Yogananda, which had been
left on the fender of the car used to buy groceries and supplies in Cody.
It was the first book I ever read on Indian religion, and it had a big effect
on me. Yogananda was a spiritual miracle worker, and I immediately
became fascinated by *siddhas*, or holy people who can perform miracles.

One summer when John and I were twelve, we were sent to Camp
Keewaydin Temagami, on Devil's Island on Lake Temagami, Ontario,

which belonged to my father's sister, Aunt Kit, and her husband, Uncle Bill Jones. I hated summer camp, but John loved it and did very well. We had to go on canoe trips portaging through the woods from one lake to the next, with two boys carrying their canoe over their heads, tormented by black flies. There was something ineffably beautiful about the lakes themselves in the early morning sunlight with the sound of the loons calling over the water. But this didn't compensate for my misery. While my brother thrived, my unhappiness erupted in a number of large boils along the left side of my body. I had to be quarantined in a separate cottage on Uncle Bill and Aunt Kit's property. Eventually, a doctor came and lanced the boils. This was my Job's travail camp summer.

When my parents came to visit, dressed beautifully for the country, they stayed in a comfortable cabin. I was amazed by it all. It was like being a prisoner and then going to visit people who were free and lived in a beautiful house. Good-looking twin counselors played bridge with my parents, and I was very impressed that they played well enough at sixteen to do so. Johnny Dalzell was another counselor. I had two cousins at the camp, and one of them had a crush on him and called him Johnny Dazzle.

To compensate for the harsh realities of camp life, I invented a transparent tent, which I furnished with a fantasy chair and lamp. In my mind's eye I would sit there and read comfortably, free from the black flies of Canada. John went on a long canoe and portage trip to an Indian village that had a Catholic mission. I asked him to bring me back a rosary, and he did. And so I recited the rosary, and that was also a great consolation for me.

From the very beginning John and I were opposites. Eventually, John went on to Deerfield and then to the University of Virginia before he left to explore a variety of occupations. After a stint with the 101st Airborne and after our mother died in 1962, he worked as a roughneck on the oil rigs in Texas before returning to college. In 1964 he came back to New York where, through our brother-in-law B. Noyes, husband of Peggy, he got a job at Bache & Company. The following year he married Anne Kinsolving and moved back to Texas to work for the Midland National Bank. Two years later, John and Anne moved to Tiburon, California, where John worked for Hilliard Oil & Gas in San Francisco and joined the management of the Oakland Clippers Soccer Team. Two years later, in 1969, John became a shepherd on the Huerto Alto Ranch, in Annapolis, California, a place so remote that during mud season they couldn't get down the road.

Three years later, in 1972, John and Anne moved to Tennessee when John became the farm manager of Wessyngton Plantation in Cedar Hill. One day while he was riding through the fields, his horse fell on him and crushed his pelvis. For a time, the doctors thought he might never walk again. Although John accuses me of being overly dramatic, after he was visited in the hospital by the pastor of the Church of Christ as well as by his father-in-law, Dr. Kinsolving, he made a quick and seemingly miraculous recovery and as a result had something of a conversion and decided to go to theological school. In 1985, he graduated from Vanderbilt Divinity School and was ordained deacon in the Episcopal Church. The following year, he moved to Shelbyville, Tennessee, to become rector there of the Church of the Redeemer. Later, he became rector of St. Augustine's Episcopal Church in Washington, DC, while Anne, who had studied Russian and could speak the language, worked teaching business practices to companies in Eastern Europe and Russia. In 2004, John retired to Old Saybrook, Connecticut, where he lives today.

It was not until we were in our thirties that John and I began to get along. We became telephone buddies and talked mostly about religion. Although John was very nice about my Buddhist studies, he said more than once, "I've always considered you a Christian."

Meanwhile, John and I entered kindergarten at Buckley School in New York City, a K–9 day school for boys, when we were five. Meanwhile, Peggy and Polly went to Miss Hall's School, a boarding school in Pittsfield, Massachusetts. Peggy went on to Sarah Lawrence, and Polly attended Vassar. I was intrigued by their studies and the textbooks they brought home. Polly told me about the novels of Tolstoy and Dostoevsky, and I quite worshipped my sisters because of their knowledge.

Once my mother asked Nanny why John and I were so much more affectionate than the girls. Nanny replied, "Mrs. Talbott, you were never here when the girls were growing up." I adored my mother unconditionally, but my sister Polly, who ordinarily had the nature of an angel, once said to me, "Mother was the most selfish person I have ever known." I was shocked by the harshness of her judgment. My sisters had no desire to lead the very social life of our parents. They had no interest whatsoever in the world of the Windsors, which my mother found so compelling, and in fact thought that our mother was heading for a train wreck. In a certain sense I have to agree and have always thought that my mother might have died of glamour.

Possibly because Mummy didn't stick around when they were growing up and instead went on trips, Polly may have had a sense of being abandoned. And indeed, my mother loved to travel, often going to South America, where she had a number of friends. In Argentina she often stayed with friends—Cora Cavanaugh in Buenos Aires and at the Nelson family's ranch on the pampas. Once, Eva Perón invited my mother to one of her daily audiences when she gave money to the poor. Of course, she was revered and loved by some of the Argentine people for her generosity, but I think it may have been a public relations ploy. On a trip to Cuba long before Castro, my parents dined with the Countess Camargo, who had become a papal countess after giving a lot of money to the Vatican. The countess said to my mother, "This is the one hundredth Dior of the season that I'm wearing." According to my mother, her jewels were absolutely fantastic as well.

During the week John and I lived the lives of typical New York City boys. Dressed in short pants, bomber jackets, and peaked caps with a B on them, we were delivered to Buckley every morning by either Nanny or Pascal the chauffeur. John excelled at sports, while my interests were more intellectual as I loved poetry and writing children's books. I was a fairly good student, but John often had trouble, for he seemed to have little interest in studying. At this stage we led quite separate lives and if truth be told got along very badly. Our fights were constant and vicious, often leaving one or both of us bruised and bloody. John was the stronger, so to even things up I would sometimes stand behind a door and stick my foot out so that he would trip over it. It annoyed our parents and drove Nanny, who had to cope with us, to despair. When things got too violent, she would threaten to leave, but before she reached the door, we always managed to intercept her and promise to mend our ways.

While I enjoyed my studies at Buckley School, what I found more enjoyable were my friends. The first friend I made at school was George Baker, known as Button Baker. He was the grandson of Edith Baker, my mother's great friend who owned Horseshoe Plantation. Button and I had a lot of fun together. As I mentioned earlier, tragedy seemed to stalk the Baker men. Button was killed when the twin engine Beechcraft Baron he was flying disappeared off Nantucket. He was only sixty-six. Three years later George's brother Anthony was killed when the light sport plane he was testing crashed into the Tennessee River.

While I was still at Buckley, I became great friends with George Hobson, who had a big influence on my life at boarding school. In fact, I later went to St. Paul's School against my father's wishes, simply because George was going there. My father had said to me, "You can go to any school you want except St. Paul's because it's so snobbish." Polly's husband, Jonesy Toland, who had gone to Saint Paul's, also told me not to go there. He said that because Saint Paul's was a hockey school, I would not enjoy it. But I was determined to go because George was going. Although his mother had told George that I was homosexual, it had no effect on our friendship. A few years later when we were both at St. Paul's, George would come have lunch with us at my parents' apartment, and once my mother said to me in a melting voice, "George is *so* handsome." And indeed, he was very good looking, almost Byronic, and very popular with the girls. But I never for one instant thought of him in erotic terms. By the time we got to Harvard, we had gone our separate ways. George eventually became the pastor of the American Cathedral in Paris.

Another friend at Buckley was Arthur MacArthur, an absolute hothouse plant, a rare bird. Nobody was like him, and of course nobody could be because he was the only child of General Douglas MacArthur.

He was the most flamboyant homosexual I've ever known, right under his father's nose. But in his father's eyes, he could do no wrong. As the general wrote in a letter when Arthur was still very young, "[my son is] the complete center of my thoughts and affection." As MacArthur's biographer, William Manchester, put it, "In the end his suffocating adoration enshrouded his son's soul."

Arthur and I had a lot of fun together. I went to see him at the Waldorf Towers, where he lived. We would often cross Park Avenue to go to the old Liberty Music Shop on Madison Avenue, where he bought a lot of records. Sometimes I would have to stop him in the street and say, "Now Arthur, get a grip on yourself, because if you carry on in public the way you do, I'm going to walk away." Although I tried to be strict with him about his mannerisms, he couldn't help himself. Extreme camp was just a part of him.

When he was as young as four years old, Arthur displayed exceptional musical talent and would come home from a concert and play by ear what he had heard. I thought that he played the piano technically very well but without much emotional depth or musical expression. Nevertheless, I admired him, for he had extraordinarily agile fingers for things like Chopin waltzes. Arthur always had to dominate those around him. No doubt it was owing to his father, but it got a little boring after a while, for he always had to outdo you. Once while my father was Secretary of the Air Force, he accepted an invitation to speak at Buckley. Afterward, Arthur came up to me and said, "You know, my father was asked to speak today, but he was too busy, so that is why they asked your father to speak."

While his father was in charge of the Allied occupation of Japan, Arthur lived with his family in Tokyo until he was twelve. When they returned to America, his father was given a ticker-tape parade in New York. Arthur and his mother were with him in the convertible as it was driven through the cheering crowds along their route. This went to his head. He said to me once, "Oh, I'm a has-been at the age of twelve!" And I said, "That's all right, Arthur, I'm a has-been too." And he replied, "You, you're a has-been that never was!" Arthur and I got up to a lot of mischief at school. We would bring in small beautiful objects from home that we had no business borrowing. Once I brought to school a jeweled ring from my mother's jewelry box. I don't know how I got hold of it because it was in a case in her bedroom. But when I brought it in, the school telephoned home to say that somebody should come get it because it was so valuable.

During my school days in New York, my brother and I studied piano at the Diller Quaile School. Neither of us had musical talent, but the school was the best for children in the city. Although I never became very good, perhaps thanks to my piano I have had a lifelong love of music. One afternoon a week, dressed in obligatory dark-blue suits, we were taken to Mr. Willie de Rham's dancing class across the street from our apartment at the River Club. Mr. de Rham and his wife and dancing partner, Miss Chapin, would teach us what was considered correct behavior and as a sideline how to dance with little girls in frilly party dresses and black patent leather Mary Janes.

Occasionally my mother would take me to the Metropolitan Opera in its old house on Broadway and 39th Street. I loved the red plush seats and the opulent gold decorations that were the setting for so many nights during the Gilded Age. When friends of my mother's like Ailsa Bruce and Thomas Watson couldn't use their box at the Met, they would lend it to my mother, and because Mrs. Bruce's was the center box, I became very spoiled. Ailsa Bruce was the daughter of Andrew Mellon and one of the benefactors of the National Gallery in Washington. It was she who made possible the acquisition of many old masters, including the portrait of Ginevra de' Benci, the only painting by Leonardo da Vinci outside Europe. She had originally intended to leave her collection of French impressionists to the Metropolitan Museum, but when they wanted to choose the ones to take, she gave her whole collection to the National Gallery in Washington. When I was taken to see her, her paintings were all lined up on the floor, propped against the walls. She never managed to make up her mind where to hang them.

Mrs. Harry Payne Bingham, whom we called Aunty Mo, also had an extraordinary collection of impressionist paintings, including

The Dance Class by Degas, which she left to the Met. Many consider it Degas's finest painting. We used to go to birthday parties for her daughter, Burks, at her Park Avenue house on 69th Street. After the Binghams sold the house, it became, for a time, the Russian consulate. When Khrushchev came to the United Nations and banged his shoe on the table to show his anger with the West, he stayed at what had once been Mrs. Bingham's house.

My mother allowed me to go to a school of drama and painting called the King-Coit School. I auditioned for a part in a play with a cast of children like myself called *The Golden Cage*, based on the paintings and poetry of William Blake. When I auditioned, Miss Coit said that I must learn to move properly and assume the poses represented in the Blake paintings. However, because my reading of the lines was good, she cast me as the lead, that of the shepherd who recited, "Piping down the valleys wild." The part of Lucifer was taken my old friend Dierdre, Loretta Howard's daughter, whom I knew from the summers she spent at Hawkeye Ranch near Deer Creek.

We rehearsed the play for months. Finally, we performed in the auditorium of Hunter College, where our parents and friends came to see it. *Vogue* magazine wrote an article about the play, with wonderful photographs of the children performing in diaphanous costumes, fashioned after Blake's paintings, some of the children sporting angels' wings. My father disapproved of my acting in this very aesthetic children's play, and I'm not sure whether he came to the play, but my mother certainly did. Mrs. Beach, my teacher at Buckley School in Junior One, came to see it, and I was very proud to perform the leading role in front of her and my mother.

CHAPTER FOUR

St. Paul's 1953–1956

Ea Discamus in Terris Quorum Scientia Perseveret in Coelis
(Let us learn on Earth the knowledge that will prevail in Heaven)
—St. Paul's school motto, from St. Jerome, Epistle 53

In February 1953, President Eisenhower appointed my father Secretary of the Air Force. Having been a member of the War Production Board in 1942 and 1943, my father knew something about the military. For years my father was active in politics, serving as a Republican presidential campaign fund-raiser in 1940, 1948, and 1952. When members of the Republican Party started a Draft Eisenhower movement, my father and several other businessmen went to Paris, where Ike was based as Supreme Commander of NATO Forces in Europe, to persuade him to run. Although Eisenhower was a Democrat from Texas, he finally agreed to become the Republican candidate. After Eisenhower won the election, he offered my father one of two posts, either the Secretary of the Air Force or ambassador to the Court of Saint James. My father called the family together and asked us which post we would like him to take. Everyone but me said that he should choose the air force. I've always wished that he had chosen Great Britain.

My parents rented a beautiful house on P Street in Georgetown and were soon at the center of the Washington world that revolved around politics. By that time Eisenhower and my father had become friends, and they usually played bridge together one night a week. When John and I visited our parents after school, the president would often have us over to swim in the White House pool, and sometimes he would come out and talk to us while we were swimming.

When I entered St. Paul's in Concord, New Hampshire, the autumn of 1953, the school was only three years shy of celebrating its centennial. Although I was a bit homesick at first, especially for Nanny, I took to the place at once, not only to my teachers and fellow students but also to the whole atmosphere of the school. I was charmed by the old brick buildings and the ponds, woods, and open fields of the campus. I even enjoyed the New England climate, so different from that of New York. When I opened my window in the early morning, there would be frost on the lawn. I could smell the autumn leaves and see the mist hanging in the air above the pond. I began to enjoy the solitude of being at the school and ceased to be homesick. I just felt that I was at home in two different places—New York and St. Paul's. The carillon that rang the hours from the chapel of St. Peter and St. Paul made me imagine that I was a member of a monastery, and I loved that. Religion was an important part of school life. Every day my friend George Hobson, who like me was a devout Episcopalian, and I would take Communion from Reverend Webb in the school's Old Chapel.

Like most boarding schools, St. Paul's was a world unto itself with its own traditions and terminology. Boys were fitted into categories according to their activities and characteristics. Jocks of course were the athletes. Brains were very good students. Fairies were effeminate boys, and by some miracle I was called that only once. Rocks were muscular boys, such as the brawny Chris, hero of the first- and second-form boys whom he supervised. It was said that he was so muscle bound that it was hard for him to brush his teeth. Regs were the regular guys, who bought their clothes at Brooks Brothers. They wore well-cut suits and blue shirts with white collars fastened with gold safety pins to make the tie stand out at the correct angle. Regs were admired but sometimes mocked. Then there were the Grubs, who had body odor or whose room smelled.

I loved my classes, at least most of them. From the start my favorite course was French with André Jacq, who had a genius for teaching. If it was medieval history, he would become a medieval Frenchman and describe building the cathedrals, the church, and the medieval mind so vividly that one felt that one was actually there. For the Renaissance he would become François Premier, and then on through the Age of

Enlightenment, the French Revolution, Napoleon, and finally the twen-
tieth century. Monsieur Jacq grew up in a village in Brittany. While he
was still a boy, the village priest had encouraged him to become a priest.
Although he never did, I think that he was a religious man. He always
attended all the services in the chapel even though he was a Catholic.
And I think that he was, like many Frenchman, a freethinker. When
he first came to America, he had studied at a music conservatory.
Sometimes I would find him reading musical scores by the likes of Bach
as though they were books. He also loved Berlioz.

One of my greatest pleasures was reading in the evening after I
finished my homework. Sitting in a comfortable secondhand armchair
I'd bought in Concord, I started with *War and Peace* before going on to
the novels of Dostoyevsky. I must say that I liked all my courses except
mathematics, at which I was a complete failure. It really almost sank
my boat at St. Paul's; in fact, eventually it did. I did not enjoy sports.
There were nine hockey teams at the school leading up to the varsity,
and I became the only member of the tenth team because I skated on
my ankles the way a seal moves on his flippers.

One of the few times I had any trouble about being effeminate
happened when I was running down the field. A boy shoved me to the
ground and said, "Get out of my way, you little fairy." I was so enamored
with Oscar Wilde that I tried to emulate him by being as flamboyant as
possible until a group of boys came to my room, held me down, and cut
my fingernails. For the speech contest my fourth-form year, I walked
slowly down the aisle to the podium carrying a large Easter lily, which I
held reverently before me as I gave a talk on art for art's sake. I won. In
addition to Oscar Wilde's writings, I read transcripts of the poet's three
trials. I also managed to obtain a first edition of his play *A Woman of
No Importance*. I really got a lot out of reading Wilde before going on to
other writers. For one thing, I learned how to write dialogue.

I must admit that it was a miracle that I wasn't hazed at the school
or given any trouble despite my effeminate personality. In part I was
spared because I was respected as a good student. And the fact that
my father was Secretary of the Air Force gave me considerable pres-

tige. Once when my father was inspecting an airplane facility near the school, he had the pilot of his government helicopter land on the St. Paul's football field. I went down to see him and found students and people running from all directions to look at the helicopter. When my father, who could be very imposing, stepped out, I got a lot of credit.

I was also respected because I lied—telling my classmates that I was a cousin of Grace Kelly's, on whom all the boys had a crush. In actuality I had embellished a story about my uncle Jack Thayer and Grace Kelly's father. Uncle Jack was a member of the University of Pennsylvania crew, but when he discovered that the son of a bricklayer was in the same shell, he refused to row. The bricklayer was Grace Kelly's grandfather, and the recipient of my uncle's snobbishness was her father.

In the autumn of 1954, I lived at Foster House as a fourth former with a number of very sophisticated and jolly fifth formers. Not only had my grades improved, but I also enjoyed both my studies and extra-curricular activities. I became a member of the Concordian Literary Society, the Debating Society, and le Cercle Français as well as an editor of *Horae Scholasticae*, the literary magazine. All in all, I was very pleased with my life at the school.

One of the highlights of my fourth-form year was the competition for the best play written by a student. My one-act play, called *The Valetudinarian*, was one of the plays entered by students. Reverend Johnson's wife, whose father had produced *Oklahoma*, agreed to direct it. It had a rather complicated plot enlivened with what I thought were some witty lines. Of course, I played one of the leads. Alexander Fortescue, the hero of *The Valetudinarian*, and his wife, Marsha, controlled the lives of several friends who had to come to live in apartments in their mansion on Fifth Avenue. As the curtain rose, Fortescue, played by my friend Benjie Nelson, was sitting center stage in an imposing, almost regal armchair while his wife, played by me, arranged flowers in a vase just as my mother did. Marsha's sister was married to Toby, a doctor who was an alcoholic. I gave her a number of lines including: "You can lead a horse to water, but if it's water you can't make him drink." In the script I had someone say quite rightly to Marsha, "You bitch!" but the director, Mrs. Johnson, told me that I couldn't have that line in the play because the rector would disapprove of a swear word. So to my great disappointment, I had to change the line to "You witch!"

Marsha Fortescue was plotting to get rid of all the guests in the house. Her sister, who had lived in Paris as a portrait painter, was once given a commission to paint someone's portrait. Instead, she painted a portrait of her lover, who later became her husband, which I considered a very snappy element of the plot. Marsha managed to persuade Mr. Fortescue to get rid of the tenants but not before he had a heart attack while sitting onstage in his chair. His brother-in-law Toby managed to sober up enough to save him. That element of the plot came from my father, who by that time had had two heart attacks. Once they were rid of all the tenants, Marsha spoke the last line of the play. "We must be very *happy*." Mrs. Johnson said, "No, no, no. The line is, 'We *must* be very happy.'" I was pleased that she was directing with such concern for detail.

I was proud and honored that several members of the fifth form who also lived in Foster House chose to be in my play. Incidentally, Benjie was soon elected president of the school. I was thrilled that not only was he in the same house as I but that a friend of mine was president of the school. My only competition was by a fifth former, John Parsons, who had written a serious play that I thought was rather ponderous and pretentious. After the judges declared *The Valetudinarian* the winner of the competition, John Parsons came back stage, I thought to congratulate me. He did so, but then said, "I see that you're going to have a great future in soap operas." *The Valetudinarian* was printed in the 1954 spring issue of *Horae Scholasticae*. I gave it to my mother to read, and when she had finished it, she looked at me over her glasses and said, "This play is written by a misogynist. You are just like Somerset Maugham."

For some time I had been trying to persuade my father to allow me to spend a summer in France. Finally, he agreed, albeit reluctantly. As Secretary of the Air Force, he knew General Pierre-Marie Gallois, assistant to President de Gaulle in La Force de Frappe, the French nuclear defense program. Several years later, General Gallois came to speak on the *force de frappe* at Harvard when I was there. The general arranged for me to stay with Nicole Bouchet de Fareins, who took paying guests at Le Bois Normand, her house in Honfleur, on Normandy's Côte de Grace.

When I arrived in Paris, I stayed for a few days with my parents' friends General Norstadt and his wife, Isabelle. At the time, General Norstadt was serving as commander in chief of USAFE as well as commanding general of the Allied Air Forces in Central Europe, under the Supreme Headquarters of the Allied Powers in Europe. When Isabelle Norstadt drove me to Honfleur, we were followed by another car driven by an officer with the luggage.

Le Bois Normand was a large house with a thatched roof. French doors opened from the salon onto a terrace surrounded by banks of hydrangeas with a view across the bay to Le Havre. It was a lovely property with beautiful gardens around the house, and across a meadow there were deep mysterious woods where we would walk. Another walk led along sandy lanes bordered by hedges. Nicole and I soon became fast friends. I also liked her sister, Françette, who often came to stay with her daughter, Christine, who was a bit younger than I. After Françette's husband was put in a French concentration camp, she did her best to get him released, but to no avail, and he finally died. General Gallois's wife, Françoise, and her two sons, one my age and the other eleven, were also paying guests.

The most interesting visitor that summer was A. J. Ayer, who had been Nicole's lover. Freddy, as everyone called him, was a well-known philosopher of the logical positivism school of Bertrand Russell. Every day Freddy would write at a card table in the garden, and in the evening, if he had managed to complete fifty words, he would reward himself with a scotch. He was friendly and elegant and wore beautiful casual clothes and often a sweater in the evenings. Occasionally, he might do a soft shoe tap dance on the stone dining room table. The following winter back at St. Paul's, I went to see the math teacher, Mr. Slesnik, who was a keen logician. As I was looking through the books in his

library, I spotted A. J. Ayer's book *Language, Truth and Action.* "Oh, you
have Freddy's book!" I said. Mr. Slesnik said, "You would know A. J.
Ayer and call him Freddy." Sometime later Freddy was knighted.

Nicole's eldest daughters, Janie and Claire, were grown up and away,
but Marie-Ange, who was seventeen and studying in England that
year, was home for the summer. When Janie and Claire were young,
many boys, some from noble families, would come to spend the day
or evenings playing billiards or ping-pong. It seems the young Duc
de Noailles was good at sardines and hide-and-seek. One afternoon
the French ambassadress to India, Ratton de Gatine, came to tea and
gave a fascinating account of her life in India. The large salon with its
high ceilings was sparsely furnished with Louis XV chairs. Above the
salon was a balcony with a very comfortable sofa where Nicole and I
would often sit and talk. She told me about her life ten years before
when she was a heroine of La Résistance. Her husband had been an
airplane manufacturer, but after he collaborated with the Germans,
she divorced him.

Nicole had various jobs during the war, including that of a courier.
Because there was no petrol, she rode her bicycle long distances along
the coast taking messages to Caen and other towns in Normandy.
Sometimes she would stay overnight with fellow French Resistance
fighters, and once she spent the night in a farmhouse with a group of
communists. Although it worried her to be a woman alone with very
tough men, she was essentially fearless. Even though German officers
were billeted in her house, she continued her work in the Resistance.
Once when several Canadian paratroopers landed on her property,
Nicole hid them in the woods until she could slip them into the house
and hide them in the attic. At the same time, she was raising her three
daughters. She told me that one day she was sitting outside in front of
the house shelling peas when the postman came by on his bicycle to
deliver a telegram. When she opened the envelope, she read that her
lover had been killed in the war. She folded the telegram and put it in
her pocket and said to herself, "I have to get the children their lunch.
I'll think of that later." When the mayor of Honfleur asked Nicole if

he could cut down a tree in her forest to use as a flagpole to fly the French tricolor in defiance of the Germans, she said no because Corot had painted the forest and it was under national protection. The mayor said that he would return. When he did, Nicole finally gave permission to cut down a tree for their very tall and impressive flagpole.

Each September, Nicole would return to Paris for the winter. From her apartment at 5 Rue de la Manutention across from the Musée Guimet in the sixteenth arrondissement, she continued her work in the Resistance. Nicole and a friend would often go to a nightclub run by Russian exiles. Chez Novi, as it was called, was popular with German officers who came to drink and dance and meet French women. Nicole and her friend would take turns dancing with an officer while the other would rummage through his coat pockets to steal his wallet, hoping to find papers that might give an indication of the German troop movements.

Joining the Resistance took courage and quick thinking. A friend of Nicole's, Pierre d'Harcourt, (later he became the Duc d'Harcourt) was on a mission when he was spotted by the Gestapo. Trying to escape down the stairs of the metro, he was shot in the leg. He was taken to a hospital where he memorized the layout before jumping out a window only to hurt his other leg. However, he managed to escape but was finally caught and arrested and sent to a concentration camp in Germany. Amazingly, when the d'Harcourt family begged Pope Pius XII to intervene on his behalf, he was freed from the camp.

Toward the end of the war Nicole noticed that the Germans were working in the chalk mines along the coast. Suspecting that they were up to something besides mining chalk, she went to investigate and discovered that there were small-gauge railroad tracks leading into the caves. She reported this to fellow members of the Resistance, who passed the information to the Allies who were planning the Normandy landings. It turned out that the tracks were for moving big guns in and out of the caves. Because the Allied forces were alerted to these gun emplacements, they took out the cannons before storming the beaches, no doubt saving the lives of countless American soldiers.

After the war, the government of de Gaulle awarded medals to Nicole for her work in the Resistance. Every year she attended the anniversary gathering of Resistance members, not because she wanted to go but because so many members of the Resistance were communists, and she wanted to show that non-communists fighting for the cause had also won medals. I once said to Nicole that I would probably have collaborated. She replied, "*Non, il y avait un contagion de courage.*" (No, courage was contagious.) Because I spoke nothing but French that summer, my French became very good.

Freddy Allen, with whom I had become friends at St. Paul's, although he was a year behind me, invited me to lunch at his parents' house not far from Honfleur. Mrs. Allen picked me up in a wonderful Quinze Cheveaux car and drove me to the family's lovely chateau in Quetteville. As I walked into the house, I came upon Freddy's sister, Sabette, and young Charlie de Mortemart, the future duke, playing billiards in the foyer. I was amused to be introduced to Charlie because his ancestors were some of the people I had enjoyed reading about in French history. The Mortemarts had a certain kind of wit that was characteristic of their family. Louis XIV's mistress, Madame de Montespan, was a Mortemart. Freddy's father, Julian Allen, was the head of Morgan Guaranty Trust in Paris. He'd been an ambulance driver at the age of sixteen in World War I, and he was greatly admired by the French for his bravery. I had a wonderful day seeing Freddy and meeting his sister, parents, and friends.

At the end of the summer my mother telephoned Nicole to say that my father had had to resign as Secretary of the Air Force. He was accused of writing a letter on air force stationery to solicit air force business from Mulligan and Company, a management consulting firm of which he owned a substantial percent. According to my brother, John, when my father's secretary, Stephany Saltys, brought him the letter to sign, he did so, never thinking there was anything wrong.

The background to this story is rather murky. It seems that Joseph Kennedy, the former ambassador to Great Britain, disliked my father for some reason. When his son Bobby became the counsel to the Senate ethics committee, Kennedy told Bobby to "get Harold Talbott." When Bobby found my father's letter, which was to be presented to the ethics committee, he gave it to his friend Charlie Bartlett, who published it on the front page of the *Chattanooga Times*. The following day the *New York Times* ran the story on their front page, and immediately all the major European papers picked it up. Perhaps the animosity between my parents and Joe Kennedy began at an event at Madison Square Garden where my parents were sitting in the box in front of Kennedy. When he said something disagreeable about someone my mother liked, she turned around and said to him, "Oh Joe, you should be in jail, you know."

When my father appeared before the Senate committee, he was exonerated of any misdemeanor. However, President Eisenhower, who had said at the outset of his administration that he would not tolerate any scandal or even the semblance of one, insisted that my father resign. To the reporters who were constantly hounding my father outside his house in Georgetown asking him, "Where are you going and what will you do now?" my father replied, "I'm going back to New York to make some dough."

My father was very courageous about the situation. He said to me once, "It's a dog-eat-dog world in Washington, and they were smarter than I was." He had loved his job and loved the air force. He did a great deal to cut waste and overspending and managed to reduce the cost of supplies. He also obtained new housing for servicemen and officers. I'm told that the air force really appreciated him and the job he did, and the servicemen felt that he had their interests at heart. And my mother was very popular with the air force wives, whom she often had to the house.

Returning to New York and losing Washington was a catastrophe beyond anything for my mother. As a political hostess while my father was in office, she was in her element giving beautifully arranged parties for diplomats and officials and the Washington elite, all of which she had to leave behind when she returned to New York. She used to say that she found her friends in New York so frivolous and their lives so meaningless because they had never done anything to serve their country.

CHAPTER FIVE

St. Paul's 1957–1958

Bliss was it in that dawn to be alive,
But to be young was very heaven!
—Wordsworth

In the fifth form everything seemed to be going my way at school. Except, that is, for my bête noire, geometry. In one marking period when all my grades were over ninety, I got a fourteen in geometry. Mr. Slesnik, my geometry teacher, called it "a courtesy grade." That year I lived in Conover House with George Hobson, my old friend from Buckley, and Ian Baldwin, an athlete and a scholar who became a close friend. I think that I may have become a little conceited because I was having such a good time and doing so well. After George's stepfather took George, Ian, and me out to lunch at the Casserole, he told George that I was arrogant and said, "Pride goeth before a fall." A bit later on, his prophecy came all too true.

My fifth-form English teacher, Mr. Montgomery, was an extraordinarily good teacher who gave us many wonderful books to read, including E. M. Forster's *A Passage to India*. He assigned us an essay on the topic "the limits of difference." Our efforts were to be judged by someone outside the school, and the winner would receive the Williamson Prize. It could be any kind of writing: narrative, expository prose, fiction, or poetry. I chose to write the following sonnet, which won the prize and was published in *Horae Scholasticae*. I was terribly pleased with myself.

High up on golgothas of woven steel,
Vicariously they toil, and know not why.
Sharp nails called Duty pin them, palm and heel,
To little wooden desks until they die.

Below, the joyous wanderer plays his part,
Who hates those little men and shirks the fray.
He lives for beauty and his useless art,
And spurns the cruel nails, which stud the way.
The debt he owes those little men remains,
And yet he wends his careless way alone.
And shall his debt, the debt which he disdains,
Repay those little men, and him atone?
Or does the love of Beauty supersede
The toil of those who for the wanderer bleed?

A frequent visitor to our room was Freddy Allen. Our friendship had grown stronger over the summer after I visited him in Normandy. Freddy's family, who had lived in Paris for several generations, seemed to have stepped out of a novel by Henry James, although Freddy himself was even more elegant than the hero of *The Ambassadors*. He spoke flawless French and had dual citizenship, both French and American, when the practice was not as common as it is today. He had two middle names as well as a last name—Frederick Harding Stevens Allen—evidence that his roots were in prominent old New York families. But really, he was French. Although he was small, he was very fast and brilliant at soccer, which he had played at Le Rosey, in Switzerland.

Freddy would often come to our room for tea, when we would listen to recordings of Baroque music. Freddy believed that good music ended with the seventeenth century. It was very daring for him to agree that Mozart was the equal of such composers as Bach, Corelli, and Vivaldi. Freddy would sometimes spend part of his holidays with my family in New York, while I would visit him at Bolton Priory, his family's house in Pelham Manor outside the city. It was an old, dilapidated, and very comfortable house with battlements in quaint imitation of a castle. We would sit in front of the huge fireplace drinking sherry and talking late into the night. The Allens served extraordinary French food. Nanan, Freddy's childhood governess, was part of the household, and there was also a butler and chauffeur. His mother spent more of her time in Paris than in America. Occasionally Mr. Allen, who was head of Morgan & Cie in Paris, would be there. Also living in the house was Freddy's uncle, for whom Freddy was named. He was a homosexual, and Freddy often made fun of him. The Allens also had a farm in Vermont. Freddy said that he was determined to make enough money to keep the farmhouse in Vermont, Bolton Priory in New York, and the house in Paris. I did not share what I thought was an extraordinarily materialistic ambition. I was much too impractical to have such ideas.

My classmate, Bill Ruger, introduced me to Max Beerbohm's comic novel *Zuleika Dobson* about life at Oxford in the Edwardian era. One winter day Bill and I went to a Friday afternoon concert of the Boston Symphony featuring Eugene Istomin performing Beethoven's Piano Concerto No. 5. We came out of Symphony Hall to find the cars parked along the street buried in snow. It was beautiful walking in the silent, empty streets, especially with the thrilling prospect of a night away from school. Bill guided us to the Ritz, but it was full, so we walked to the Copley Plaza, where we got a room. From room service Bill ordered a brandy for himself and a martini for me. I hid in the bathroom so the waiter wouldn't see me, as I looked too young to drink. Then we went down to dinner. Bill sent a telegram to the school saying that the blizzard made it impossible to return that night but that we would get back the next day, "*Deo volente.*" He signed it William Batterman Ruger. When the rector got the telegram, he said that nobody but Ruger, known for his elegant wit, could have sent it.

One day, Ian's younger brother, Michael Baldwin, who was in the fourth form and who would become one of my dearest friends, came to see him at our room at Conover House. I wasn't there, but Michael looked in my desk drawer and found my checkbook, which had a balance of five thousand dollars. It was typical of Michael to find out exactly how much money everyone had. The reason I had so much money was that my father had been required by law to divest himself of his stocks, put them in a blind trust, and stop doing business while he was in office. But he gave stock tips to some of his friends, including Uncle Charlie Cushing, who further enriched himself because of my father's tips. So

Uncle Charlie had given my brother and me five thousand each, and we were allowed to put the money in our checkbooks and spend it.

Graduation was held on the lawn in front of the chapel of St. Peter and Paul. Parents and friends who came to celebrate were seated with the students in front of the stage, where the rector stood to award prizes. I was very happy to win the Dickey Prize for French—I was given leather-bound volumes of Molière and Racine—as well as the Malbone Prize for French, which I shared with John Parsons. The judge said that my French was the best but that John's analysis of the plot of the book *La Condition Humaine* by Andre Malraux was the better of the two. We both received leather-bound volumes of *Les Fables de la Fontaine*.

Before the summer break, my housemaster, Ronald Clark, who was head of the mathematics department, called me to his room and announced that because I had failed geometry I would not be allowed to enter the sixth form unless I went to a tutoring school during the summer. He gave me the option of either taking the final exam at the tutoring school or else arriving the day before the beginning of school in September and taking the exam then.

That summer my father was in New York working hard to make money, having not being allowed to do business while serving as Secretary of the Air Force. My parents had been living on the money he'd made before taking office. Now that he had resigned, he could resume his businesses. Late one afternoon while Ian and I were sitting in the upstairs living room of our apartment, my father strode into the room after work. Both of us rose, as one did out of respect when an adult entered the room. Afterward, Ian said that I had leaped to my feet as if charged by an electric force. He said that he had never felt anything like my sense of terror in my father's presence.

At the New York Tutoring School, I studied with a Mr. Szabo, a Hungarian and a gentle and cheerful teacher who made it possible for me to pass the tests he gave me. Nonetheless, I realized that I would never be able to pass the required exam that summer and told Mr. Szabo that I would take the test at St. Paul's before the beginning of school. In order to get back to school a day early to take the exam, Bill Ruger agreed to drive me up in his antique fire engine, which he was allowed to keep at the school for his sixth-form year. His father owned the Ruger Firearms Company—his motto was AAA, or Arm Another Arab—and collected antique cars.

Though I had managed to arrive in time, I did not take the makeup exam as I was supposed to. Because I had so looked forward to being in the sixth form—I was now the head of all the clubs I'd been in and had so many friends among the boys in my form—I recklessly decided to pretend that I had already taken the exam at the tutoring school. Of course, I knew when it was discovered that I had not taken the test and therefore had not passed geometry, I would probably be expelled. But at the time it seemed worth the risk. Occasionally Mr. Mecham, the vice rector who was also in the mathematics department, would question me suspiciously about the exam, but I continued to lie and say that I had taken the test at the tutoring school. I had expected the truth to come out in a matter of days, but in fact nothing was said, and I remained in a state of anxiety from the beginning of term until almost Thanksgiving. The issue was resolved only after Mr. Szabo, my New York tutor, who had been in Hungary and hard to reach, finally wrote to say that he "remembered tutoring Harold Talbott. He was a nice boy, but he never took the exam."

The rector, Dr. Matthew Madison Warren, soon summoned me to his office, where he made me wait in a state of great anxiety while continuing to work at his desk. After what seemed an interminable length of time, my parents arrived, having flown up in my father's plane. They swept into the rector's office, my mother wearing a mink coat over a beautifully tailored suit and pearls. After my parents were seated, the rector told them that I had lied about the mathematics exam. "Your son is a demon disrupting the peace of my school," he said. Then he looked at me and announced in his thick southern accent, "Harold Talbott, I expel you from St. Paul's School." When my father asked the rector if he could speak to him in private, the rector sent my mother and me out of the room. I felt terribly sorry for my mother, who was almost in tears. Most of all I was mortified. Weeks later my father told me that he had tried to bribe Dr. Warren, but the rector had refused. I thought to myself, "Not enough money."

After packing my bags, I drove to Concord Airport with my parents. The first thing I did was buy a pack of cigarettes from the cigarette machine to officially start celebrating my freedom. It was something of a relief to have been found out. Throughout the fall term, I had felt like Raskolnikov being hounded by the detective inspector and waiting in limbo to be discovered. It had been a nightmare.

When we arrived at the apartment, we were met by Nanny, who was very sad. She never reprimanded me, but I could see that it disturbed her that I had brought this trouble upon myself. She was a very moral Scottish Presbyterian and felt that I had failed the family and her. The servants were all very kind to me, and no one mentioned the reason I had been sent home. They were so discreet, and I appreciated that very much.

That evening at the dining room table, I found a telegram waiting for me on my plate. It was from Bill Ruger and it read, "Your Grace, last night two black owls perched upon the battlements of Castle Tavvel Tacton," a quotation from *Zuleika Dobson*. For the family of the Duke of Dorset, a character in the novel, this was an omen of the duke's impending death. I was supposed to telegraph back the duke's reply, "Prepare the vault." But I wasn't in the mood for writing witty telegrams.

Some years later my former English teacher Mr. Montgomery told me that after I had been expelled, there was a fractious faculty meeting in which a number of the masters said that the whole matter had been mishandled; Mr. Clark, head of the math department, should never have threatened me with expulsion, and I could have been tutored in geometry throughout my whole sixth-form year, which would have given me a good chance to pass the exam. They said that the school had lost their most exceptional student. You can imagine how wonderful Mr. Montgomery's words made me feel. Though I did not hear of this meeting until after I had graduated, in March the rector telephoned to tell me that I would be allowed to return to St. Paul's in September, providing I take the geometry exam again. So it was back once more to the New York Tutoring School.

At the same time my father gave me a job as receptionist at his office and would sometimes take me to lunch at the nearby Le Chambord. I find it interesting that I was not the slightest bit ill at ease with him at this time. One day he took me to the Cloud Room at the top of the Chrysler Building, where he had his office. He was president of the club, and he talked about some of his far-flung investments, such as tin in Bolivia. Then he pushed back from the table and said, "Jesus, I know a lot!"

After he had to resign as Secretary of the Air Force, my father suffered two heart attacks in just a matter of months. Nonetheless, he kept working ferociously. One night in March 1957, he came home from the office with his secretary, Stephanie Saltys, to finish something they were working on before he left for Florida the following morning. They set up a card table in the downstairs sitting room where they worked together on a deal to run an overland pipeline from Texas to the St. Lawrence Seaway that would obviate the need to transport oil to the Northeast by sea. Aristotle Onassis, who owned many oil tankers, managed with the help of his fellow ship owners to obstruct the deal. As a result, my father, who owned property in Texas, was able to sell the land. My mother was in Palm Beach staying with her friend Melissa Bingham, and John was at Deerfield, so apart from the servants it was just me, Nanny, and my father at the apartment.

Shortly after Stephanie left, my father stood under the sitting-room door with his arms stretched over his head, grasping the lintel. He had turned absolutely gray. He told me to call Dr. Levi and ask him to come over at once. After Dr. Levi examined him, he said that my father had had a small stroke. He told him to go to bed and said that I should stay with my father and keep a vigil. So we stayed together that night.

The following morning my father was up early and left for his office before seven. When he returned at midday we had lunch, which turned out to be our last meal together. He told me that he regretted that he no longer had a company to leave to my brother and me but suggested that I become a lawyer because I was smart. "Half my money each year goes to lawyers," he said. "They make a lot of money."

"No, I'm not going to become a lawyer," I told him. "I'm going to be a writer."

"If you were going to be a writer, you would be writing now," he replied.

I said, "If that's what you think of me, let me tell you what I think of you. I don't have any respect for you or your businesses."

I have no idea where that came from. It certainly wasn't true. Perhaps it came from bitterness and cruelty. Perhaps I was paying him back in some deluded way for what he had just said to me, which happened to be absolutely true. After lunch I went into the library to read, while his valet packed his bags. As he was about to leave, he asked if I was coming to the airport to see him off. I said, "No, I'm not coming," so he said good-bye and left for the airport alone. I have always deeply regretted my anger and lack of love.

That evening, my parents played bridge after dinner in Palm Beach and then went up to bed. In the night my father had a cerebral stroke. My mother was in bed with him, and she held him in her arms. He was seventy-one. The next morning my mother called and told me that my father had died; she said that she would return to New York as soon as she could. I put the phone down, went into the nursery, and lay down on the couch and cried. All my negative thoughts about my father, my alienation from him, and my fear of him had vanished, and I could only remember the good things he'd done for me and how much he'd loved me and what a good father he had been. I regretted that I had failed to take advantage of the many times when I might have become closer to him. Unfortunately, once you lose such opportunities in life, you can never have them back no matter how much you may regret their loss. But at least in this case, my negativity was at last replaced by very strong feelings of love and appreciation.

Something strange happened right after my father died. While I was mourning his death in the nursery, my eye fell upon the *Apologia Pro*

Vita Sua by John Henry Cardinal Newman, which was sitting on a pile of books waiting to be read. I was forcibly struck by the book and had the sense that my destiny included Catholicism. I had been attracted to the Catholic Church ever since attending Mass at my godmother Loretta Howard's Hawkeye Ranch when I was very young. I loved the Latin of the Mass as well as its splendor and ceremony. I soon became captivated with the book and many of the aspects of the Catholic teachings, especially the view that the apostolic succession in the church had only belonged to the Roman Catholic Church. It had been broken by the Reformation, so the sacraments were not valid in the Protestant churches. In the nineteenth century, when the *Apologia* was written, this was the view of the church. It has since changed.

The *Apologia* had a great impact on my life and prompted me to study Catholic doctrine and dogma. In the late fifties, it inspired me to write a letter to the prior of Portsmouth Priory, Dom Aelred Graham, who was an outstanding Thomist theologian. We later became fast friends, and it was he who facilitated my study of Buddhism. He also introduced me to Elsie Mitchell, who would become the patroness of the Buddhayana Foundation, which Michael Baldwin and I founded in 1980.

Soon after my father died, I began wandering the streets late at night, looking for the homosexual bars that I was certain must exist. One morning while shopping at Brentano's, I noticed a young salesman who was obviously homosexual. I went up to him and said, "Pretend you're selling me a book." His name was Charlie, and I invited him to have dinner with me that night at L'Aiglon. After dinner Charlie took me to Regent's Row, a gay bar that required coats and ties, unlike some of the other bars I found later. As it turned out Regent's Row belonged to Jimmy Donahue, the son of my mother's friend Jessie Donahue. He had a very young lover named Lucky, who was sitting on a table swinging his legs. Lucky was one of the most beautiful boys I had ever seen. Sadly, his luck ran out. He became a drug addict, and one weekend in Palm Beach, he died of an overdose that might have been administered by Donahue—an older man who was part of international society. At any rate, rumor had it that Lucky was murdered.

I soon heard of another bar, not far from our apartment, called The 316, where you could dress casually. One night, the moment I walked in, I saw a black boy who smiled at me and before long invited me to his apartment in the East 50s. He was so gentle and loving, it was a revelation to me, the culmination of years of longing. Later in the taxi, going home before sunrise, I repeated to myself a favorite passage from Stendhal, *Ah, c'est ça, l'amour!* Since it was my first experience of sexual love, of course my emotions were very tender, and I was enamored of the friend of the night. He worked for TWA, but when I tried to find him, it was to no avail. New York giveth and New York taketh away, leaving only the memory of nights on the town and dawn rides home with the big trucks thundering down the avenues of the city.

When Freddy Allen was home for spring vacation, I went to lunch at the Allens at Bolton Priory. Monsieur Jacq, who tutored Freddy in French literature, was there and said to me, "Something is different." I knew he had realized that I had experienced homosexual love. For my next foray into New York's world of homosexual romance, I fell in love with Jonathan Watts, a dancer in Balanchine's corps de ballet who was, like me, in his late teens. I sent him some roses with a note asking him to have lunch with me—again at L'Aiglon. When Jonathan arrived, he laughed and said, "Oh, you're so young! I thought you'd be much older."

Talking to Jonathan about the company and Balanchine's ballets, I learned a lot about the dance. He invited me down to the Village, where he lived with a man who was a *maître de corps de ballet.* After the three of us listened to *Swan Lake*, they took me out for a steak dinner. I became very fond of Jonathan and soon invited him to lunch with my mother and Nanny. During lunch he told us that he had a younger sister who was disabled and whom he was helping to support. Jonathan became, as it were, three people for me: a real person with human sufferings, a wonderful dancer whom I would see in performances, and the person for whom I had sexual longings. We became very affectionate with each other, but we never became lovers; I was too young for him.

One day Ian Baldwin, who was about to begin his sophomore year at Columbia, came to stay. After dinner I said to him, "Tonight I am going to go to a bar where Puerto Rican boys dance together. It's called The 415. Would you like to go with me?" And he very kindly said, "Sure." So we went to the bar and danced together for hours. The Puerto Rican boys were all beautiful, and I thought they'd be jealous of me dancing with Ian, who was also very beautiful, but nobody looked at us at all. It was as if we were from two different worlds and never the twain should meet. I was very grateful to Ian for being so broad-minded and understanding.

As it happened my father was equally broad-minded and tolerant. Our trustee Clayton Irwin was gay. In the 1940s he had gone to a gay bar on Staten Island when it was raided by the police. Clayton was taken to jail, where he used his one phone call to call my father, who got him out. In the car on the way uptown, my father said, "Jesus, Clayton, you've got to be careful." But he never criticized or admonished him. Later, when he was Secretary of the Air Force, an airman was outed. Although some in the organization demanded that he be dismissed, my father refused and said that his military service had nothing to do with his sexuality. Another time my father met Billy Baldwin, the hugely popular designer, in an elevator. My father asked him what he did, and when Billy said that he was an interior decorator, my father said, "That's all right, just so long as you're the best."

Nonetheless, it was only after my father had died that I openly declared my homosexuality. Perhaps I was subconsciously afraid of what he might think, but I think it was more out of concern for family respectability. My brother's godmother, Dumpy von Lichtenstein, helped me find the courage when, the day after my father's death, she asked me to visit her at the Waldorf Towers, where she was staying. I went over before lunch and found her making up her face at her dressing table. She looked at me in the mirror and said, "Nobody cares what you do so long as you don't talk about it."

At St. Paul's all my friends were straight, and they accepted me with no reservations. At the school you were allowed to be different if you somehow fit in. I was a very good student, and I could be funny. Moreover, they thought that I was a sophisticated New Yorker and as such somewhat glamorous. More importantly, I stood up to the masters on behalf of the individual rights of the students in contrast to the establishment of the school. At one point we were asked to sign a paper agreeing to report any student whom we found cheating or otherwise flouting the rules. Even Monsieur Jacq told me to sign the paper and not make trouble. Although it might mean being expelled, I refused to sign, saying that the school did not have the right to deprive any of us of freedom of speech. My father liked my refusal so much that he told Charles Lindberg wasn't it wonderful that I had done this at St. Paul's. Nothing came of my rebellion.

Freddy Allen, however, was less broad-minded and tolerant. I had finally managed to pass the geometry exam and so was going back to St. Paul's in September. Freddy came to stay the day before we returned. My mother took us to Stratford to see Shakespeare's *Measure for Measure*, and later, as we had done so many times in the past, we sat talking by the fire at 450 East 52 Street long into the night. That summer Freddy's stepbrother, Billy Pell, had died after a long illness. Freddy had been very upset and written me many letters telling me that he was reading *Jude the Obscure*, which I thought was a poor idea because it was such a morbid story. He was also taking forty-kilometer bicycle rides throughout the country to take his mind off his grief.

Because Freddy had written me so frankly about what had been happening to him, I decided to tell him that in the course of the summer I had become active as a homosexual and had gone to bars to pick up boys for the night. Although I had known that I was gay for years, it was the first time I had told a friend—anyone for that matter—that I preferred my own sex. Freddy was silent for a long time. Then he said that he was going to spend the night with his cousins. When I said, "But you were going to stay here as you always do the night before we take the train to St. Paul's." He insisted on staying with his cousins. After Freddy left I was very confused and felt that I had shocked him and that my confession had been a serious blunder. In the morning after boarding the train, I walked through the cars looking for Freddy. I found him sitting with some friends and asked him if he wasn't going to sit with me as he always did. "No," he replied, "I'm sitting here." I was devastated and have always regretted taking Freddy into my confidence and rupturing our friendship. I have only spoken to Freddy one other time in all the past sixty years. But recently he sent me an e-mail, which made me very happy. Back in the 1950s no one would have dreamed of admitting that he was homosexual. For someone to learn that one of his closest friends was gay must have been very difficult, especially for Freddy, who had been brought up in such an old-fashioned way.

The evening after we arrived at St. Paul's, Freddy was in such a catatonic state that Monsieur Jacq took him to his room and asked him what was wrong. Freddy told him the entire story. Monsieur Jacq asked the rector for advice, and Freddy was taken to the infirmary. A few days later I went to see Freddy; I brought him his record player and some of his favorite records. He didn't speak but seemed in a trance. Soon after, he left St. Paul's for his parents' house in Vermont, and a bit later he went back to France and their house in Neuilly. Come the snows, he went skiing in Switzerland. The following year he returned to St. Paul's, by which time I had gone to Harvard.

At the start of my senior year, the rector had me see him in his office once a week for what I suppose was moral instruction. In fact, we had a wonderful time, talking mostly about the philosophy of Kierkegaard, the Christian existentialist. As I discovered somewhat to my surprise, Dr. Matthew Madison Warren was a highly educated and very sophisticated man.

Early in the sixth form I became fast friends with Michael Baldwin and Christopher Clark, who were also in the sixth form. I was always grateful to Ian, Michael's brother, for asking his younger brother to befriend me my sixth-form year because I might be lonely and not know anybody. They would invite me to their room in the third-form house, where they were supervisors, and we would have marvelous talks and laughter. Chris was a hockey and tennis star; Michael was a great mimic with a fabulous sense of humor. Somehow, I fit in as a third friend. It didn't matter that I flaunted my campiness as a homosexual. They found my imitations of Barbara Stanwyck or Joan Crawford hilarious.

It was such a tonic for me to make these friends laugh and to be able to be camp without any censure. Sixty years later we are all still very close friends. Michael and Chris talk on the phone several times a week, and Chris calls me on Sundays. When he and his wife, Bunny, come to stay with Michael and his wife, Margie, in Marion, it's as if we were back in the sixth form.

During this year I resumed my membership in a number of clubs, including the Debating Society. I was also the editor in chief of *Horae Scholasticae*, as well as head of the French club Le Cercle Français, supervised by Monsieur Jacq. I was in my element and had a splendid year; at graduation I won a number of prizes. When you entered work in a competition you took a nom de plume so that the submission was anonymous. At commencement the rector would announce the winner's nom de plume from the stage in front of all the students, parents, and friends. When the winner came up to receive his prize, his identity would be revealed. For one of the prizes the rector read out the name I had chosen, which was Pizzazz, the word Diana Vreeland had invented for high fashion. That got a good laugh.

CHAPTER SIX

Religious Beginnings

I first became interested in religion when I was five and my mother showed John and me photographs in *National Geographic* of Tibet before the Chinese invaded the country and everything changed for the Tibetan people. I was so captivated, I vowed that I would go to Tibet when I grew up and study Buddhism with Tibetan lamas. A friend of my mother's, Suydam Cutting, had made two expeditions to Lhasa in the 1930s, when he met Tibetans as well as some lamas. I asked my mother if she would write a letter to Mr. Cutting for me because I wanted to follow in his footsteps. He kindly wrote me back and more or less said, "Go for it!" Later, when I read *Seven Years in Tibet* by Heinrich Harrer to my mother, we both cried at the account of the Dalai Lama's flight in 1950. Leaving Lhasa in the dead of night just ahead of the invading Chinese, he escaped over the mountains to Yatung, near the Indian border. This account only increased my fascination with the country.

Though other religions also captured my interest, I was mostly fascinated by Buddhism. Once when I was eleven or so, Nanny, John, and I were walking along Madison Avenue, and I saw a Buddha image in the window of an oriental shop. I begged Nanny to buy it for me, and she very kindly did so. In another shop I got a little black silk Japanese kimono with a red lining and embroidered with chrysanthemums; in a different shop I got incense and a handbell. On a school trip to Bermuda with some friends from Buckley, I went into an Indian store and got the owner to string 108 beads as a rosary for me.

I asked Nanny to put the Buddha on the top of a highboy in John's and my bedroom. Then I'd light incense, sit in the lotus posture (which I could do in those days, but no longer), and with my rosary recite *om mani padme hum*, the mantra of the Buddha of compassion, while looking at the Buddha on the highboy. Thus, I started my lifelong Buddhist practice, invented at the outset by myself.

At about this time my friend Arthur MacArthur lent me a book called *Magic and Mystery in Tibet* by Alexandra David-Neel. After I read it I was even more fascinated by the civilization of Tibet and especially with Buddhism. Sometimes people said that David-Neel's claims about the mysterious powers of lamas were preposterous. But later I myself witnessed what lamas did with their siddhis, powers they attained through many years of meditation, sometimes in isolated caves.

In the fifth form I began reading Alan Watts on Hinduism, Buddhism, and Taoism. I also did a retreat at the Monastery of the Society of St. John the Evangelist, built by Isabella Stuart Gardner. It was the first time I had heard a Gregorian chant, although it was in English and not in Latin, formerly the mantric language of the church that has always made such an impression on me. Here also I heard the monks chanting the hours of the monastic day: matins or lauds, prime, terce, sext, none, vespers, and the final absolutely beautiful evening-hour compline devoted to the Blessed Virgin Mary. My first introduction to the monastery was through Father Walter P. Morse, a monk who belonged to the society and who had become a missionary. He had a clinic in an abandoned temple in Kalimpong, a town in the Himalayas that would later become very important to me because my chief guru, Dudjom Rinpoche, lived there.

The summer of 1957, before I returned to St. Paul's in the sixth form, my mother got me a job, through her friend Roy Howard of Scripps Howard, at the *Commercial Appeal* newspaper in Memphis, Tennessee. During those few months in Memphis, I stayed at the YMCA, where my life was transformed from a very worldly and sensual New York person to a solitary wanderer working at a modest job in a city where I knew nobody. I entered into a mood of religious zeal that was quite different from my lustful quests in New York. Every day on my knees, I recited many Psalms for the repose of my father's soul. I did a lot of reading in Dr. Daisetz T. Suzuki's books on Zen. I also read the *The Story of a Soul*, the autobiography of St. Therese de Lisieux, first published in 1898. She was named by the church the Little Flower, and her teaching of a method of sanctity was and still is called the Little Way. She is considered a great teacher of the church in mystical theology. She was a deeply humble person who taught that it was not possible for everyone all the time to do great acts of holiness, and instead if you used the little events of your life to aspire to holiness, that was an effective way of living. I had gone to visit her basilica in Lisieux with my friend Nicole, so she already meant something to me before I read her autobiography.

I also read some of Thomas Merton's works, including *The Seven Storey Mountain* and *The Sign of Jonas*. Through him I fell in love with the monastic life. I also read books by Aelred Graham including *The Love of God* and *The Christ of Catholicism*, which were much more difficult theologically because he was a Thomist theologian. Every morning I went to Mass at a wonderful church. I can still remember the blazing summer heat, the effigies of the saints, and the ceiling fans.

At the end of my job and close to the end of summer, I got on a bus in Memphis and went to Bardstown, Kentucky, to the Abbey of Gethsemani, where Thomas Merton lived as a monk. I asked to see him and have an interview with him. First the abbot, Dom James Fox, received me and told me that I would be permitted to meet with Thomas Merton. I asked him if I could enter the monastery as a postulant, and he said, "No. Go to Harvard first and then come back and speak to me, and I'll allow you to enter the monastery." However, as it turned out, Father Merton could not see me after all.

That winter during my sixth-form year at Saint Paul's, I wrote Alan Watts to say how much I admired his writing. I invited him to have lunch with me when next he came to New York (he lived in Sausalito, California), and he wrote back that he would soon be in town to give lectures with Susanne Langer, a lady who taught yoga, and would be delighted to meet me for lunch. During my spring vacation, we had lunch together at L'Aiglon Restaurant.

In his memoir *In My Own Way*, Alan described our lunch "at one of the best French Restaurants in town."

[Harold] appeared to know the headwaiter and ordered the luncheon and the wine with the taste of an experienced gourmet. Thereafter he engaged me in a theological discussion of quite amazing profundity, in the course of which he disclosed that, after going to Harvard, he intended to become a Trappist monk. I considered that such a remarkably cultured young man was much more of a Benedictine than a Trappist, for most Benedictines I have known have an urbane and assured serenity which comes both from being the oldest order in the Church and from the preoccupations with scholarship and art as well as the spiritual life.

I found Alan completely natural and easy to talk to. I told him that I was so interested in his teachings on nonduality and especially Buddhism that I wanted to study it but that I had become a Catholic and was going to apply to enter the Cistercian Abbey of Gethsemani in Bardstown, Kentucky, where Thomas Merton was a monk. He said, "Well, if you're interested in Buddhism as a Catholic, the only Catholic I know who knows something about Buddhism is Dom Aelred Graham, the prior of Portsmouth Priory in Rhode Island. If you write him, tell him you have an introduction to him from his friend Alan Watts." So I wrote to the prior, and we made contact. I asked him to stay with me when he would next be in New York City. A couple of years later he did so, and that made an enormous difference to my life.

At St. Paul's it was the Christian religion that was an important part of my life at the school. During the winter George Hobson and I would walk together through the snow to the chapel of St. Peter and St. Paul, where Reverend Webb would give us Communion.

After graduating from St. Paul's just before leaving for Harvard, I came around the corner of 94th Street near my mother's apartment and saw a sign in front of a house reading "Ramakrishna-Vivekananda Center—Sanskrit lessons available." Swami Nikhilananda, master of the monastic order of the center, taught Sanskrit and Indian studies including the Hindu religion and the Vedanta at Columbia University and was known for his translation of the *Upanishads*. His order in India, the Ramakrishna-Vivekananda Order, was made up of scholars and practitioners of the Vedanta meditations. It was like a lightning bolt of good fortune for me that I had found Swami Nikhilananda and the Vivekananda Center right around the corner from our apartment.

Coincidentally, when Alan Watts and I had had lunch together the year before, we had talked about the Vedanta philosophy of Shankara Acharya, the Hindu master of the thirteenth century. He was the greatest commentator on the scriptures of the *Upanishads* as well as a teacher of the philosophical and religious principle of nonduality, one of the things that fascinated me about the Indian religion. Alan Watts had written a wonderful book on the nonduality of the Vedanta titled *The Supreme Identity*.

Despite my conversion to Catholicism, my main reason for want- ing to go to Harvard was the Sanskrit and Indian studies department, which included the study of Tibetan. When I was in the sixth form, Skiddy von Stade, Harvard dean of freshmen, whose family were friends of my family, came to St. Paul's to interview the boys who had applied to Harvard. He asked me what I was reading, and I replied *Secret Tibet* by Fosco Maraini. At Harvard you first took Sanskrit, and when you were able to read the *Bhagavad Gita* in Sanskrit, you were allowed to study Tibetan. In my SATs during my sixth-form year, I got 800s in French, English, and Latin, which allowed me to skip freshman year and enter Harvard as a sophomore. I decided to take sophomore standing because Sanskrit and Indian studies and the study of Tibetan were not offered to freshmen.

When I got into Harvard, I wrote the professor of Buddhism, Dr. Kenneth Chen, and asked if I could study with him. He wrote back saying that he was sorry but he would be teaching at Berkeley and referred me to Professor Masatoshi Nagatomi, who was replacing him. I wrote to Professor Nagatomi, and he said to come ahead. The Sanskrit class was a wonder. As only five of us were taking the course, it was really like a seminar. Professor Nagatomi, a Pure Land Buddhist, sat at the head of the oval table. To his right was the Reverend Matsunami, a Japanese Pure Land Buddhist priest from Hawaii. He was a little chubby, and as Michael might say, he was *tunsin,* or cute. Both men had shy and embarrassed Japanese laughs.

Although compassionate, the professor was a very strong and emphatic person. I'd been told that when he was a young man in Japan, he had come under suspicion by the military dictatorship and been taken into custody by the much-feared Kempetai secret police and questioned. Across the table from Reverend Matsunami sat Steven Proskauer, a brilliant freshman; to my left was Professor Whatmough, who was famous in the field of linguistics. On my right was Wendy Doniger, who would become the University of Chicago's head of the religious department specializing in Sanskrit, Indian studies, and Hinduism. These two geniuses on either side of me would amuse themselves by comparing Greek paradigms to the conjugations of Sanskrit verbs. They were inspired in this activity by the great grammarian Panini, who had used Sanskrit, which had only regular verbs, to create a lot of irregular verbs, thereby making the language even more wildly sophisticated. So their paradigms showing the derivation of many Indo-European words from Sanskrit gave them a lot of pleasure.

Meanwhile, I was struggling with yesterday's homework, elementary sentences such as "The king dismounted and the rishi poured ghee on the fire." We used Lanman's *Sanskrit Reader* as our textbook for grammar and vocabulary. One had to learn two principles of grammar in Sanskrit that were the means of elision of words. Because words in the Sanskrit script are all tied together by a bar above them, without a gap between them, you had to separate them in your mind. These two principles of elision are called *guna* and *vritti,* and I had a lot of trouble with them. Sanskrit was a lark for Professor Whatmough and Wendy Doniger, but for me it was a steep mountain of a challenge. My main mistake was expecting that Harvard and the study of Sanskrit would be the academic romp that my last year at St. Paul's had been when, for example, my English teacher, Mr. Burnham, gave me a 98 for the last term's marking period, telling me that he just couldn't give me a 100. And then there had been those three 800s on the SATs.

Michael and Chris were more diligent students than I was, but all three of us felt the pressure of Harvard. I had few opportunities to see old friends or meet new ones because everyone was working so hard. Besides Sanskrit, my other favorite course my first year was Drama Through the Ages, given by Professor William Alfred, my adviser, who was the most marvelous teacher imaginable. He himself was a playwright. His course began with the *Oresteia* of Aescalus. I was fascinated to discover that the source of ancient Greek drama and comedy was derived from elements of sacred rituals. To be heard in the vast stadiums, the actors held small copper megaphones in their mouths so their voices were broadcast in an eerie way. Professor Alfred set the scene of the *Oresteia* so vividly and brought everything to life as he read and acted out the parts. He evoked the terror that is so much a part of the play yet at the same time, he could be very funny. He had such warmth and sympathy for his students and such a yearning to educate them that it was a joy to be in his class.

He had a great laugh, an embarrassed one if there was anything off color in the conversation. He was sophisticated and simple. He wore his Phi Beta Kappa key with his dark three-piece suit and gray hat. Professor Alfred's mother lived with him on Athens Street, coincidentally opposite a miniature castle built by William Randolph Hearst, as his undergraduate residence. Later it became the offices of *The Harvard Lampoon*. Across the street was the large red brick Church of St. Paul, where both Professor Alfred and I went to daily Mass. When Michael became a Catholic, we went together to St. Paul's. Michael used to imitate the soprano who sang in lieu of a choir. Of course, I followed attentively the Latin liturgy with its mantric power. Incidentally, my favorite hymn of the monastic hours of the church, sung at night at the end of compline, is "Salve Regina." I loved St. Paul's Church, especially the stained-glass windows depicting various saints, including St. Augustine. My favorite was St. Jerome with his lion in his cave sitting at a table on which are spread the folio-size pages of his Latin translation from the Hebrew of the Old Testament and the Greek of the New Testament, which he is writing.

At the same time Catholicism played an important part in my life my first year at Harvard. The only decoration in my room at Hurlbut Hall was a large crucifix over my desk. Inspired by my visit to Gethsemane, I had become a zealous Catholic and felt that owning a crucifix was the monastic thing to do. Danny Cheval, a beautiful French Israeli boy with curly black hair and a dazzling smile, lived across the hall from me. He was amazed to discover his neighbor had nothing in his room but a bookcase, a bed, and a large crucifix. Danny was a romantic who rode his motorcycle all over Cambridge, sometimes even going into Boston. He was killed on his motorcycle in the first days of school. I was inconsolable.

The Catholic chaplain, Father Porras, was a Spaniard and a member of Opus Dei. He served Mass and taught the Catholic students the doctrines and dogmas of the Catholic Church. He gave readings from a book by Father Escrivá, the founder of the order, in a small darkened chapel with only a single light trained on the book. When I bought a crucifix for the chapel like the one I had in my dorm room, Father Porras was grateful. Daniel Sargent, a prominent Bostonian with a great deal of money who became a convert to Catholicism, had bequeathed his vast house in Boston to Opus Dei. Father Porras took his Catholic students to see the house chapel with its huge ivory triptych, which had been a wedding present from Catherine of Aragon to Henry VIII. Aelred soon enlightened me about Opus Dei; he said that it was a Spanish fascist organization.

In November my beloved Catholic godmother, Loretta Howard; Agnes Dawson, my mother's maid; and Eleanor McLaren (Nanny), who consented to be present although she was Presbyterian, all gathered around the font at Saint Ignatius Loyola Church at 83rd and Park Avenue as Father O'Pray baptized me into the Roman Catholic Church. Afterward, I went to confession (that was a doozy). Loretta gave me a beautiful missal, and Agnes gave me a leather missal cover. Father O'Pray, a brilliant and sophisticated man, had given me wonderful instructions to enter the Catholic Church as well as insight into the Jesuit mind. He said that the doctrines of the Catholic Church were "the party line."

I went to Gethsemani over Thanksgiving vacation and had my confirmation in the Catholic Church and took Holy Communion at the monastery. I was staying in a room in the guesthouse near the church, when Father Merton, who was the novice master at the time, knocked on my door and came in. He said to me, "I'm always very glad to meet someone who has just come into the church because they're full of grace, and the grace overflows on me. I have only one thing to say to you, the church is a very big place. Always remember to go your own way in it."

Harvard was demanding. Michael, Chris, and I invented the word *neuro*, as in, "I'm feeling neuro about the coming test." To escape from being neuro we would take what we called a "reality break," often going to the movies either at the Brattle Theater or occasionally in Boston. Our two favorite movies were the English comedy *Carry on Nurse* and *Le Bourgeois Gentilhomme*, a 1958 French film based on Molière's five-act comedy ballet. Chris and I were convulsed with laughter watching the actor Louis Jourdan because we thought that he was just like Michael. The favorite film of the college was *Casablanca*.

Our other reality breaks included visiting Michael's grandmother, Mrs. Katherine Saltonstall Weld on the North Shore, or Chris's family in Hamilton, also on the North Shore. The seven Clark children, two adopted nieces, and Mr. and Mrs. Clark made all their friends feel welcome. From an enormous silver cocktail shaker in the form of a lighthouse, Mr. Clark would dispense the most delicious—and intoxicating—drinks. Michael borrowed this shaker for the huge parties he would give at the Frick, as we called our rooms in Kirkland House because they were so elaborately decorated by Michael, who would go round the room pouring whiskey sours, which were always a great hit. At Harvard Chris was on both the varsity hockey team and the tennis team. When he was at St. Paul's, *Newsweek* ran a story on Chris in an SPS hockey game; the caption of the photograph of him read "The fastest in fast company."

As the heavenly New England autumn gave way to snow ("*Mais ou sont les neiges d'antan?*"), I could say with Catullus, "*Odi et amo*" ("I love and I hate"). I was stricken with depression and wracked with anxiety over my self-imposed course load. I began to skip classes and sleep until noon or later, a sure sign of deep depression. I balked at taking end-of-term exams. Things were going from bad to worse. My only consolation was Chris and Michael. I hoped that one day I could say with Virgil, "*Forsan et haec olim meminisse iuvabit*" ("Perhaps one day we shall look back on these things and laugh," *Aeneid*, Book 1).

Meanwhile, by winter I had become increasingly desperate because of my heavy course load. Finally, I threw in the towel and decided that I was having a nervous breakdown. In desperation, I went to see Professor Alfred, my adviser, and told him I was sick and that my mother was mentally very ill and that I had to leave Harvard.

He said, "Well, go home, take a job, get some rest, and we'd very much like to have you back next year, when you can go into your real sophomore year. And when you return it would be wise to see a psychiatrist on the staff of the Harvard Health Services. And God be with you." I was so lacking in self-awareness that after seeing Professor Alfred and explaining the situation, I thought that I might be faking it. But in fact, I was in deep trouble. Soon we were to begin the reading period for the end-of-term exams, and I was terrified that I'd fail. So I spiraled into a state of deep depression and anxiety.

One snowy winter day before leaving, I walked through Harvard Yard and across the campus to the Yenching Institute of Asian Studies, which I had hoped might be my stepping-stone to the Tibetan Buddhist lamas in exile in India whom I'd been fantasizing about since I was a child. I found Professor Nagatomi in his smoke-filled office, sitting at his desk piled high with papers and books. In what little space remained, he was writing a letter in Japanese. I told him that I was leaving because I was sick, and my mother was so ill that I had to be with her. His eyes filled with tears. With compassion and sincerity, he said, "Oh, I'm *very* sorry. But you're coming back." He sounded so assured, it was as if he was uttering a prophecy. "I plan to," I replied. "And you'll take my courses." "I plan to. The Sanskrit and the course on Buddhism." "Good. Well, good-bye for now, Mr. Talbott." "Good-bye, Professor Nagatomi, and thank you so much."

I walked back to Massachusetts Avenue through the snow elated, "on gossamer wings," to quote Cole Porter. I went to Hayes Bickford, a popular cafeteria on Mass Ave nicknamed the Bick, to meet Chris and Michael for lunch and to say good-bye. We planned to room together the following year. Michael promised to visit me in New York, and the three of us said good-bye. Leaving Harvard and the company of Michael and Chris was a great sadness to me, but at the same time, I felt an overwhelming sense of relief at being free from the pressure of studies and exams. As I left the university I thought to myself, as General Douglas MacArthur said when he had been forced to take his army out of Manila, "I shall return."

CHAPTER SEVEN

1959–Gap Year

The shuttle from Logan Airport to La Guardia cost twelve dollars in those days. As the taxi approached the city, I saw the bridge that my grandfather Thayer had built for the Pennsylvania Railroad, and then my breath was taken away by the New York skyline. I was thankful to find that my mother was her old self. She didn't scold me for dropping out of Harvard. Although my parents had sent Polly to Vassar and Peggy to Sarah Lawrence and John to the University of Virginia, they were never terribly interested in our education apart from seeing that we went to good schools.

When Peggy was graduating, Professor Joseph Campbell, with whom she was studying myth, agreed to take her on as a graduate student. Our father wouldn't let her do it, saying that she had had enough education and that she should get a job. He used his influence and got her a job writing feature articles for *Vogue*. She loved the work and was able to live at home without the commute to Bronxville. She was imperious about being driven to and from her office. Our chauffeur called her "the duchess." Our father had left college after his first year at Yale and had gone into business, and our mother never went to school at all but was tutored at home.

My mother would sometimes call me up at college and ask me to come down because she was giving a dinner for the Windsors. I'd say that I had to study. "But you do so well," she would reply. She wasn't that bothered by my dropping out for nine months, especially since it meant that I'd be staying with her. She was lonely after my father's death and liked having me at home, although I had been diligent about writing or telephoning her as often as I could. She said of me to my sister Polly, "He's such good company!" In the evenings I would often go to the opera or the theater with my mother. One night we went with

Loretta Howard to a concert the duo pianists Arthur Gold and Bobby Fizdale were giving at Carnegie Hall, little knowing that one day they would become an important part of my life. I would also often read to my mother, which was an old custom of ours.

I had meetings with Swami Nikilananda at his center around the corner and attended the Hindu ceremonies he would perform on the weekends. If my mother wasn't home for lunch, or if she was working at her volunteer job as vice president of the New York Infirmary, I would go to Mass at St. Patrick's Cathedral before having lunch across the street at Hamburger Heaven. Naturally I did a lot of reading on my own. I went to bookstores and bought books. One shop was devoted entirely to books on ballet, memoirs of dancers, and books on Balanchine. I bought international newspapers at a store on 57th Street and Madison Avenue. However, this leisurely self-indulgent life had to stop at some point.

Even though my mother had never been to school, she was a brilliant fund-raiser and was on the board of trustees of Sarah Lawrence. Turner Catledge, managing editor of the *New York Times*, was chairman of the board, and after board meetings in Bronxville, he often came back to our apartment for a drink or a cup of tea. Often, I would join them. Mr. Catledge knew Judge Ruth Apfelberg at the Domestic Relations Court. He got me a job with Judge Apfelberg's approval as an assistant to the probation officers. Now I was part of the real world with a real job downtown. In the morning I took the Lexington Avenue subway to Grand Central, then the cross-town subway to the West Side, and finally the Seventh Avenue IRT down to 23rd Street. I enjoyed the ride even in the summer's scalding heat and loved the surging New York crowds. I don't know why I liked the subway so much. Maybe it was the feeling that I was part of the real world.

Judge Apfelberg was a warm and cozy person, very natural with no pretentions. Nonetheless, she was an imposing figure as she sat on her high seat at the podium. She listened carefully to everything the parents said so as to decide whether they could keep their children: Were they meeting their obligations as parents? Was there violence at home? Did the children have proper accommodations? Were they being well fed? If not, she gave the judgment of Solomon, and the children were removed from the family and taken to foster homes.

When I took the subway home, I would realize the contrast between the life I was leading and the lives of the families I saw at the Domestic Relations Court. I was an assistant to the Domestic Relations Court probation officers, who were good people but under a lot of pressure because of the amount of work. Once one of the women supervisors was late because the pipes had burst in her kitchen, and she had to arrange with the landlord to have it attended to. She was terribly upset by the situation, and I felt very sorry for her. Although I could tell that Judge Ruth Apfelberg liked me, I often felt heartbroken. One day I had to accompany a little boy who was being put into the Cardinal Spellman Home. On the Staten Island ferry, he told me that his mother was a prostitute who received her clients in their one-room apartment. There were rats. Sorrow was there in that courtroom every day. There was another probation officer who was a nice man, I thought. He came to my little cubicle one day and said to me, "You know, you have to develop compassion for the families being judged. It's very important to not just do your work in a mechanical way."

Meanwhile, my mother was busy with her work as vice president of the New York Infirmary. Many of the ladies there later told me that she had been the most wonderful person to work for. Every year, Lucky Luciano would have my mother to lunch, and she would tell him how many beds in the hospital had been occupied by Italian Americans that year, and he would give her a big check.

Although she was a brilliant fund-raiser, it was not all smooth sailing. At about that time a very wealthy woman from Canada came to New York City. She was so rich that, even in a place as accustomed to wealth as New York, she made a great splash. It was precisely what she wanted to do. Her name was Gwen Cafritz, and she wanted to befriend my mother. The nouveau riches were always captivated by my mother's graciousness and hospitality. In turn, my mother wanted her money for her hospital. One of the things about Mrs. Cafritz that caused amusement and wonder was the way she went about decorating her apartment. She told her decorator, "I want you to make my apartment perfect, and when I walk in, I want every ashtray in place." Another thing that fascinated my mother was that when Mrs. Cafritz came to dine, her jewels were so valuable that she had to have a bodyguard standing in the hall. Her diamond ring was so enormous that at the bridge table she could hardly lift her cards. Ethel Merman played her on Broadway in *Call Me Madam.*

I do not know if my mother was successful in raising money from Mrs. Cafritz. She rarely failed to obtain money for the hospital. In one case, however, the patience and tact that you must exert in fund-raising were tried to the limit. Vivian Beaumont kept telephoning her and asking what face cream she used. My mother stopped taking her calls. Rebuffed, she gave the money to found the Vivian Beaumont Theatre. My mother's greatest triumph came from her friendship with the Duke and Duchess of Windsor. "Sir and Duchess," she said, "you know how popular you are in America. Think how people would love you if you were to make a contribution to the New York Infirmary." In this way the hospital added the Duchess of Windsor Wing.

Walter Hoving, who owned Tiffany's, offered my mother the job as head of the department that oversaw and displayed the table settings. She would choose the glass and china and silver and arrange the tables and the centerpieces. My mother was a friend of Mrs. Hoving's and had worked as a volunteer in her shop within Bonwit Teller's, which did the same thing with table settings. As buyers, my mother and Mrs. Hoving had gone to a porcelain manufacturing factory at Este in the Veneto for the tables at Bonwit's. Mummy was well known for her impeccable eye and good taste in New York, Washington, London, and Paris. The Tiffany job sounded made for her. When she met Mr. Hoving—and I can visualize the big window where they sat looking out onto Fifth Avenue and 57th Street—she told him that she couldn't take the job. She was at the time mildly depressed (although not so low that she couldn't give a pre-Christmas party for the Windsors). She was spending too much money and could certainly have used the job. Like my uncle Jack Thayer, I was a snob, and I didn't like her working for a shop-keeper. I was totally out to lunch back then.

Mrs. Hoving was interested in Christian mysticism. Knowing that I was too, when she came to dinner one evening and gave me a book titled *The Cloud of Unknowing* by an anonymous fourteenth-century Christian monk. I was very grateful to her and curious that she took such an interest in Christian mysticism.

Although I had had a nervous breakdown at Harvard and was home recovering, I was happy and free of anxiety because I was with my mother. We bucked each other up. The only problem was that I was so sorry to see her suffering from her depression. For a number of years, Christmas had included a visit to Mrs. Baker's Horse Shoe Plantation in Tallahassee. That year, my mother was too sick to go.

For several years, she had swung between manic highs and deep depressions—the hallmarks of what is now called bipolar disorder. Although little was known about it then, the cause was largely chemical, triggered by my father's death. She began falling apart about one year after he died in 1957. She went to several institutions, including the Institute for Living in Connecticut and the Payne Whitney in New York, where she was given shock treatments, which she hated even more than she did her psychiatrists. Of one of these she told me, "My doctor is a rat and is living in a nest under my bed." Still her insight into the problem was remarkably accurate. "You know," she once told me, "in the future this mental illness is going to be treated by chemicals." Unfortunately, that day lay too far in the future to be of any help to her.

That winter Dom Aelred Graham finally came to visit us from Peru, Illinois, where he had given a lecture. He imitated the Midwesterners and pronounced it "Peeru" and was passing through New York on his way back to Portsmouth Priory. In the past he had always stayed with my godmother, Loretta Howard, in her splendid town house on 74th Street. She was only one of Dom Aelred's rich patrons, whose lavish hospitality he had become accustomed to in his sixteen years of running Portsmouth Priory. Nonetheless, he found our apartment perfectly comfortable.

Dom Aelred Graham had a double title as prior of Portsmouth Priory and head of the Governing Body of Portsmouth Priory School. My mother's chauffeur Pascal took me to meet his plane. I waited for a long time as everyone disembarked. No prior of Portsmouth. Finally, he emerged, and we shook hands, and I said that I was so glad that he had arrived because he had gotten off the plane after a long pause at the end of the line. Quoting from Matthew, Aelred replied, "Well, you know what is said? 'The last shall be first.'" And he laughed heartily.

Aelred suggested that we have a drink at the airport before going into town. We ended up having a couple of martinis with some snacks that Aelred called "blotting paper." I had recently received my ID card from the military proving that I was eighteen, so I could join Aelred in our first getting-to-know-you session. Later he told me that he didn't like the sensation of getting drunk, but he did like martinis. Once he had been out in Detroit staying with Mr. Fisher (of Fisher Body, an automobile coach-builder), who was a donor to Portsmouth Priory School. Mr. Fisher and his guests were having martinis by the swimming pool. Someone said to the bartender, "Stir, don't shake. It bruises the gin." Aelred loved that.

Aelred, whom I referred to in public by his title, Dom Aelred—Dom meaning lord, from medieval Latin—saw that I was reading a book by the French theologian Garrigou-Lagrange about the Blessed Virgin Mary. Aelred said that Garrigou-Lagrange was *vieux jeu*, old-fashioned, and that in general the French theologians were doctrinaire. Being a zealous young convert to the Catholic Church, I lapped up theology that was doctrinaire. At that time Aelred was writing a book titled *Zen Catholicism*. When I asked him how he squared being a prelate of the Catholic Church with his attraction to Buddhism, he replied, "I have come out the other side of Catholicism." When someone asked him, "Are you a Catholic or a Buddhist?" he was known to reply, "No labels."

When I told Dom Aelred that one of the probation officers had told me that I needed to develop compassion for the families who came to the court, Dom Aelred said, "How did that probation officer know whether you felt compassion or not?" And so he eased my mind in his astute way. We quickly became fast friends.

Often that year I'd stay the weekend with Aelred at Portsmouth Priory. Everything about the journey was pleasant—Grand Central Station and the Oyster Bar, the train, and the stout at the Biltmore in Providence before the lovely ride to Portsmouth Priory, where at the head of the lane, a black-robed monk or sometimes even Aelred himself would meet the bus. We would take long walks in the grounds of the monastery. Sometimes we'd go down to the beach on Naragansett Bay to the place where Aelred practiced yoga asanas, which I called "the yoga ridge." We'd also have long conversations in the gazebo, or in Aelred's rooms, conversations on Zen, Buddhism, Hinduism, the Upanishads, and Shankaracharya (788–820 CE). When Aelred was writing his book on Zen Buddhism, Father Hilary Martin, another monk at Portsmouth Priory, who was a fine gardener, created a Zen sand garden with rocks and a few shrubs outside Aelred's window so that he could have a view to inspire him.

One precious thing about my visits was studying the *Summa Theologica* of St. Thomas Aquinas with this acclaimed Thomist, sometimes in the Latin text and sometimes in the English translation. Aelred had been taught Latin as well as Latin composition at his school in Liverpool. Of all the sayings of Thomas that Aelred taught me, my favorite was "*Gratia non tollit natura sed perficit,*" which means "Grace does not destroy nature but perfects it."

Another spiritual writer whom I enjoyed hearing Aelred talk about was Meister Eckhart. Many years later I visited Blackfriars, the Benedictine house of studies at Oxford where I went to see a monk of Ampleforth, who, for his doctorate in divinity, had done a strict retreat for a year to meditate on the mystical teachings of Meister Eckhart. His name was Cyprian Smith, and he wrote a magnificent book on Eckhart titled *The Way of Paradox.*

Aelred was popular and often had visitors, including William Buckley and Michael Novak. It was quite courageous of them, because they were conservatives and Aelred was definitely left wing. Evelyn Waugh once said that he'd sent his son, Auberon, to Downside instead of to Ampleforth, one of the two great Catholic schools in England, because "the red monk was there," meaning Aelred. Robert Fitzgerald, who translated Virgil's *Aeneid*, came to see him, as well as Elsie Mitchell, the founder of the Cambridge Buddhist Association. Rose Kennedy came, as did John Walker, the first director of the National Gallery in Washington, and his wife, Lady Margaret.

Father Hilary Martin, who was worldly and social, also had many visitors. As a young man in Boston working as a city planner, Father Hilary had shared an apartment with Michael's great uncle, Nathaniel Saltonstall, and because of that relationship, Michael became a close friend of Father Hilary. So from Harvard, Michael and I would go down for the weekend, I to visit Aelred and Michael to visit Father Hilary. Father Hilary was a housemaster. He had a little monk's room, and when he had people to dinner, he would cook up the most delicious meals on a little stove placed on a plank over the toilet. His most amusing guest was Alan Pryce-Jones, a Welshman who had been the editor of the *Times Literary Supplement*. One night, Alan brought Molly, the Duchess of Buccleuch, whose husband was the largest landowner in Scotland. Aelred came down from the monastery and said, "I had to see a real duchess."

My weekends spent visiting the priory were a different world from my weekdays in New York working for the Domestic Relations Court. During the evenings after work, the people I usually saw were Ian Baldwin, who was in his second year at Columbia University, and my friend Carlotta Marshall, who had become engaged to Peter Prestcott.

I had first met Carlotta while I was at St. Paul's. After she graduated from Wheaton College, she had broken away from her parents, who lived in Jacksonville, Florida, and had come to live in New York City. Carlotta was something of an adventuress. One of her first jobs was in the children's book department at FAO Schwartz. That same Christmas, Peter was wrapping packages, which Carlotta said looked like jewels. Soon after they met, Carlotta and Peter became very attached to each other. Photographs taken of her at the time—one appeared on the cover of *Infinity* magazine—show her beauty and great style. She also had a remarkable quality of romantic yearning. One evening I took

Carlotta to a coming-out party at the St. Regis Rooftop Ballroom. At some point we went over to a window and looked out at the building across the way. The building was illuminated, and trying to be mysterious I said, "Behind each of those lights is a person." Of course, it wasn't true at all; there was no one in the building but the janitors. However, Carlotta thought that I was a mystic.

Serena and Carlotta had been at the Ethel Walker School in Simsbury, Connecticut, together. Although not in the same class, they knew of each other but did not become friends until one day they came across each other waiting in line at the American Express in Paris to collect their mail. They have been great friends ever since. Carlotta, who had multiple sclerosis since the early '70s, and Serena lived near each other in New York and often got together for dinner or takeout.

I first met Peter Prestcott at a party for his engagement to Carlotta. When I rang the bell, Peter opened the door. I looked at him, and instead of introducing myself and asking if he was the groom, I asked, "Is Serena Stewart here?" He replied, "Yes, she is right there," but he never forgot my rudeness. Nonetheless, we became and continue to be close friends. During my gap year, Carlotta, Peter, and I would go out to dinner together and often go on to hear Mabel Mercer, who was a friend of Carlotta's, sing at the Carlyle.

After Peter and Carlotta broke off their engagement, Carlotta became Ian Baldwin's girlfriend, which was another link between Carlotta and myself. We had very strong mutual karma, and she was a truly loyal friend to me my entire life. She had a genius for friendship; it meant an enormous amount to her, and she inspired friendship in others. Carlotta and Peter always remained great friends. Peter had many homosexual friends whom Carlotta adopted as part of her world. Although she liked straight boys like Ian, she also had a penchant for gay boys. She once said to me, "You know, I didn't know what homosexuals were. I thought a homosexual was a young man who loved poetry." Serena set her straight.

Peter, too, has remained a great friend throughout my life. His father was consul general from Poland to Yugoslavia before the war. Peter was born in 1939, the year Hitler invaded Poland. His family, who were in Yugoslavia at the time, fled to London, where Peter's father joined the Polish government in exile and was much appreciated by Winston Churchill. However, Peter's family had no money. His mother had been a chemist in Poland, but she had no license to practice her profession in England. In order to send Peter to public school or boarding school, she worked in an ABC, one of the restaurant chains found in every British railroad station. She sent Peter to Charter House, the public school Winston Churchill had attended, where Peter turned into a real English gentleman, complete with a public school accent. Because Oskerco-Maslowski, his double-barreled Polish name, proved difficult to pronounce at school, he changed it to Peter Prestcott.

In his late teens, Peter came to America, where there was a network of Polish refugees, among them Arthur Rubinstein, the great pianist. Peter and his mother came to America at the invitation of Helena Rubinstein, the owner of the cosmetic business named after her. She hired Peter to work for her, and that was his first job in this country. Peter went on to have his own business called the Bead Shop. He and a partner made beaded objects. The apogee of their creations was the beaded headdress Katharine Hepburn wore as Cleopatra. Peter is also a terrific cook, and at one point he had his own television show teaching people to cook. But the good times seldom lasted. Even when he had a good job, something would invariably go wrong, and he would be out of work again.

At one point he came to me in the most terrible state of depression and anxiety because he had no money, no work, and no place to live. Fortunately, I knew someone who was a friend of the medievalist Anne Freemantle, who wrote about Christian theology of the Middle Ages and whose husband was a famous Gurdjieffian. They had a railroad flat on Third Avenue, which I was able to rent for Peter, so at least he had some place to live. Twice in his life Peter has had serious automobile accidents in which the person in the passenger seat has been badly hurt. First, when driving Carlotta to Cape Cod while they were still engaged, he fell asleep at the wheel. Carlotta had to have many stitches on the side of her face and neck that fortunately no longer showed, so her beauty stayed intact.

Years later in the 1970s, Peter went to California, where he worked for Rock Hudson. They became great friends, and because Peter did such good work, Rock decided to buy him a Porsche by way of thanks. Peter begged Rock to give him cash instead, saying that he really didn't want an automobile. But Rock insisted, so Peter accepted the car. Unfortunately, while Peter was driving with a friend from Hollywood to Las Vegas, he had a horrendous accident that left his friend a quadriplegic. By that time, I was living in Marion, Massachusetts, and hadn't seen Peter for several years because I'd been away in India. Dodrup Chen Rinpoche, the great lama, was staying with me, when I sensed that Peter was in trouble. I am not the least bit psychic, but perhaps because of the strong karma between Peter and myself, I sensed that something was wrong. I went to see Rinpoche in his room and explained that I was very worried about a friend, who I thought was in trouble. The lama said, "Yes indeed, he is in trouble, and you must try to find him." But I had no idea how to get in touch with Peter.

I called a number of Peter's friends to find out where he was, and each one would give me the name of another friend. Finally, the trail ended with a great friend of Peter's and mine, Marian Fenn Witte. When I reached her in California, she told me about the accident and said that Peter had been very ill with serious internal injuries. After leaving the hospital, Peter had gone to stay in Wilmington, Delaware, with Vicki Sharp, who was married to one of the Du Ponts and was looking after him while he stayed in her pool house. I called Vicki and apologized because it was so late at night. She said, "Oh, don't be sorry. Peter talks about you all the time." She told me that earlier that evening, Peter had gone out for a walk and hadn't returned. She and her husband finally found him lying facedown in the snow and carried him back to her pool house. She told me that Peter had had some brandy before going out, which had kept him from getting frostbite.

The following morning, I told Dodrup Chen Rinpoche what had happened and said that I was so surprised to have sensed that Peter was in trouble. Dodrup Chen Rinpoche said, "That's right. This sort of thing will happen to you more often if you continue to give money to lamas." And then he laughed and laughed. The following afternoon, I telephoned Peter at Vicki's house, and he told me that in the spring he would return to live in New York. He telephoned me as soon as he got back to New York, and we met at the King Cole Bar in the St. Regis Hotel, where we shared a booth beneath the mural by Maxfield Parrish. We both had martinis—gin for me, and Peter, being Polish, vodka.

He told me that he was staying with a woman in her suite at the St. Regis Hotel. She was a psychiatrist from Wilmington, Delaware, who had a number of patients from the Du Pont family. He invited me up to meet her. She was one of the most remarkable people I've ever seen. She had flung a glorious mink coat on the arm of a chair and was wearing a beautiful diamond ring. She was from Argentina and had enormous flair and a very strong character. I was so thankful that she had some- how appeared out of thin air to look after Peter when he needed it so badly. I was relieved that my dear friend was being looked after by such an assertive, oddly apropos character.

My grandmother, Katherine Houk Talbott.

My father, Harold E. Talbott, Jr, his brother, Nelson, and grandfather Harold E. Talbott.

Christmas dinner at the Runnymede Playhouse.

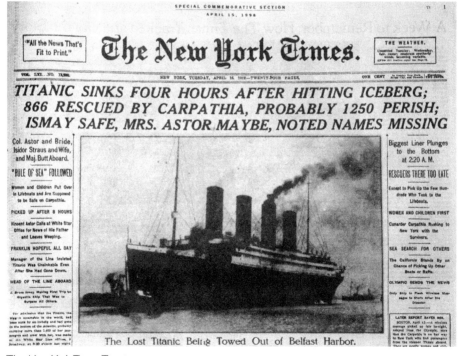

The *New York Times* Titanic story.

My grandfather,
John Borland Thayer.

Grandmother Thayer
("Gaga") as a widow,
with her four children,
PTT, Jack, Polly,
and Teddy.

HET with his seven sisters: Elsie, Lilah, Daisy, Marnie, HET, Lil, Marianna, and Kit.

Runnymede, the Talbott home in Dayton.

HET playing polo.

Wedding day, Harold and Peggy Talbott, August 11, 1925.

Nanny, Polly, Peggy, and PTT at the Boardwalk Atlantic City.

Gaga Thayer with Peggy and Polly on Christmas in Philadelphia, 1931.

HET with "Paula Negri"
at the Pillars, 1931.

Peggy Thayer Talbott.

My father on "Round the Clock" in a polo match at Roslyn.

Peggy and Harold at the Conde Nast dinner before the Opera Ball.

PTT and "The Phantom."

PTT on "Black Magic" at The Meadowbrook Drag.

HET and PTT.

HET, Polly, Peggy, PTT, The Family Class at Piping Rock.

Harold, PTT, and John, Fall 1940.

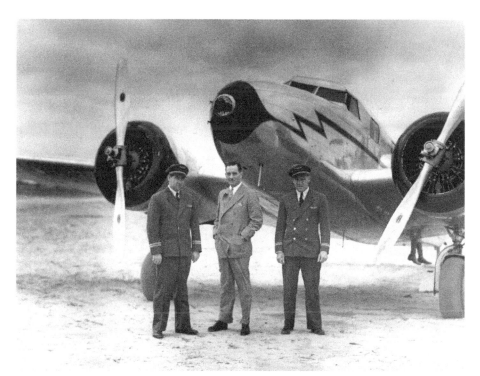

Ed Maloney (pilot), HET (owner), Ed Seymour (mechanic) with "The Lockheed."

The Pillars, Old Westbury, NY, our weekend house.

Harold, Peggy, PTT, Polly, John, 1941.

The 20th Wedding Anniversary — The Meadow Club, Southampton, August 11, 1945.

CHAPTER EIGHT

Back to Harvard

In September 1959, I returned to Harvard for another attempt at sophomore year. Michael, Chris, and I went to see Master Finley of Elliott House to ask if we could live in his house. He said, "No, you're Paulies, and I have enough preppies." So we decided to lodge next door at Kirkland House. Michael set about decorating our rooms (numbered F32). He got some furniture at a shop in Boston he liked, and each of us had something sent to us from home. I got some porcelain, which later I found out was very valuable, and Michael had a beautiful mirror that he put up over the fireplace, which unfortunately was no longer working. He filled the larger of our rooms with flowering plants—cyclamen and gloxinia were his favorites. The other two rooms were tiny monk-like cells. We crammed the double-decker bed and the single bed provided by the university into one of the small rooms so we could use the other one as a cozy place for afternoon tea.

Unlike St. Paul's with its woods and sweeping lawns, Harvard was plunked in the middle of Cambridge, where the only grass was the center of Harvard Yard. Coming from Boston, your first glimpse was Widener Library, built with a gift from Eleanor Elkins Widener in memory of her son, Harry, who had perished aboard the *Titanic* along with my grandfather Thayer. On early mornings, one sometimes saw Harry Wolfson, the medievalist, Jewish scholar, and linguist, holding onto his daughter's arm, just as Oedipus held on to his daughter Antigone's, as he walked into Widener Library to start his day's work. Harry Wolfson did for Greco-Roman and Jewish philosophy what Etienne Gilson did for medieval Christian philosophy. Eventually, I attended a seminar of his arranged by my tutor, Professor Elizabeth Brown, known as Peggy by her peers, for the students of the department of medieval history and literature, in which he gleefully mocked what he considered to be the shallowness of Christian philosophy compared to Greco-Roman and Jewish philosophy. I was shocked!

If you stood on the steps of Widener facing the Yard, to your right is Sever Hall. In the course of the countless lectures I went to in Sever, I grew to be very fond of the old Victorian building designed by the architect H. H. Richardson in the 1870s, although it was rather dilapidated. Next to Sever is Emerson, where I once went to an extraordinary and inspiring lecture on the *Summa Theologica* of St. Thomas Aquinas. The lecture, as I recollect, may have been given by Frederick Copleston, S.J., who wrote a history of philosophy from the early Ionians to Heiddeger.

Across the Yard from Widener is Memorial Hall, a nondenominational church where various university events were held. I never set foot in it, but I did love the look of it. Behind Memorial Hall across Cambridge Street is Sanders Theatre, an old Victorian citadel where you went to hear concerts or great lectures. Years after I had graduated I went with Tulku Thondup, a Tibetan lama and great friend, to hear the Dalai Lama speak at Sanders Theatre. It was the first time since my Indian travels that I saw the man who had been my spiritual hero since I was five years old.

On Quincy Street was the Fogg Museum, my favorite building of the college. My favorite painting there is a portrait of Madame de Pompadour by François Boucher. She sits in her boudoir holding a powder puff gazing into a mirror perhaps at the people gathered around her waiting to receive their orders to work on those aspects of the French civilization she presided over. Not far from the Fogg is the Swedenborgian Church, my second favorite building at Harvard. It was always closed, and I'm not sure if there were parishioners anymore. Across the street was the Busch-Reisinger Museum, which housed a collection of German art that I didn't consider especially beautiful.

According to Professor Alfred, the beautiful yellow house down Mass Ave from Widener was once a stop on the underground railway. It had also belonged to Henry Clarke Warren, the Harvard scholar of Buddhism who wrote the masterpiece *Buddhism in Translation*.

Although Professor Warren was so ill that he had to live under a gauze tent, he managed to write his *Compendium of Buddhist Scriptures* in translation from the Pali.

A little ways farther along Mass Ave was the Bick, where everyone would meet for endless cups of coffee and conversation. Then came J. Press, a clothing store where many boys ran up bills that took months to pay off. Fortunately, I was a dowdy preppy with no interest in fashion, so I didn't run up much of a bill at J. Press. Nearby was Schoenhof's Foreign Books, a favorite haunt of mine for French books that weren't as expensive as they are now. Also in Harvard Square was the Coop, where we bought all our textbooks and just about anything else we might want. Next door to the Coop was the University Theater, and in the center of Harvard Square was a newspaper stand selling periodicals from around the world. Down a bit from the Coop was Brigham's Ice Cream Shop, where it was said that jimmies (chocolate sprinkles) originated. Brigham's was a favorite of Chris's, who loved their frappes.

Over on Brattle Street was the Brattle Theatre, where we'd go on many a reality break. Bryant Haliday owned the theater as well as the Casablanca bar next door, known as the CB, which was a popular gathering place for friends of mine. Next door was the Window Shop, a restaurant that also played a big part in my Harvard life. A few streets south of Harvard Square one comes to the Charles River. The Larz Anderson Memorial Bridge was built by a relative of Michael's, and next to it is the Weld Boathouse, named after a member of Michael's maternal family. There were two snappy restaurants in Cambridge, one being Chez Dreyfus, where it was great fun to eat or have a martini at the bar. Later, when Michael became interested in Catholicism, we had a martini at the bar and lamented that our friend Chris wouldn't join the Catholic Church with us. The chicest of all the restaurants was the Henri IV, where you took a Radcliffe girl if you wanted to make a good impression.

Michael and Chris both chose to major in fine arts. Although I wanted to continue studying Sanskrit to become eligible to study Tibetan, I had a sense of impending danger, so I backed off. Once burned, twice shy. Because of my previous downfall, I was trying to be sensible about what courses I signed up for. In addition, I was going to take a course on Buddhist studies given by Professor Nagatomi, and I felt that was enough for the time being. I could study Sanskrit and Tibetan later on. Professor Nagatomi's survey of Buddhism was the best course I took at Harvard. On his reading list was the best book I studied and wrote a paper on—*The Central Philosophy of Buddhism: A Study of Madhyamika System* by T. R. V. Murti. Several years later at Benares Hindu University, Aelred and I had a conversation with Professor Murti, which is recorded in Aelred's book *The End of Religion.*

I decided to major in medieval history and literature because of my devotion to the saints of the church, including the anonymous author of *The Cloud of Unknowing*, Dame Juliana of Norwich, and other great medieval mystics. Because of continuing my weekend visits to the priory with Dom Aelred Graham, where I'd continue my Thomist studies, I didn't plan to write a thesis on the *Summa Theologica* of St. Thomas Aquinas or on Meister Eckhart at Harvard. I got plenty of teaching about both outside Harvard.

One of the most important events of our sophomore year was punching season, when the social clubs took prospective members to dinner at alumni members' houses or to restaurants. The Porcellian, founded in 1791, was the most exalted of the clubs—and solidly old Boston. The AD was mainly a club for New York boys while the Fly had many foreign students among its members. Although you could go to the Hasty Pudding for lunch or dinner, the club was best known for its annual musical always written and acted in by the members, many of whom played the parts of women. The Signet Society was for intellectuals and literary people.

Invitations for a dinner were sent through the mail on heavy cards. If you wanted to join the club, you would accept one of these dinners. Chris and Michael were what are called legacies to the Porcellian Club because their fathers or grandfathers had been members, but I had no connection with the club. But they punched me—probably because I was rooming with Michael and Chris. I was also asked to join the AD, the Fly, the Hasty Pudding, and the Signet Society.

One evening I was taken to dinner at a restaurant in Boston to be looked over by members of the Fly. I was seated next to Amyn Khan, the brother of the Aga Khan. At one point, Amyn asked me if I liked Kandinsky. I replied, "I must confess I'm not very fond of modern art." He said, "Oh, I love Kandinsky. Whenever I get a chance, I buy one." When I asked Amyn if he knew our classmate Sharam Pahlevi, a nephew of the Shah of Iran, he exclaimed distainfully, "The Pahlevis! They were tribesmen in the hills when my grandfather was racing at Biarritz."

I would have loved to join the Fly, but Michael and Chris said that we must stick together, so all three of us joined the Porcellian. After having once gone to Harvard for a weekend, my mother felt that the club was terribly snobbish and told me if I went to Harvard I mustn't join the Porcellian Club. When I did join, I told her, and she replied with a telegram saying, "All is forgiven, come home to mother."

It is still a most secret institution, although I can at least divulge its address—1324 Massachusetts Avenue. I can also say that the front door opens into a narrow room known as the Bicycle Room, empty except for a bench and table. A staircase leads up to the club's locked door, which only members know how to open. Guests are not permitted, and certainly no women, who if they visit are restricted to the Bicycle Room. That's all I can say about the club.

As it happens, an article in the *New York Times* ("Social Club at Harvard Rejects Calls to Admit Women," April 13, 2018) reported that some students were up in arms because the club stated publicly that it would not admit women. I am very uncertain about what is right. Allowing women as members would radically change the atmosphere of the club and make it unrecognizable. But perhaps women feel that they must push for political correctness and storm the bastion of the old Porcellian Club. Anyway, it's something to think about in terms of justice. I wonder why women aren't satisfied with the three or four women's clubs that have been founded at Harvard?

At the beginning of the fall semester, Chris joined the varsity hockey and tennis teams. I was very proud of him. It was wonderful that someone so cultivated and civilized was also a very fine athlete. He was almost like the Greek ideal of a young man. Michael continued to decorate the Frick, and we would go into Boston to Courtright House, which was owned by Mrs. Carter, the wife of the composer Elliott Carter, and buy all sorts of objects for the room.

One day in March 1959, I was standing by the newspaper stand in Harvard Square when I happened to look down at the headlines of the *New York Times* to see, "Dalai Lama Escapes to India." On Saint Patrick's Day the twenty-three-year-old lama, disguised as a soldier, had made his escape from the Chinese communists who were occupying his country. With only a small retinue of loyal supporters, he crossed the Himalayas on foot traveling only at night to avoid detection. *Time* magazine later reported a rumor that, thanks to the prayers of Buddhist holy men, mists and low clouds had hidden the little party from Chinese search planes. It was a thunderbolt for me. I was thrilled to learn that he was safe.

My favorite book throughout my Harvard career in history and lit was *The Mediaeval Mind: A History of the Development of Thought and Emotion in the Middle Ages* by Henry Osborn Taylor. Other books on medieval history that Dr. Brown taught me that I liked were *The Origins of Modern Germany* by Geoffrey Barraclough and *The Love of Learning and the Desire for God* by Dom Jean Leclerc, O.S.B. Also of interest was the *History of the Middle Ages* by Strayer and Munro.

Along with Dr. Elizabeth Brown, Dr. Charles Witke also tutored me in medieval literature. His wife, Roxanne, was a scholar of Chinese language and history. She was the only Westerner ever to interview Jiang Qing, Mao Tse-tung's wife, who was the leader of the Gang of Four. Madame Mao told Roxanne Witke, "Power is the greatest aphrodisiac."

Dr. Witke had me read Joinville's *The History of St. Louis*, about his crusade and his imprisonment by the Arabs. He also taught the works of Froissart, the medieval historian of the Hundred Years War and, as literature, the Arthurian romances of Chrétien de Troyes, who lived in the latter half of the twelfth century and wrote in Old French. Chrétien wrote five romances: *Erec and Enide, Cligès, Lancelot, Yvain,* and *Perceval, the Story of the Grail.*

My greatest pleasure that sophomore year was Professor Nagatomi's course on Buddhism. I wrote a paper on the philosophy of a first-century Buddhist thinker, Nagarjuna, who fascinated me. His philosophy is called the Madhyamaka (middle way). I was disappointed to only get a B plus on the paper. When I went to Professor Nagatomi, he said, "Oh, don't be bothered because I didn't give anybody else a higher mark. You did a good job." So I was encouraged in my lifelong study and practice of Buddhism.

In my junior year Dr. Witke and I discussed the topic for my thesis at length. Because I wanted a literary text, I decided to write on one of the Arthurian romances by Chrétien de Troyes. Of the Chrétien romances, I chose *Erec and Enide,* a story about the love between a husband and wife who go through a bad patch and then joyfully reconcile, because of its ending, which is steeped in ambiguity. Although Erec is passionately attached to his wife, he blames Enide for the loss of his knightly reputation. Two problems in *Erec and Enide* make it a fascinating work of art. The first problem was why Chrétien de Troyes wrote *Erec.* At the time of writing, Chrétien had as his patroness Marie of France, Countess of Champagne, whose mother was Eleanor of Aquitaine, the patroness of the troubadours. Marie's great-grandfather, Bertrand du Guesclin, was the first troubadour. Could it be that *Erec* was an entertainment for the court of Marie of Champagne on the occasion of her marriage?

Dr. Witke was more interested in the second problem. The story culminates in a celebration after Erec vanquishes a mysterious knight who dwells in a garden with a skimpily dressed girl. The garden contains a row of heads on spikes on which are resting the shields of the knights whom the mysterious knight had slain in joust. Erec defeats him, and then everybody participates in an event called *la joie de la cour* (the joy of the court), which is never explained. Is it a secret ceremony or ritual? I suggested that it could be a druid ritual of which there are traces in the Arthurian romances or a Celtic rite. The romances are known to be partly derived from Celtic material. Another source of the romances is *la matière de Bretagne* (the matter of Brittany). Or is it derived from Cathar rituals or from Hindu or Buddhist Tantras? Dr. Witke was pleased with my idea, and we became great friends. He told me that he was a Catholic and that he recited daily the six hours of the Catholic Church.

During my junior year I once again found it difficult to keep up with the obligations of a Harvard education. A couple of obstacles prevented me from properly doing my homework and studying for my monthly hour exams. The first was that I fell into the circle of homosexual students around Ed Hood, a "section man" in the English department. He was a tiny little gnome of a man with strange slanted eyes and a bald head. He lived in a ground-floor apartment in a slum building off Brattle Street, where he entertained a coterie of boys who were magnetized by his literary intelligence. One could say that his circle was intellectually gay, for he had very high standards and would throw you out if you were ignorant. I was very careful to keep separate the gay world from that of the clubs, and Ed Hood was part of an underground that I repudiated when I was with straight friends. He once said, "You are so compartmentalized between your PC friends and ourselves. You should mingle them." He would have liked to meet my club friends, although he was totally persona non grata.

Some of us called him the Marschallin from *Der Rosenkavalier* or Edwina instead of Ed. He held nightly salons at his rundown apartment, which I often went to, and wasted much time hanging about this particular circle of people. It made me think of T. S. Eliot's line "Ridiculous the waste sad time / Stretching before and after," from *The Four Quartets*. I very much regret it and believe that it led to my second downfall at Harvard. Eventually, Skiddy von Stade, dean of students, called Ed to tell him that he had been sanctioned and forbidden to stand on Harvard territory for trying to solicit boys from Harvard. At that Edwina went and peed in the corner of von Stade's office to express his outrage.

Despite being attracted to this homosexual world, in my junior year I decided to propose to Gillian Walker, thanks in large part to the influence of Dom Aelred. Gillian was a devout Catholic, which led Aelred and Father Hilary to say, "The thing we think would be good for you is to marry Gillian." They had apparently spoken to Gillian's parents, who were appalled that she was thinking of marrying William Alfred, the professor whose lectures on the *Oresteia* I had so enjoyed my first year at Harvard. He was not only in his forties and much older than Gillian but also a professor at Harvard and was just a man of letters and so was hardly someone they wanted their daughter to marry.

During a walk along the beach in Portsmouth near the monastery, I asked Gillian to marry me. She started to cry and said, "I feel so badly that I can't marry you because the kind of man I want to marry is like Stephen," who was exceptionally handsome and masculine. As we were leaving the monastery to go back to Harvard, Gillian said that she thought we shouldn't continue to see each other because it was too painful. When I got back to my room, the phone was ringing, and it was Gillian to say, "OK, let's see each other," and we remained the fastest of friends. I learned years later much to my gratification that when Stephen returned from Vietnam he brought a little Vietnamese boy with him as his lover. Years later, long after she had married Al Maysles, the film director who made *Gimme Shelter* and *Grey Gardens*, Gillian and I were swimming at Fishers Island when she told me that she had been a failure in the eyes of her parents. When I asked what she meant, she said, "My mother wanted a coronet and a small grouse moor."

In retrospect it seems to me that in the winter of my junior year, I again fell into a deep depression partly because of my mother's illness. I now sought to avoid the work I should have been doing for medieval history and literature and instead would go to Schoenhof's Bookstore and buy French novels that were not on my reading list. I would take them back to the Frick and sit on the sofa wrapped in a blanket reading to escape my life and homework. I loved Colette, Cocteau, Gide, and Roger Peyrefitte and was hooked on Marcel Proust.

Michael and Chris would come back to the room and ask what I was reading and if it was for any of my courses. I would say no, and they would shake their heads, knowing what the effect would be on my marks. I was taking a class on Chaucer given by Professor Alfred that was perfectly wonderful, but I didn't do very much work, and that's how the year went on. I knew that the following year I'd be writing my thesis, so vowed that over the summer I would do some more reading in the Arthurian romances just to situate *Erec and Enide* in the context of the five romances. Dr. Brown was teaching me from two books: *The Carolingian Empire* by Heinrich Fichtenau and *Church, State and Christian Society* by Gerd Tellenbach about the Investiture Controversy between Pope Gregory VII, Hildebrand, and the emperor Henry IV of Germany, known as Barbarossa (Red Beard). Before the pope would lift his interdiction of all the churches of Germany, causing the refusal of the sacraments and the excommunication of the emperor, the emperor was forced to stand barefoot in the snow before the pope's palace at Canossa and beg for forgiveness. Even more dramatic was Ernst Kantorowicz's book *Frederick the Second: 1194–1250*, about the thirteenth-century emperor of the Holy Roman Empire.

For students of medieval history and literature that year, Harvard held dinners with experts on the Middle Ages. The first one was with Christopher Dawson, a professor in Roman Catholic studies who was the Chauncey Stillman chair. The position had been offered to and turned down by Aelred. He didn't want to leave Portsmouth Priory, where he had the peace and quiet to write.

The next dinner was the Ford Foundation dinner in a private room at Kirkland House. Shelley Winters, the guest of honor, began the evening telling us that she was nervous coming to Harvard. Not having had much education, she found it daunting to be talking to Harvard students. Very cleverly, she went around the table asking each student what he was studying and what he planned to do after he had gotten a degree. Kevin Klose, who said that he wanted to be a journalist, became a news correspondent in the Soviet Union and later the head of PBS. When Shelley Winters came to me, she asked what I was studying, and I said, "Medieval history and literature." And she said, "Well, what will you want with that? What do you want to become later?" And I said, "A medieval man."

Another wonderful occasion was Dr. Elizabeth Brown's seminar with Harry Wolfson on Philo, the Jewish philosopher who was born in 30 BCE and died in 45 CE. He was very influential among students of philosophy in the Middle Ages. Dr. Brown also ran a seminar on Plato's *Timaeus*. The Middle Ages took a great deal of its theories from *Timaeus*, and cosmology most definitely was not my subject. But I loved the two dialogues of Plato on pederasty, or love between a man and a boy. Nonetheless, I was in a slump for much of my junior year.

Our senior year Chris had changed his major to music and was playing tennis on the varsity team. Michael continued to major in fine arts and gave fabulous parties of up to one hundred people in our three small rooms amid lavish arrangements of potted plants and vases of flowers. Unlike Ed Hood's parties, Michael's were limited to boys from the Porcellian and girls from Radcliffe.

My mother came up one weekend, and we went out to Clarkville to see Chris's family. Amazed at the stables filled with horses, the swimming pool, the tennis courts, and the big house, she said, "I didn't know people lived like that anymore." She spent the night in Boston at the Copley Plaza Hotel before returning to New York the next day. Meanwhile, I was out carousing with friends from Ed Hood's circle. The following morning, I overslept, and I had to rush to get my mother to the airport. She was in the blackest of moods because I had kept her waiting so long. I was very cold to her because of her mood, and when she got to New York, she wrote me to say, "Please do not be angry with me. I couldn't bear it." I was very sad when I realized the effect I had on her mind.

My senior year I continued to evade work and escape into French novels. Remembering that year, I think of the line in Shakespeare's Sonnet 30: "My dear time's waste." Because I had studied the Arthurian romances over the summer and made copious notes, I was ready to write my thesis on *Erec and Enide*. But somehow, I became totally blocked. I think it must have been another depression because it was followed in the spring by a tremendous burst of manic energy. At that time, I hardly slept, and I walked through Harvard Square and Mount

Auburn Street, and at four in the morning I would go to the Hayes Bickford for ham and eggs. Then I'd go back to the Frick for an hour or two of sleep before going to classes.

I took Harry Levin's celebrated course on Shakespeare. He had a special way of explaining the text, which I used to my benefit in my future education and also in my study of Tibetan scriptures. But instead of writing my thesis, I read Stendhal for the first time. I loved Stendhal. My reading, which included modern novels, was part of my downfall. Not writing my thesis made me extremely anxious. I had a meeting with my tutor, Elizabeth Brown, who said, sadly, "We expected you to get a summa cum laude and then a Ph.D. and then teach here at Harvard. We are all very sad and disappointed."

That year Dr. Brown gave the inaugural address in Sever Hall to all the students studying history and literature. The lecture was a manifestation of the substance of the writing of history. At that time the trend in historical research was to concentrate on a small aspect of the civilization or era being studied. In her lecture, Dr. Brown explained that the tax rolls in France in 1305 could be a means for understanding the whole society and culture of the time. I was dismayed at the thought of history being such a precise and detailed study. I much preferred the old-fashioned way of Henry Osborn Taylor, who wrote *The Mediaeval Mind* in two vast volumes that surveyed the whole scope of medieval history. It was the sweeping viewpoint I was after.

Seeing that I was very troubled, Dom Aelred took it upon himself to help me get through Harvard. He went to see my housemaster, the medieval historian Charles Taylor, and told him that he realized I sometimes balked at the prospect of exams. He asked if I could take my exams in his office at the priory. I was allowed to do so because Aelred was admired as a great educator. Because I had neglected my work, I graduated without honors and only by the skin of my teeth in an honors department. Our final exam lasted three hours and covered the entire range of studies in medieval history and literature for the past three years. I managed to answer all the questions fairly well, but the question I answered miraculously well concerned the sources of

Dante's *Commedia Divina*. At that time, it was fashionable in the world of scholarship to attribute Dante's vision of the inferno, purgatory, and heaven to a large extent to Arab writings. However, I suggested that the visionary writings of two nuns, Hildegard von Bingen and Hroswitha of Gandersheim, were much closer to Dante's world and could therefore be sources of his vision of hell, purgatory, and heaven. When my exam was corrected, it was discovered by Peter Stanskione, one of the medieval history and literature department graders, and others that, not only was my answer a brilliant speculation, but it was also less like an answer on an exam and more like an essay to be published in a medieval studies journal. So that one answer on that exam saved me big time! I was saved by two nuns.

Our graduation ceremony took place in the quad of Kirkland House in early June 1962. Among Professor Alfred's talents was that of a poet, and for the event he recited a poem that was very apropos of our moving on to a new era in our lives. My mother came up from New York for the graduation. Michael's grandmother, Mrs. Weld, who knew my mother, was there as well. Sadly, my mother was in such a terrible state of mind that she was unable to answer Mrs. Weld's questions. She must have appeared strange or rude.

CHAPTER NINE

Mummy Dies: Aftermath

When I got home from Memphis the autumn of 1959, I found my mother in a state of great anxiety and depression in part because she was trying to find buyers for the duplex apartment at 450 East 52nd Street that she'd lived in since 1925. Sometimes she was manic, and this typically showed itself when she suddenly gave large dinner parties. It would not be long before she entered for the first time the Institute for Living, a sanatorium for the mentally ill near Hartford, Connecticut, in 1959, the first of several such visits.

Prince Ali Khan had made a bid for the apartment but was turned down by the board of the co-op. The eldest son of the old Aga Khan, the prince was a playboy who had been married several times, including once to Rita Hayworth. He was considered irresponsible and unfit to assume the office of king of the Ismaili Muslims. The Aga Khan, knowing this, had passed him over and made his grandson, Ali's son Karim, the heir to the Khanate, a ruling family of Ismaili Muslims in Pakistan. Incidentally, when Michael, Chris, and I were at Harvard, Karim Aga Khan was the head of the varsity soccer team. He was fantastically good looking with almond-shaped eyes and very sexy. To see him playing soccer was "very heaven" to me.

After receiving the bid from Ali Khan my mother had to assemble all the residents of the apartment building to get their agreement to accept the prospective buyer. Greta Garbo, who lived above us, was staying on the Riviera along with her friends George Schlee, who was also her business manager, and the *couturière* Valentina. Some said that this was a ménage a trois. Garbo refused to answer my mother's telephone calls as did Schlee and Valentina, which was terribly upsetting to my mother, who was in a state of great frustration. Finally, the three returned home and there was a meeting of the residents. Ali Khan was turned down because of the loud parties for which he was known.

My mother then received an offer from Benjamin Buttenweiser, a partner at Kuhn Loeb and president of many Jewish philanthropies in New York. Mr. Buttenweiser's wife, Helen, was the first woman ever admitted to the New York Bar Association and the first chairwoman of the Legal Aid society. After receiving their bid, my mother had to get an agreement from all the residents of the building to accept them. At the co-op board meeting to discuss the Buttenweisers's offer, George Schlee said to my mother, "Your husband was anti-Semitic," referring to the years my father had been head of the co-op board. My mother replied, "George, you know perfectly well that you wouldn't be here if my husband hadn't gone to bat for you." The Buttenweiser offer was accepted.

Now that the apartment was sold, our lives seemed terribly imperma-nent. As I looked around the beloved rooms, I realized that before long I would never see them again. I stood on the balcony off the living room and watched the tugboats shepherding their barges through the strong current of the East River. Down to the right I could see the great hole where construction was just beginning on the United Nations. The views at night were especially beautiful. The lights on the 59th Street Bridge twinkled like skeins of fairy candles, while across the river on Welfare Island the Pepsi-Cola sign cast its neon red glow high into the sky.

Some of the beautiful paintings in the living room and the dining room would probably have to go. The large painting by Bellotto of a piazza in Venice was sold. Some years later I spent the weekend with Arthur Loeb and his family in Purchase, New York. As I was sitting alone having breakfast in the dining room, my eyes fell upon my moth-er's Bellotto hanging on the wall across the table. When Mr. Loeb came down for breakfast I said to him, "That painting belonged to my mother." His only reply was a little smile. However, the Boudin paint-ing of the rocks and seashore on the Normandy coast went with my mother to her new apartment.

My mother's depression and anxiety during this difficult period had changed her so much that at times I found it difficult to recognize her. But there were happy times as well. Once Michael Baldwin came to visit us from Mount Kisco, and I enjoyed showing him around the apartment. In those days the profession of interior designer had yet to be invented, and women like my mother decorated their houses themselves. Michael had a tremendous sense of style and admired everything my mother had done in furnishing the apartment. My mother adored him. She had known his family since she came out in Philadelphia in 1916.

If selling the big apartment where she had lived for so much of her life was not hard enough for my mother, she also had to look for a suitable replacement. Her search took her all over the city; in fact she looked at forty-three possible apartments, most of which she would say were like "rats' nests." Finally, she found one she liked at 1133 Fifth Avenue and 92nd Street overlooking the reservoir and Central Park West. It was the most beautiful view of New York that I've ever seen, and she decorated the apartment wonderfully. Sadly, there was no longer a room for Nanny, which was yet another break with the past. To celebrate the new apartment my mother started giving fabulous dinner parties. Her extravagant entertaining was characteristic of the manic phase she had now entered.

After my Harvard graduation in 1962, I stayed for a couple of weeks with my mother in New York. One weekend in the middle of June, I accepted an invitation from Michael to visit his first cousin, Nat Reynal, in Nantucket. Michael's cousin, Stephen Baldwin, whose mother was French and who was great company, was also part of the group. We were swimming shortly before lunch when Nat called us out of the water and told me that I should telephone Dom Aelred immediately. Aelred told me that my mother had died. When I asked what had happened, he said, "She jumped out of the window, and you must come back at once."

When I got back to New York, my brother and my sisters and their husbands were already at the apartment. A little while after we finished planning the funeral, Aelred arrived and spent some time with us before leaving to stay at the Roosevelt Hotel. My brothers-in-law, Jonesy and B. Noyes, were staying at B.'s family's suite at the Ritz, while John and I, along with Polly and Peggy, remained at the apartment. That evening I went out with Harvard and New York friends, and they did their best to comfort me.

Although I don't think you can blame yourself for things you couldn't control, I felt badly about having left my mother to spend the weekend in Nantucket. I had never realized how she depended on me to help her remain stable and bear her suffering. As I was leaving for the weekend, she came with me to the elevator to say good-bye, which she had never done before. She was wringing her hands. It made me very sad, but I left.

Earlier that year my mother's son-in-law B. and her other trustee sat her down and explained the state of her finances. Of the $7 million she inherited when my father died (equal to $61 million today), only one million remained. She had spent $6 million in just five years. B told her that if she continued at the same rate, in a year's time she would be left with nothing. I am convinced that this contributed to her suicide.

The funeral at St. James was presided over by the Reverend Arthur Lee Kinsolving. No one has ever equaled the majesty of Dr. Kinsolving's "I am the resurrection and the light." Aelred said that he thought it the finest service he'd ever attended.

After John and my sisters and their husbands left New York, I spent some days in the apartment by myself. Soon, however, we all assembled to choose who would take what furniture, paintings, ornaments, and carpets. My mother left one of her needlepoint rugs to each of us with the porcelain that went with it. I inherited all the porcelain vegetables. I sold these piece by piece over the next years to support my extravagant lifestyle following my mother's death.

Soon after my mother died I went to Paris for a week or so. Although it was pleasant being in Paris, it was also sad, for it reminded me of the many wonderful times my mother and I had spent there together. I was fourteen the first time we went to France to stay with a great friend of my mother's, Princess von Lichtenstein, who had a villa at Cap Ferrat.

The princess was known as Dumpy because, with typical British humor, she was so thin. She seemed a figure from the twenties with her bobbed peroxide blond hair, silk pajama suits, and a long cigarette holder. She was high spirited, with a raspy voice and a delightful laugh. Everybody loved Dumpy, whose real name was Dorothy and who was American. She was godmother to my brother, John, as well as to Serena Stewart.

Dumpy's first husband, Hermann Oelrichs Jr., was the heir to a Nevada silver fortune. They spent their summers at Rosecliff, one of Newport's more opulent stately homes built at the turn of the century by Stanford White and modeled on the Grand Trianon of Versailles, albeit somewhat smaller. When Oelrichs died he left Dumpy a great deal of money. Many years later *The Great Gatsby* starring Robert Redford was filmed at Rosecliff.

When Dumpy was in her early fifties, she married her second husband, Ferdinand von Lichtenstein, said to be the black sheep of the Lichtenstein ruling family because he had once bounced a check. He had Austrian charm and liked to ski and shoot. When Dumpy married him, he was living in Rome, where most of his friends were members of great families and as such were papal chamberlains who were not permitted to receive a divorced person.

As a consequence, Ferdinand and Dumpy lived partly in Kitzbuhl, so Ferdinand could ski, and partly in America, although Dumpy couldn't stay too long because of taxes. Some of the time they lived apart, and Dumpy spent her summers in the South of France without him. I remember one summer when they were both together in Wyoming at Deer Creek Ranch. Dumpy's house at Cap Ferrat on the French Riviera overlooked the harbor, which was always filled with sailboats and motor launches. When I awoke in the early mornings, the walls of my room shimmered in the reflected play of brilliant sunlight, while the houses of Ville Franche across the water were blazing white beneath their red roofs.

When my mother and I arrived, the art dealer Betty Parsons, who had been a girlhood friend of my mother's in Philadelphia, was staying with Dumpy. She was very thoughtful and liked to be alone. She spent a good deal of time in a room at the top of the house that she had turned into a studio, where she painted watercolors of the view. We had long talks leaning against the balustrade of the terrace. It was from her that I first heard about Zen Buddhism. She had been introduced to Zen by Jackson Pollock, one of the artists whom she showed at her gallery in New York.

After Betty left, another old friend of Dumpy's, Tookie Zoppola, came to stay. Like Dumpy she was an American who had married a European count. Something had happened that made Dumpy and my mother feel very sorry for her. Even to me Tookie seemed fragile. Much later I learned that she had recently been at the wheel of a car and had hit a man and killed him. After dinner the four of us would play cards. I don't think I paid as much attention to the cards as to the undercurrent of feeling swirling around the table.

Dumpy's house had a dock for sunbathing and swimming. Lady Kenmare lived above Dumpy at the Villa Fiorentina, the celebrated property that she and her son, Rory Cameron, known for his exquisite taste, had restored to perfection. Because the house had no access to the sea, Dumpy let her use her dock. One morning Claudette Colbert, who was staying with Lady Kenmare, came down to swim while I was reading on the dock. She introduced herself and asked me what I was reading. I told her *War and Peace*, and she said, "Oh, I read it just at your age. How wonderful." And with that she dove into the water. I was sorry she was wearing a bathing cap because she was so beautiful.

Lady Kenmare deserves a brief mention because at the time she was quite famous, or perhaps infamous is a better word. She was a celebrated beauty. It was said that people stood on chairs in the lobby of the Hotel de Paris in Monaco just to catch a glimpse of her as she walked by swathed in clouds of gray chiffon with a bunch of violets at her tiny waist. She was also celebrated for her four marriages—two to immensely rich men, three of whom had titles. All of them died before her, two less than a year after she married them, causing her neighbor, Somerset Maugham, to call her Lady Killmore. Lady Kenmare was said to be a legally registered heroin addict. Apparently, opium was her drug of choice. "I don't think Enid killed anybody," said a friend of her son, Rory. "But she may have given them drugs and helped them along."

During our visit Dumpy gave a cocktail party. Among the guests was the former Lady Kathleen Manners, who two years before had divorced Lowell Guinness, heir to the Guinness Brewing fortune, after fifteen years of marriage. He had visiting rights that summer over their two children, a boy and a girl who were then twelve and fourteen and who were staying with him on his extremely large yacht, which was anchored some distance out in the harbor. According to their mother, Guinness was taking advantage of a general strike to extend his time with the children and prevent Mrs. Guinness from seeing them. She made a bit of a scene at the party, going on at length about the situation. It sounded heart-wrenching to me, although I noticed that none of the other guests seemed the least sympathetic.

Suddenly, she looked at me and said that she needed me to take her out to the yacht on a *pedalo*—a raftlike contraption still popular in the South of France that two people peddle like a bicycle. I looked at my mother, and she told me to go ahead. By the time we reached the yacht, she had become hysterical. Although I was somewhat mystified by the lady's predicament, I was absolutely on her side and hostile to the man who was cruelly keeping her from her children. I saw myself as her champion. When Mrs. Guinness called up to the crew, they lowered a rope ladder so that we could climb aboard. When we reached the deck, we found the large crew in crisp white uniforms and several beautiful children, including a tall girl with long hair. Standing with the children was the former Gloria Rubio, who, it was said, had clawed her way out of a Mexican brothel to become Lowell Guinness's third wife. The moment Mrs. Guinness boarded the yacht, she rushed across the deck crying, "My darling children!" She hugged them for a very long time indeed, and I thought that they both seemed embarrassed, as she begged their father to let her take them away with her. No doubt they were having a very good time on the yacht. However, Guinness was adamant that they remain with him, so in tears she left the boat, and I peddled her back to shore.

Several days later Dumpy and my mother took me to lunch with Somerset Maugham at the Villa Mauresque in Ville Franche. While the grown-ups played bridge, I lay on the lawn and continued making my way through *War and Peace*. Some days later, my mother and I left Cap Ferrat, and on our way to the airport, my mother turned to me and said, "I'm never going back to the Riviera. The people are so unattractive." And she never did.

No doubt she would have agreed with Bill Paley, who once described the society of the South of France as "the cream of the scum."

In 1961, Michael, who had been sailing on a boat in Norway, joined my mother and me in Paris, where he traveled with us through the Loire Valley in an old limousine driven by Leon, a quintessentially courteous Frenchman who loved good food and wine. When we left Paris, my mother refused to give up our rooms at the Hotel Vendôme, although we would not be using them for a week. When asked about this extravagance, she simply said that it was the height of the season and if we let go of the rooms, we wouldn't get them back.

Between my sophomore and junior years, my mother and I sailed to Italy with Dom Aelred on the *Vulcania*. The Sunday morning we were on board the ship, Aelred celebrated Mass in the *Vulcania*'s chapel. When my mother went up to take Communion, Aelred told her to return to her seat. Although she knew that only Catholics were entitled to take Communion, she thought that she should be an exception and was hurt and angry at his refusal.

We went first to Ravello, where Dom Aelred left us to stay with his old friend Father Ralph Vellardi in Amalfi. My mother and I were driven to Vienna, and from there we went to Florence and on to Venice, where we "did Venice," as they say. As I was walking alone one evening near the Piazza San Marco, I spotted a very good-looking young blond man. I pretended to look in a shop window while I waited for him to catch up. When he asked if I was German, I said, "No, I'm American. Do you speak English?" He said, "No, let's speak French." So in French we made an engagement to meet the following afternoon. When I asked him why, as a Venetian, he had blond hair he explained that he was a Lombard and that many Lombards have blond hair. The Lombards, he told me, came down and conquered Northern Italy. He said that his name was Luciano Tempo and that he worked in the office of the Bauer Grunwald Hotel.

Before we separated he took me under the shadow of Teatro La Fenice, and we were intimate in a passionate but gentle way. I left him in a state of high anticipation of our next meeting. I told my mother that I had run into Button Baker at the American Express and that we had agreed to go the following afternoon to an island festival and that I'd be home late. I walked along the little streets of Venice the next afternoon and found my new acquaintance waiting at the Rialto Bridge. He had rented a little boat and rowed us out along the canal, where he was very loving to me in the middle of the boat traffic. I admired his *desinvoltura* but felt a little uneasy that our small boat might not be unnoticed. Later we went to the Lido for a swim, and that was a great treat as it gave me a chance to see Luciano's beautiful body. I hoped that we would soon be in bed together. We recited together the poem of Alphonse de Lamartine that takes place in a skiff off the coast of Lebanon. We spent an incredibly beautiful night, and early in the morning, we stopped at a little chapel and said a prayer. I walked back to the Danieli and joined my mother at breakfast. She asked, "How was Button?" I said, "Oh, Button was great!" That was one of the most beautiful encounters of my life.

From Venice my mother and I went to Paris and stayed at the Ritz. One day we went to lunch with the Windsors at their house in the Bois de Boulogne. Suddenly the duchess said to me, "I think you belong in the foreign office." When she mentioned that she had to make an appointment with Monsieur Alexandre, the coiffeur, for the following day, I said, "Oh, let me make the appointment for you." So I telephoned and in French said, "I'm speaking on behalf of the Duchess of Windsor. May we have an appointment for tomorrow?" The duchess laughed and laughed and said, "Yes, you really do belong in the foreign office."

Another time we lunched with the Windsors at Le Moulin, their old mill just outside Paris, which they had turned into a lovely country house. When we arrived, the duke took us around his garden, of which he was deservedly very proud. He then led us to a house on the property, which consisted of one big room he used as his study. He showed us memorabilia from the days when he was king of England, including an enormous drum that had been presented to him by his regiment; he had turned it into a table.

We joined the duchess in her sitting room until we were called in to lunch, which was served in an outdoor dining room. During the lunch I made something of a faux pas. At the time the duke was preoccupied with the Mau Mau uprising and the rebellion in Kenya against the British Empire. He asked my mother what she thought, and she gave a very diplomatic reply. When he asked me how I felt about the rebellion, I said, "Well sir, I come from a different generation and I think differently." To which the duke replied, "If I had known he was going to talk that way, I wouldn't have invited him." But it was all covered over by the waters of good humor, and we were sent off affectionately at the end of our visit.

During that same visit I went to see my friend Nicole Bouchet de Fareins, with whom I had spent the summer in 1955. She asked me where we had dined the previous night, and I told her that we had dined with Héli de Talleyrand-Périgord, who was the fifth Duke of Talleyrand, his wife, and Leila, a rich American friend of my mother's, at St. Brice, the Talleyrands' house at St. Denis, which had once belonged to Edith Wharton. Nicole asked how we had gotten there, and I said, "We went in the car of Princess Cora Caetani." Nicole said, "Well, all of your mother's friends are collaborators!" As a heroine of La Résistance, Nicole was quite sensitive about the matter of collaboration. Héli's distant and most distinguished ancestor was the Talleyrand who was Napoleon's foreign minister. After the fall of the empire, Talleyrand survived the Bourbon Restoration. With Metternich he headed the Vienna Congress, which redistributed the kingdoms and principalities disrupted by Napoleon, and resumed his position as foreign minister of France.

That summer after my mother's death in 1962, I stayed with Nicole, who very sweetly came up to Paris, which was empty during the summer. She had sacrificed some of her wonderful Normandy summer to give me hospitality at her apartment. We had long talks together. In my grief and confusion, I felt very supported by her. It turned out that my aunt

Polly was also in Paris. We met at her hotel, the Meurice, and had lunch together at the Eiffel Tower. I told her about Nicole and her extraordinary adventures in the Resistance during the war. And she said, "You should write about Nicole." And now, fifty-six years later, I have.

Several years later in 1963, when I was staying with Nicole again, she told me that she was going to have to sell Le Bois Normand. I was so distressed at the thought of her losing the house that I sent a telegram to my brother-in-law B. Noyes, who was my financial trustee, and asked him to send Nicole $10,000. He telegraphed me back to confirm it, and I gave the OK to sell some stock. She used most of the money to repair the thatched roof at Le Bois Normand. Unfortunately, it became impossible for her to keep the house because of taxes, and she had to sell it the following year. Among the prospective buyers was the novelist Françoise Sagan, who had written several best-selling novels, including *Bonjour Tristesse* followed by *Un Certain Sourire* and *Aimez-vous Brahms?* When Nicole told Sagan that the film of Alain-Fournier's novel *Le Grand Meaulnes* had been shot at Le Bois Normand, Sagan said that it was not a very good novel. Nicole replied, "Alain-Fournier had the good taste to die after his first novel." When I was visiting Nicole, Gerald Maurois, the son of the great French writer André Maurois, was also staying at Le Bois Normand. He had taught French at Middlebury College in Vermont and had a malicious sense of humor. He wrote down the telegram from B. Noyes over the phone about my raising some money for her, and he gave me the news, but called Nicole Tata (auntie), meaning that she had obviously won my affection.

Earlier that year before leaving for Paris, I had applied for a course at the Harvard Summer School in my favorite subject, the French novel. When I returned to New York from Paris, I took the shuttle to Boston, then the subway to Cambridge and the house where rooms were provided for summer school students. To my astonishment I found several large gray mail bags filled with letters of sympathy from friends about my mother, including one from the Windsors.

My course was taught by a Monsieur Bénichou, a French Algerian who was among the best French teachers I'd ever had. Among the novels we studied were *La Princesse de Clèves* by Madame de La Fayette, *Les Liaisons Dangereuses* by Choderlos de Laclos, *Manon Lescaut* by L'Abbé Prévot, and *Le Père Goriot* by Balzac. I was thrilled to get an A in the course. It went on my Harvard transcript and was very helpful as things turned out.

In our first lecture a student sat down next to me and introduced himself as Issam Azzam. For some reason, perhaps because I was in need of a friend, we immediately became close friends. Issam lived with his parents at the Plaza Hotel in a suite provided by the Egyptian government that he called Our Tent. His father, Abdul Rahman Hassan Azzam, had been appointed Egyptian ambassador to the United Nations by Nasser. He had previously been foreign minister of Egypt under King Farouk, and before that the first secretary general of the Arab League. I introduced Issam to all my New York friends, who adored him, and we all saw a great deal of him. He was extremely funny and very social, but underneath he was a devout Muslim and a Sufi. His book on the Sufi poet Al-Maari begins with the proverb "Only he who understands is sad."

As soon as I got back to New York after summer school in September 1962, I went to see Nanny, who was living at the West End Hotel. My second visit was to Vera Somoff, to whom I often went for tea and to talk about my mother. She had known our family since the 1930s when she had been a model for the dressmaker Hattie Carnegie. My parents became very fond of her, and as she was a talented artist, they had invited her to the Pillars in Old Westbury to paint my sisters' portraits. It was the beginning of a close friendship between my mother and Vera, and she came every year for Christmas lunch with us. Elsa Maxwell, society's hostess, also came to these lunches, which made my sister Peggy very angry, as she disliked people who she thought were social climbers.

I was very young when I first met Vera. One day I came into the living room where she was sitting with my mother, who introduced us. I said, "Nanny and I go out for walks in the park. Would you like to come for a walk with us?" She laughed and said that she would be delighted. That is how we became lifelong friends. Now, twenty years later, Vera was a great comfort to me after my mother died. During our visits she would tell me about Russia before the revolution and the life of her family, making it all so vivid that even now whenever I read about Russia everything seems familiar to me.

Vera's father had been a member of Tsar Nicholas II's Conseil d'État. The Somoffs were descended from the Mongols who invaded Russia in the thirteenth century. In time they became completely Russian and served the tsar for centuries rather like the Yousoupoffs, who also started out as Mongols but became important members of the Russian aristocracy. Mr. Somoff was also the Maréchal de Noblesse of St. Petersburg, the official who settled disputes among members of the nobility. As Maréchal he was asked by the tsar to organize the last great Russian Imperial Ball in St. Petersburg in 1913. The ball was opened by the tsarina dancing with Mr. Somoff and the tsar dancing with Vera's mother.

Mr. Somoff was also a member of the board of the Conservatories of Music in St. Petersburg and Moscow when Tchaikovsky was the leading Russian composer. After his death the board appointed Glazunov as the new composer in residence. Vera said that music was always part of her childhood, for her father loved to play the piano, especially the German romantic music of Shubert and Schumann; the Grieg piano concerto was a particular favorite. Before the revolution, Vera was a great heiress because both her parents owned vast estates. One day just before the revolution, her mother took her to one of the family's properties, and Vera, who was already a good draftsman, made drawings of it. When she told her mother how much she loved the place, her mother said, "It belongs to you."

In 1918, shortly after the revolution began, the Somoffs fled from St. Petersburg to the Crimea, where they stayed in a house belonging to the Yousoupoffs. The Dowager Empress Marie Feodorovna, daughter of King Frederick of Denmark and mother of Tsar Nicholas II, had also escaped to the Crimea along with many other members of the court. When her nephew George V (who was also first cousin to the tsar) dispatched the dreadnought *Marlborough*, along with a flotilla escort, to rescue his aunt, the empress refused to leave unless everyone who wanted to go would be given safe passage. Some people decided to stay in Russia, which was a very poor decision. While they were still in the Crimea, Madame Narishkina, one of Vera's relatives who was lady-in-waiting to the Dowager Empress, presented Vera to her majesty. After Vera, who had been too young to be presented at court, and Madame Narishkina were given tea, the empress appeared (the tsar's family never had tea nor meals with people) and after talking to Vera for a time gave her a photograph of herself. When she died in 1990, Vera left the photograph to me.

In 1918, Vera sailed from the Crimea with her parents and her brother and sister on one of King George V's ships. While still in St. Petersburg, she had fallen in love with Count Muraviev Amursky, and they planned to marry. They each left the Crimea on separate ships, and as the ships passed each other heading out to sea, Vera caught a glimpse of her fiancé. It was the last time they ever saw each other. The count had a villa in Florence, where they had planned to settle, but he died suddenly, before they could meet again. Vera said, "Something good happens to me and then it is always taken away." I think she was bitter about her exile and deeply missed the Russia of her youth. Although there was an aura of sadness about her, she nonetheless had enormous charm and humor.

The Somoffs went first to Turkey, then to Malta, and then on to Italy, where they settled for a time in Rome. By that time Vera's mother was very ill. The queen of Italy was one of three Montenegran princesses, one of whom married the king of Italy, while the other two married grand dukes of Russia. Through her sister, Madame Somoff knew the queen of Italy, who arranged for her to have the best medical care. Unfortunately, it was to no avail.

After her mother died, Vera and her father went to Paris, where her father hoped to earn some money. In Paris speculators often lent money to Russian refugee landowners, gambling that the refugees' properties would be restored to them when the Bolsheviks were driven out of power. However, Paris proved too expensive, and Vera and her father moved to Munich, where a rich American from Chicago named Shaw-Kennedy asked Mr. Somoff for permission to marry his daughter. Vera's sister, who had escaped with them from the Crimea, had had a nervous breakdown and was in a hospital in Nice, which was costing more than Mr. Somoff could afford. When he begged Vera to accept the rich Shaw-Kennedy, she reluctantly married him and went to America, where she lived for the rest of her life except for a few trips to Paris to see her brother.

The wedding took place in Munich in 1923 during Hitler's Putsch, which was put down only after a great deal of fighting in the streets. Vera, in her wedding dress, had to step around barricades of bricks and debris to get from the hotel to the church. In the wedding liturgy of the Russian Orthodox Church, a man holds a crown over the bride's head, and the man with the crown for Vera was the son of Prince Gorchakov, who had been minister of the interior under Tsar Nicholas II. It was he who distributed the notorious false document called *The Protocols of the Elders of Zion*. Vera was pro-Nazi and anti-Semitic, as so many exiled Russians were, because they believed that if Hitler conquered Russia, their properties would be restored to them.

After a few years in New York, Vera asked Shaw-Kennedy for a divorce. When he asked her to return the jewelry he had given her, she collected them and threw them in his face. Subsequently, she went through all her scrapbooks and in every photo in which he appeared she cut out his face with a pair of scissors.

Vera then moved to a two-room apartment on East 63rd Street just off Fifth Avenue. I think her rent was thirty-five dollars a month, and because the apartment was rent controlled, she was able to stay in it until she died. When I was eighteen Vera and I started going to the Balanchine ballet together, and it was thrilling to talk to a Russian who had been familiar with the Mariinsky Theatre and the Imperial Ballet before the revolution. Her artistic standards were lofty, however. When I once asked her what she thought of Dvorak as a composer, she answered, "That cheap little Czech!"

After visiting Vera Somoff, I returned to the apartment at 1133 Fifth Avenue. Agnes Dawson, my mother's maid, was still staying there, as was Mary Reilly, the cook; Delia, the maid who served the meals; and Margaret, who washed the pots. We all remained there until the apartment was sold. Meanwhile, I had been accepted at Columbia Graduate School to study for a master's degree in French literature starting that autumn.

Some years before at a party, Serena Stewart had introduced me to Dennis Deegan. Dennis and Serena once came for lunch at the 52nd Street apartment with their friend Michael Smith. Afterward, we all went across the street to the River Club for a swim in the club pool. With Serena riding on Michael's shoulders and I on Dennis's shoulders, we had a brisk game of water polo. Through Arthur Loeb, I later met Dennis again when he was fresh out of Yale; he had only stayed there a year. When he heard from Serena that I was in New York, he telephoned and came around to see me while I was still living alone in the apartment on Fifth Avenue. No furniture was left except for one chair, and I sat in that chair as long as I could. I told Dennis that I had to leave the apartment because it was soon to be sold, and I had no idea where to live. He said, "Oh, that's simple. I'll just get a *New York Times* and we'll look at the real estate section, circle what sounds promising, and go to see them. I have no place to stay so I could stay there with you." I was relieved that someone was willing to take charge of this worldly transition, as I had no experience with the practicalities involved.

We soon found an apartment on the top floor of a small apartment house on East 19th Street, just around the corner from Gramercy Park. Down the street, which was known as Block Beautiful, lived Lincoln Kirstein, the patron of Balanchine's ballet; next door to us was a tiny house owned by Lillian Gish and her sister Dorothy, great actresses of the silent screen.

I brought some of the furniture and porcelain I inherited from my mother to the new apartment but put most of it in storage because the apartment was so small and the vegetable porcelain was too precious to risk breakage. Meanwhile, Dennis moved into 1133 with me and took over the household. Before long Agnes came to me in some distress and said, "You've got to get rid of him or I will leave. I can't stand him!" So I calmed her down and told her, "Agnes, you stay, and I will leave with Dennis." I had become possessed by him, to put it mildly.

Dennis was not particularly good looking; in fact, he looked like Cocteau's drawing of Dargelo in *Les Enfants Terribles*. He had a cruel streak, and I suspect what attracted me to him was what the French call *nostalgie de la boue*—a craving for the gutter. The whole thing was masochism. He stole things and spoke ill of my friends; he humiliated me in many ways and used me without ever trying to be nice. Moreover, we only had sex once; afterward, he refused anything remotely intimate. In fact, he was nothing but a leech, but I seemed to need that. Nonetheless, he had a kind of raffish quality that was not without charm. Once he and I were lunching at the Plaza, where John Gielgud was holding court at a table full of young men. Dennis went over and introduced himself to Gielgud, who said, "Saucy beauty."

Dennis took charge of decorating the 19th Street apartment. He turned the front hall into a bedroom for himself. In the sitting room, which looked out onto 19th Street and which he also took over for himself, he installed a long marble-topped table with two magnificent Chinese porcelain geese, which were the best things in my mother's exceptional collection of porcelain.

A long corridor led to the back of the apartment where there was another sitting room with pots of palm trees. One entire wall was devoted to my books, arranged on shelves that Dennis had built. On the floor was one of the rugs my mother had needle-pointed. There was an unusual Dutch coffee table with a beaded top and a brown couch with Marquet's impressionist painting of the Pont Neuf above it. Farther along at the end of the flat was a small bathroom with an old bathtub with claw feet and my little bedroom. So, we had two sections to live in.

Meanwhile, I was going uptown to Columbia, where I was taking courses in French literature. I had several good teachers, especially Madame Jeanne Plesants, a linguistics professor who taught a course on the French language. She also taught us the art of pronunciation by giving examples of how the French sentences rise at the end, whereas English sentences descend (other than questions of course). A genius among the teachers was Monsieur Riffaterre, who after being tortured by the Gestapo had managed to escape. He taught the novels of

Stendhal using an unusual method of analyzing a page of the novelist's prose, a method the French call *explication du texte*. It was an almost mathematical way of studying a writer's style by examining how they employed each word, whether they tended to use repetitions, and so on. Learning about Stendhal and his novels came in handy and quite literally saved me later on. I will tell that story soon.

When the time came for me to present my thesis topic, I told Monsieur Riffaterre that I wanted to write on "De l'amour," Stendhal's philosophical and psychological essay that was the basis for his many novels. The professor was pleased, so I was in business. However, once again circumstances forced me to suspend work on a thesis.

At about this time I was asked to fly out to Colorado Springs to the US Air Force Academy to present the prize given in honor of my father to the outstanding cadet of the year. I arrived at the ceremony wearing a new white linen suit, which I had had made for me by an Italian tailor on Madison Avenue and that made me look, I thought, like one of the actors then popular in Italian films. It was worthy of Oscar Wilde. After I presented the prize to a very handsome cadet—I thought to myself that I would like to receive him as a prize—the commandant asked me to stay for the evening reception. I rather grandly refused, saying that I had to get back to New York in time for a dinner party.

Dennis had come to New York to direct a play, *Save Me a Place at Forest Lawn* by Lorees Yerby, which was being funded by Arthur Loeb, who became a friend of mine. Shortly before the play opened, Marian Fenn, producer John Houseman's secretary, came to New York to assist Dennis. Marian was from Norfolk, England, charming but plain and hyperefficient. We became close friends. She found an extraordinary apartment consisting of a one-room cabin on the roof of an apartment building on the West Side, which she furnished with a few pieces of my mother's furniture that I'd loaned her. Out on the roof she set up a large dining room table where she would give dinners for a small group of us involved in the production or who otherwise were appreciative well-wishers. An invitation to one of her parties read, "Come to a roof."

Like me, Marian understood Dennis's grave shortcomings but put up with them. The three of us often went to Pete's Tavern, a restaurant around the corner from our apartment. Of course, I paid because that was part of being Dennis's friend. Occasionally to be extravagant, we went to Orsini's. One night, Marian and I went to Orsini's, and Dennis arrived a couple of hours late. We were angry and scolded him, but he simply said, "That's the way I am, and if you want to be my friend, you'll just have to put up with it."

Dennis was something the French call an *entremetteuse*, a brothel keeper who introduces girls to boys or to men. Dennis would bring people together. For example, he knew the French popular singer Charles Aznavour, who was short but liked tall American models, so Dennis filled the apartment with tall American girls for him. Once when Dennis stayed at 1133 before it was sold, my sister Peggy answered the phone when we were out. Virgil Thompson was on the other end and asked for Dennis. Peggy was simply amazed that we knew Virgil Thompson.

Sometimes we would transform my sitting room into a dining room for parties, many of which were very big, rather like those Michael gave in the Frick when we were at Harvard, with lots of people all squeezed together. Not all our parties were gay. There were plenty of models, actors, and Hollywood types, many of whom could be found shooting up in the bathroom. At one of Dennis's dinners for John Houseman and the actress Ruth Ford, they invited me to join them—at my own table no less. Another evening Sam Barber came to a dinner I gave for my sister Polly and her husband, Jonesy.

I suppose having Dennis live with me was one of my worst mistakes ever. Although he himself may not have taken heroin, many of his friends did, which created an atmosphere of decadence that I found revolting. Dennis liked to shock people. My friends who knew him warned me that I should not be so involved with him because he was such a bad character. Father Hilary quite rightly told me to get out of the demimonde.

Dennis's play *Save Me a Place at Forest Lawn* consisted of two plays in one. The second play had three black actors, including James Earl Jones and Cicely Tyson. Dennis was her lover, and Cicely became a friend of mine. She spent a lot of time with us, especially in Dennis's bedroom. James Earl Jones was wonderful in his part, and I went several times just to watch him. There's an extra dimension to the theater when you know an actor; you feel close to them. The other play featured the great star Margaret Hamilton, who had played the Wicked Witch of the West in the film *Wizard of Oz*. She was delightful and unpretentious. In fact, all the actors were wonderful in their parts. After opening night on May 8, 1963, everyone came back to our apartment to wait for the reviews. The first newspapers were so encouraging that we thought the play might continue. However, when Edith Oliver, the drama critic of *The New Yorker*, panned the production, it folded. I was sorry for Dennis, but when I saw how well he took the defeat, I realized that in some ways he had strength of character.

When the play closed the actors went their separate ways, except Cicely Tyson, who stayed with Dennis. I gave her some of my mother's costume jewelry. A few years later as I was walking by Tiffany's with Aelred Graham, I ran into Cicely swathed in a magnificent fur coat. I was happy for her, and Aelred was amused to see me calling out to a beautiful lady hurrying along Fifth Avenue in luxurious furs. Since then I've followed Cicely's remarkable career on stage and screen. I was proud of Dennis for the first-rate cast he managed to assemble for his two Off Broadway productions. The actors taught me that at its best the stage is harmonious, not the bitchy jealous place of which one often thinks.

Before coming to New York, Dennis had been living in Venice, California, working for John Houseman. He was a sometime lover of Houseman's wife, Joan, who would come to stay with Dennis at my apartment. At a dinner we gave for Houseman one evening, he announced, "Joan is now staying with Dennis down here, but I know in a couple of days she will be at the Plaza." Another evening I came home from Columbia to find Joan and Dennis at the apartment. I went back to my library/sitting room and sat down at my mother's beautiful eighteenth-century English double desk and got to work reading Stendhal's *Lucien Leuwen* for my master's thesis. Dennis and Joan eventually came back to ask me to join them for dinner. I said that I had to study, and Joan said, "Oh, but you don't have to study *all* the time."

One of Dennis's friends, Andreas Voutsinas, was Jane Fonda's acting teacher. Dennis and Andreas were giving a birthday party for Jane in our apartment, and she was sitting in a chair in the farthest room receiving people like royalty. I was wearing my white linen suit, and when someone—maybe Leo Castelli, the art dealer, who was also very louche—introduced us, Jane shook hands and said, "You're just like my brother, Peter."

At one point, Dennis got jaundice and became depressed. He was pitiful. When he begged me to take him to the priory, I refused. I had made a firm distinction between Dennis and his New York friends and Dom Aelred and the priory. By mutual agreement, Dennis finally managed to meet Aelred when he and I were lunching in New York at Nicholson's on Second Avenue, a restaurant belonging to Dennis's friend Johnny Nicholson. Dennis arrived with a white rose, which he placed on the table in front of Aelred. Obviously, he wanted to make a good impression, perhaps because his father was an Irish American Catholic and his mother was a Polish American Catholic. His gesture made a favorable impression on Aelred, who did not, however, change his opinion of Dennis.

To cheer Dennis up I took him to Puerto Rico to stay at a hotel that Vera recommended. We had to leave after the first night because Dennis felt that the hotel wasn't up to his standards. We ended up at El Convento, formerly an old convent, which had been beautifully restored by the Rockefellers in the Spanish style. Dennis invited everyone he knew in San Juan to dine with us. I had never taken any drugs of any kind, but I decided to get high on marijuana with the rest of them. The next morning, when Dennis insisted that we leave the hotel immediately, I thought it rather odd, but I imagined that since the hotel had my address in New York, they would either send me a bill or a threatening letter. When Johnny Nicholson came to see us off at the airport, Dennis asked him to pay our hotel bill. Johnny not only said that he would, but he actually did. That's the amoral way Dennis operated.

Another time Dennis and I went to St. Thomas. I must say that in all my travels that vacation was one of the most beautiful and happy times I've ever had. We knew nobody until I ran into Priscilla, someone I'd known since childhood. She was the daughter of Polly Howe, a friend of my mother's who was such a close friend of the Windsors that she was affectionately called their lady-in-waiting. Priscilla had been in my sister Peggy's wedding, and suddenly there she was, sitting at a table in a restaurant in St. Thomas. So we had a great reunion. The waiter was named Ben Johnson, although I rather doubt he was familiar with the great English poet and playwright. Ben was the kept boy of the Englishman who owned the restaurant, and we'd go to his house to visit Ben. The Englishman, however, was so jealous that finally we were no longer welcome.

The best thing about St. Thomas was Kokie Beach, a tiny cove that Vera Somoff had told me about. We'd lie on the sand, swim in the ocean, and then return to the beach and read. Dennis was reading William Burroughs, and I continued reading Stendhal. A big outdoor bar on the street with tables reminded me of cafés in Paris.

On our return to the States, I started to crumble. Dennis and I had shared the apartment for almost two years. I was so fed up with his appalling demimonde life that I told him to stay in the apartment and I would move up nearer Columbia. So I took a room in a hotel on 116th Street and left Dennis in the apartment with all my mother's beautiful things and stopped seeing him. My trustee and brother-in-law B. Noyes finally got rid of the apartment. When he left, Dennis took a sword with a gold hilt that had been a present to my father from the king of Saudi Arabia.

Eventually, Dennis married a woman who was a relation of Henri Matisse. They lived in an apartment in Paris with Matisse frescoes on the walls. One day Dennis went out for a stroll and stopped in a French street urinal where he put the make on a young Algerian boy who stabbed him to death.

CHAPTER TEN

Aftermath, Continued

I returned to New York in September 1962 for the start of my first term at Columbia University. Among my courses was one on Henry de Montherlant, one of my favorite French authors. For one assignment we had to give an oral report on one of his works, and I chose the play *Le Cardinal d'Espagne*. It took almost an hour, and I used the method of analyzing a text that I had learned from Professor Harry Levin's Shakespeare course at Harvard. I traced words throughout the play that developed different meanings as they made their way to the end of the drama. I was pleased that the professor was delighted.

In December, I went back to Greece to see Minas, whom I had met earlier in June. I had gone to Athens, where I took the ferry to Hydra. As I came down the gangplank, I was unaware of the Merchant Marine Academy students who were checking out the passengers as was their custom. Often, they would befriend tourists who later would come to the cafés for a drink and a bite to eat. Dressed in a gray summer suit and wearing sunglasses, I must have seemed glamorous to one of the boys.

Later at dinner in a *taverna,* a small Greek restaurant, I met a boy, Minas Lekanides, who was with a girl from Alexandria named Olga. They both knew English, so we had no trouble communicating. Suddenly Minas stood up and dove into the harbor with all his clothes on. Olga said, "Don't pay any attention to him. He's always showing off." We then went and sat on the jetty where Minas put his head in Olga's lap and said something in Greek. She said, "He said you are γοητευτικός, which means 'enchanting.'" So I got my hopes up despite his having set his head in her lap.

Minas was absolutely beautiful, like a Greek god. We went swimming every day and agreed to meet in Athens. When I returned to the Grande Bretagne Hotel, Minas came and spent the night with me. At some point an employee of the hotel unlocked our door and found the two of us in bed. He said, "Excuse me," and left. It seems they were looking for people who might have sneaked in as unpaid guests. I didn't get the feeling that it was a search on moral grounds but rather for economic reasons. Nevertheless, the receptionist telephoned in the morning to say that Mrs. Lekanides was downstairs wanting to see her son.

Minas leaped into his clothes and rushed down to the lobby, where he was spirited away by his mother. Although I was embarrassed, I was relieved that Minas and I could meet again. After a heavenly few days on Corfu, we returned to Athens and agreed to meet again in December during Columbia's Christmas holiday, when I would return to Athens. We swam every day at a beach in a little cove called Paleokastritsa, where we had lunch in a taverna with a wooden terrace beneath a roof of vines. From a sensuous point of view, my life was completely fulfilled.

That December we had hoped to visit Alexandria to see my friend Issam Azzam, but alas, Minas did not have a visa for Egypt, so instead we went to Rome, where we stayed at the Hotel d'Inghilterra where Oscar Wilde once stayed. While I was there, a friend from Harvard, Colin Streeter, came to see me along with two Italian friends, Enzo and Andrea Reichlin. We all had a delightful lunch together on the Via Veneto. Minas was rather quiet perhaps because he noticed that I was quite taken by the Italians, especially by Andrea.

For New Year's Eve we all planned to go to Naples to meet with Ralph Love, another friend from Harvard. As Andrea's family was having a party, it was quite late when we picked him up and drove out of Rome, cautiously because of an old pagan custom that was still observed. People would toss glasses out of their windows as a way of throwing out the old year, and one could be pelted with glass "missiles." However, we made it safely out of Rome and got to Naples in the early hours of the morning. We made our way to a little *castello* on the seacoast where Ralph was living and knocked on the door. The young man who answered the door told Andrea that Ralph had just died of a heroin overdose and was in the morgue. Fate had decreed that our reunion with Ralph Love was not to be. He had been very attractive.

His father had been the governor of Colorado, and I think Ralph left because he was gay and ended up living in New York.

When we left Naples, I was sorry to say good-bye to Andrea, although I felt a bit guilty because I was attracted to someone besides Minas. I thought I was being greedy. Minas and I then went on to Venice, where, ironically, we stayed at the hotel Bauer-Grünwald, where Luciano Tempo, the young man with whom I had had a romance years before when I was in Venice with my mother, had worked. However, we never saw him, so perhaps he had moved on.

When we returned to Athens, Minas persuaded me to give him a car. I telephoned my trustee, Clayton Erwin, who said that financially I would need to be more careful but that he'd give me the funds because, being gay himself, he understood the situation. Then he added, "But couldn't you find someone who you didn't have to give cars to?" When we went to the bank to arrange for the car, the banker asked me why I was doing such a thing. And Minas piped up and said, "Oh, I saved his life. He was out swimming and got in trouble, and now he's rewarding me with a car." And the banker looked at me and said very ironically, "Well, thank you for what you're doing for the Greek economy."

After I returned to Columbia to continue studying Stendhal for my thesis, Minas wrote me, and I also received a letter from Andrea Reichlin, which said simply, "Why haven't you written to me, Harold?" Although I was so glad to hear from him, I somehow never got around to writing him back.

Things soon started to cave in for me, and I began to behave strangely. I roamed the streets of the city for two days and two nights without pausing to eat anything. I began hallucinating, convinced that I was going to form a government and appoint friends of mine to various offices. I ended up in the lobby of the Plaza Hotel, where I telephoned Issam and told him that I was downstairs and wanted to see him. He came down carrying a beautifully furled umbrella and took me into the dining room, where he gave me breakfast. I told him that I wanted him to be the foreign minister of the new government I was forming. He said, "Well, the first thing that somebody forming a government has to do is go to the doctor and have his health examined. So come along and we will see your doctor." We went to my mother's doctor, Dr. Santi, who became very emotional about my condition because he realized that my mother's bipolar gene had been transmitted.

As Issam had to return to work, he took me back to my hotel room on 116th Street. I telephoned my sister Peggy in Connecticut and went on and on about how we must make some recompense to James Baldwin, the great black writer, for all that we had done to the blacks. She agreed and said that she was coming into town to see me. Meanwhile, she called her husband, B. Noyes, and told him to come up from Wall Street and get me at my hotel. After taking me to lunch, B. took me to his parents' suite at the Ritz, where Peggy joined us. Peggy was very pregnant, and I feel badly that in my demented state I put her through such a terrible time. They suggested that we go out to dinner and then to a movie. Halfway through dinner I wanted to leave, so we did. And halfway through the James Bond movie *Dr. No* (I thought the whole thing was in code), I wanted to leave, and we did.

We went back to the Ritz, and B. said, "There's a closet in my room where you can hang your coat up." As I thought he had said, "Go hang yourself," I became frightened and aggressive. I sat on the sofa and said, "You don't know anything about me." Peggy said, "Well, then tell us about yourself." "That fire screen looks like a movie screen," I told them. "I can see the Dalai Lama, and I can see exactly what he's doing." Peggy said, "That's wonderful." I then ran to the desk and threw a very valuable clock out the window to get attention so that they wouldn't try to kill me. I ran to the door and out into the hall and raced up and down with B. trying to catch me. He finally grabbed my arm, and I bit him, which prompted B. to holler to Peggy, "The little bastard bit me!"

They dragged me into the suite and called the hospital. A doctor arrived with an elephant-size injection needle to knock me out. I awoke the following day to find myself in the psychiatric wing of Roosevelt Hospital, where I stayed for a week of treatment for what was called a psychotic episode. Friends, including Michael and Chris, came to visit.

Dom Aelred arrived from the priory. He asked me what book he could get for me, and I said *King Lear*. Although he thought it was not the best reading material under the circumstances, he got it for me anyway. Loretta Howard also came to see me. She had been deeply loyal to my mother when she was hospitalized, and I was grateful.

When I was still in the hospital, I had a visit from Harold Peterson, whom I'd known at Harvard and who was teaching at the Trinity School. He very kindly invited me stay at his apartment after I left the hospital, and I gratefully accepted. So I recuperated at Harold Peterson's apartment on West End Avenue and 72nd Street, where I spent most of my time lying on his sofa eating ice cream and drinking Demerara rum and tonic, while gazing wistfully at my mother's Marquet painting of the Pont Neuf. I did manage to have tea with Vera Somoff as well as with Nanny, who lived across the street.

I decided to leave Columbia in 1963 because I had become incapable of doing the class work let alone writing my thesis. I knew my limits, so I gave up my plans of continuing my French studies at the Normale Superiere or the Sorbonne. I had hoped to live in Paris, see my friend Nicole Bouchet de Fareins, and be analyzed by Princess Marie Bonaparte, a great-grandniece of Emperor Napoleon who had been recommended to me by my psychiatrist at Harvard. Marie had paid Freud's ransom to Nazi Germany and was often able to help those threatened or despoiled by World War II. When the Greek royal family were in exile or Greece was under occupation, she helped support her husband's banished relatives, including her husband's nephew, Prince Philip of Greece, now the Duke of Edinburgh.

By Christmas, I was so depressed that whenever the telephone rang, which it did constantly, I refused to answer it. I had neglected to tell my family where I was, and afterward they told me how terribly worried they were, especially Nanny. I deeply regret my selfishness. My brother-in-law B. Noyes had found a psychiatrist for me named Dr. Kloth, who, like B., was very conservative. I was still going to Mass daily, and I started to go to lectures and ceremonies at the Ramakrishna-Vivekananda Center with Swami Nikilananda.

Because I was still confused and grief stricken over my mother's death and in a state of constant depression, I saw practically no one for almost two years. In April of 1964, I was walking down Madison Avenue one afternoon when I ran into a composer I knew, Chuck Turner, who in his youth had been a lover of Sam Barber. He insisted that I come to a party to meet the German composer Hans Werner Hentze, and somewhat reluctantly I accepted.

Everyone at the party, which was held in a railroad flat downtown on Third Avenue, was a famous artist except for me. Virgil Thompson and the producer Herbie Ross were among the impressive roster of guests. Across the room I saw Robert Fizdale and Arthur Gold, the two pianists whom I had heard at Carnegie Hall in a performance I had gone to with my mother and Loretta Howard. I went up to them and said, "I'm so glad to meet you because you see I'm a twin too." For some reason I assumed they were twins.

I then said to Bobby, "Let me take you away from all this." And he said, "Where to?" And I said, "The next room." We had a wonderful talk, which led to my going home with him. The following morning Arthur came in to the kitchen, and we sat down for Zwieback and Nescafé. Although both Bobby and Arthur were master cooks, that's what they had for breakfast every morning because, as Bobby explained to me, they ate a frugal meal because of the long day of practicing that lay ahead of them. I must have charmed Arthur, for years later he said, "I knew from the beginning that I liked you because anyone who could be as funny as you at breakfast must be all right."

Although Bobby and Arthur had briefly been lovers in their youth, they continued to live together in part because of their music. Once when Bobby took up with the poet Frank O'Hara, Arthur decided that if Bobby had a boyfriend who was a poet he had to have a boyfriend who was a poet too, so he took Jimmy Schuyler as a lover. "The boys," as Bobby and Arthur were known, formed the hub of a vast circle of talented people from all walks of life—music, literature, ballet, as well as what in those days was known as society. And now their world opened for me like the unfolding of a peacock's tail.

Both their parents had been Russian Jews and members of the Communist Party who had escaped the tsarist pogroms and come to the new world, Bobby's family to Chicago and Arthur's to Toronto. Arthur was a child prodigy who began performing with Canadian symphony orchestras when he was only twelve. Bobby was a brilliant linguist and mathematician as well as a musician. By the time the pair met at Julliard, Arthur had lost his nerve and was unable to perform in public. By a stroke of good fortune, their teachers decided to pair them together, which allowed Arthur to overcome his stage fright and launched them on their way to becoming world-famous duo pianists.

Although they gave dazzling performances of classical works by such composers as Mozart, Brahms, and Mendelssohn, they much preferred persuading living composers to write something just for them. Over the years John Cage and Francis Poulenc—who called them *deux petits penguins bien elevés*—composed pieces for them, as did Virgil Thomson, Samuel Barber, and Ned Rorem.

Bobby and Arthur lived at 333 Central Park West on 96th Street, where they had managed to create an atmosphere that was both European and sophisticated yet at the same time very friendly and simple. A long hallway led to the living room with their two grand pianos in one corner. At the end of the room, a wall of windows gave a wonderful view across Central Park and the reservoir to Fifth Avenue and what had been my mother's apartment building. They had some beautiful pieces of eighteenth-century Venetian furniture and a niche with shelves painted silver. On one wall hung a painting by Willem de Kooning, who had given it to them in return for their paying his dental bills when he could not afford to do so.

Bobby and Arthur would practice a solid eight hours a day. Because I was quiet and respectful of their work, they allowed me to stay while they practiced, which was a great pleasure for me. Later when I went to a concert, the piece they were playing would be familiar to me, and it was thrilling to see them performing in front of a huge audience. Evenings when they were not performing, they would go out to dinner or entertain at home.

Soon after I met Bobby and Arthur, they invited me to a party that Jerome Robbins was giving at Snedens Landing, a hamlet twelve miles north of the city overlooking the Hudson River that was a favorite of artists and entertainers. I was thunderstruck to be included, and I realized that it was a great honor. We drove to the party with Tanny Balanchine, and on our way we stopped to pick up the author and playwright Jane Bowles at her hotel. I was sent upstairs to get her and found her hallucinating, convinced that the curtain was a snake. I tried to calm her down and tell her it was just a curtain. She was an alcoholic, and a few years before had suffered a stroke, and I think she was sometimes quite deranged. However, she got better as the evening progressed. A couple of years later I met her husband, Paul, who was also a great writer.

Tanny Balanchine, George Balanchine's fourth wife, was known to the world as Tanaquil Le Clercq. She quickly became a close friend whom I loved very much. She had been a great dancer before she was stricken with polio in Copenhagen and confined to a wheelchair. When Tanny was fifteen years old, George Balanchine asked her to perform with him in a dance he choreographed for a polio charity benefit. In an eerie portent of things to come, he played a character named Polio, and Le Clercq was his victim, who became paralyzed and fell to the floor. Then, children tossed dimes at her character, prompting her to get up and dance again. Before the tragedy, Balanchine, Jerome Robbins, and Merce Cunningham had all created roles for her.

Balanchine remained with Tanny for years until he eventually fell in love with Suzanne Farrell, a prima ballerina in his company. One night during a performance of *Don Quixote*, with Farrell playing Dulcinea and Balanchine in the role of Quixote, his love was so obvious that Tanny asked for a divorce that very night. Tanny was a beautiful woman who could be very tough, which no doubt helped her survive her illness. She could also be a little bitchy. Her father was French, and perhaps she inherited his malicious humor. Although she regained most of the use of her arms and torso, she remained paralyzed from the waist down. Nonetheless, she was able to teach and so remain involved with the ballet.

Weekends I would take the train—what Gillian Walker called the Lily Bart Special because she claimed that girls took it to Southampton to find rich husbands—to stay with Bobby and Arthur at their house on Flying Point Road in Watermill. In his book *Callas Kissed Me Lenny Too!*, John Gruen describes their lives there: "Gold and Fizdale were wonderful hosts, giving superb luncheons and dinner parties for all kinds of important people doing all the shopping and cooking themselves." He says that he and his wife, Jane, were on "the B list"—either Bobby or Arthur would ring up to say, "We're having Stravinsky, Balanchine, and Jerome Robbins for dinner tonight. Will you come and eat leftovers tomorrow?" Gruen says that he and his wife always accepted because they knew that "the food, though a day old, would still be exquisite and the gossip scintillating." As a houseguest I was fortunate to be on both lists.

One weekend the composer Sam Barber invited himself for the weekend because, he said to me, "I wanted to observe Bobby and Arthur with you because in the past Arthur has been extremely jealous, mean, and rude to Bobby's lover. I heard this rumor that Arthur is very fond of you, so I had to see for myself what was going on." I was reminded of the afternoon some years before when I was still at Harvard and had answered the telephone to hear, "This is Samuel Barber," just after Chris had put Barber's *Adagio for Strings* on the record player. So I held the receiver by the speaker and said, "Hello, Mr. Barber. Listen to the music we put on just before you called." He was amused by the coincidence and said that he had asked a friend in Philadelphia whom he might look up at Harvard who would be fun to see when he came up to receive an honorary degree. The friend told him that my sister Polly "has a brother that people talk about at Harvard." Barber invited me for a drink at the Ritz Bar and told me to bring along my roommates. Chris, although he was a wonderful musician, was too shy to come, and Michael also refused because of shyness, although in part I think it was because his parents wouldn't want him to associate with Samuel Barber because, although he was an outstanding composer, he was a notorious homosexual.

Barber introduced me to Manfred Ibel, his German boyfriend who was studying at Columbia University, his education no doubt paid for by Sam. Over martinis Sam asked about my studies and interests and told me that he was composing a series of songs related to incidents in medieval Irish history. As we talked he suddenly said in a charming way, "Oh, you know everything." After we finished our drinks, he took us to a seafood restaurant, where Sam and Manfred spoke German to each other. At one point, Manfred said, "No, that word is feminine not masculine." And Sam replied, "Gender has never been my strong suit." I loved it. We had a marvelous evening, and we became close friends.

After I went to the Far East in 1967, I saw much less of Gold and Fizdale than I had, although we kept in touch. In the late 1970s Bobby developed problems with his hands, which made it difficult for him to perform. Undaunted, the pair turned to writing and produced two delightful biographies: *Misia: The Life of Misia Sert* and *The Divine Sarah: A Biography of Sarah Bernhardt*. In 1984 they published *The Gold and Fizdale Cookbook*, dedicated to George Balanchine, "In whose kitchen we spent many happy hours."

Bobby was the only person I was with for more than three months. I was twenty-four when we began what was a semiplatonic relationship. It had very little to do with lust. Rather it was more about friendship with a very intelligent and sophisticated older man who was also charming at a time when I was very rudderless. Through Loretta Howard they knew my mother, so they were aware of the world from which I came, and although they were both brilliant musicians, they were also very snobbish and cultivated members of the upper class who were well connected. However, I was more of a protégé in a whole new world.

In June of 1964, I went to Italy with Dom Aelred. Bobby Fizdale and I arranged to write each other in secret so that Aelred wouldn't find out. Harold Peterson was designated the go-between. We would mail our letters to each other in envelopes addressed to him, who would then address the letter to the intended recipient in his handwriting with his return address.

We went first to Positano, where we met the most wonderful girl, Principessa Ornella Pignatelli, who invited us to a picnic lunch on a beautiful deserted beach. Ornella worked as a travel agent in Naples and told us she was a communist. Aelred very much approved of her politics. One evening, Ornella invited me to what she called a *spaghetini* at the Caracciolo family's *castello* overlooking the Bay of Naples. As we went up a magnificent staircase, Ornella told me that for grand parties footmen stood on each side of the steps with torches to light the guests' way. I had been told to dress casually, but when we arrived, I was embarrassed to discover all the men wearing tuxedos and the women in evening dresses. Thankfully, one of the girls in the family took me to her father's room, where she opened a closet filled with a row of tuxedos. She told me to borrow one.

As the party began, all the guests lined up and filed by a young couple who were seated on chairs so large and elaborate they were almost like thrones. They were the Bourbons and therefore descended from the former rulers of Naples. One by one, we bowed to the young man and kissed the girl's hand. It seems the Caracciolos, at one time subjects of the Bourbons, were paying homage to their former owners.

The table was covered with a crimson damask cloth, and in the center sat a magnificent piece of Capodimonte china. My mother had been a lover of porcelain, and I grew up being able to distinguish one kind from another. At the party were a couple of agents of the Aga Khan who were in charge of the new resort he was building on Sardinia's Costa Smeralda. They invited me to fly over with them the next day to see it. I thought that it would be fun, but when I got back to the hotel, Aelred told me not to go. He said, "They're fund-raising and think you're an American with money." Reluctantly, I passed up the invitation.

From Positano, Aelred and I went to Rome, where we stayed at the Hassler, the hotel Hitler had stayed at when he visited Mussolini. One morning while we were sitting in the lobby, a man came in dressed in britches, silk stockings, and a crimson jacket. Although he looked like the fish footman who presents an invitation to a game of croquet from the queen of hearts, he was actually a messenger from the Vatican where an official wanted to meet with the Very Reverend Dom Aelred Graham, prior of Portsmouth Priory. Aelred changed into his black Benedictine robes before being driven to the Vatican to meet the head of the congregation of non-Christian religions with whom Pope John XXIII had been consulting.

At that time, the Vatican Council was holding the largest gathering of bishops and cardinals in Catholic history. It had opened in 1962 under Pope John XXIII and would end in 1965 under Pope Paul VI. In 1963, Aelred had recently published his book *Zen Catholicism*, and the Vatican was so interested in his understanding of Buddhism as a Catholic theologian that they invited him to become the *peritus*, or expert, on Buddhism for the Vatican council. Instead of criticizing non-Christian religions, as they called them, the council decreed that Catholic thinkers and students of religion should take the best from these religions and apply it to Catholicism for the benefit of the church. Aelred declined, saying that the encounter between Buddhism and Catholicism could not take place at the level of the *magisterium*, or teaching body. A discussion of the doctrines and dogmas of the Catholic Church can only take place at the level of two contemplatives talking in private. Instead of Aelred, David Snellgrove, the professor of Buddhist studies at the Asian and African Institute of London University, became the peritus of Buddhist studies at the Vatican.

After Aelred returned to the States that summer of 1964, I went to Athens to see Minas as well as Carlotta, who by that time was living there. One day I invited Carlotta to join Minas and me for a visit to the Temple of Poseidon at Sounion, some forty miles southeast of Athens. Minas drove us in the car I'd given him, but at such a rate of speed we begged him to slow down because we thought that we'd be killed. I regretted that I'd given him the car, especially as Carlotta thought it was very bad for him. She had made friends with his sister, who told her how upset the family was that he had an American boyfriend who gave him a car. Oh, well. You can't always do the right thing.

In Athens, I became friends with the composer Manos Hadjidakis, who wrote "Never on Sunday," the theme song for the 1960 film of the same name. He was quite amused that I had acquired a kept boy, as he called Minas. "You must know some older men who have kept boys, and you just want to imitate them," he told me. I admit that it was rather ridiculous for someone age twenty-four to have a kept boy of eighteen.

When I returned to New York in September 1964, I got my own place in what must have been the servant's quarters on the top floor of a beautiful house on 74th Street just off Fifth Avenue. Angelo Torricini, a talented decorator from Martinique who was then Arthur Gold's boyfriend, helped me decorate the apartment with my mother's furniture, paintings, and rugs, which had been in storage. There was a living room and down a hall a bedroom, which we transformed into a dining room for parties. Peter Prescott and I would often give parties together because he was such a good cook and had a friend, Loshka Michel, who was a caterer, so all we had to do was arrange things. We would dismantle my bed, put it in the cellar, and rent gold chairs and a table, which we set with silver candelabras, flowers, and my mother's porcelain.

My parties often included friends from the Balanchine's School of American Ballet. Betty Cage was a frequent guest. In her obituary the *Times* described her as the linchpin of the New York City Ballet, who "avoided the limelight and was unknown to the ballet-going public. A woman of few words, she presided over generations of dancers, choreographers and backstage personnel with a wryly detached wit and a calm, almost uncanny sense of approaching trouble." Other guests included Natasha Molostvoff, Princess Ourousoff, and her daughter, Mrs. Glebov. Tanny Balanchine always came to these parties, and sometimes her mother, Mrs. Le Clerq, would join us. Edward Villella, one of the most celebrated male dancers of the day, was another frequent guest, as was the Mexican dancer Nicholas Magallanes.

One evening I went to the ballet with Lucia Davidova, who described herself as Balanchine's "best platonic woman friend." The two had met soon after Balanchine arrived in America in 1934 and remained friends until his death fifty years later. She was small with very black hair and a strong Russian accent. Arthur said, "She had patent leather eyes." A great friend of Leopold Stowkovski, Davidova once told me that when he came to New York he parked his tails in her closet.

The evening I went with her to the ballet, Balanchine had told her that he would come to dinner with us after the performance. Lucia had put on a pot roast to cook while we were at the ballet, so we were able to have supper as soon as George arrived. Knowing that I was interested in religion, he turned to me and said that while he was still in St. Petersburg he had thought of doing a ballet on the Book of Genesis to the music of Rimsky-Korsakov but was forbidden to put it on stage. "I'd like to tell you and show you the ballet," he said.

He explained that the ballet opened with a completely dark stage, and as a rose light appeared, dancers in rose-colored tutus came onto the stage. When the scene changed to the creation of the animals, little boys and girls from the Imperial School of Ballet in St. Petersburg took the parts of the various animals, rather the way the mice would eventually do in *The Nutcracker*. The next scene in his mind was the Garden of Eden before a backdrop by Chagall. Adam came onto the stage, and when he bent over, Eve appeared leaning on him to represent her birth from his rib. Balanchine used his fingers to demonstrate this pas de deux of Adam and Eve. Next, Balanchine explained that a dancer dressed in black showed up as the serpent and made provocative gestures that tempted Eve to pluck an apple from the tree and take a bite. At that point a tremendous wind arose and drove Adam and Eve from the stage. Then it was the turn of Cain and Abel. After Cain murdered Abel, a large group of dancers appeared, dancing fiercely to represent the birth of violence. The ballet then ended, as it had begun, in the dark.

Using only his fingers to represent the steps of the dance, Balanchine was able to bring the ballet that existed only in his mind to life in the most extraordinary and vivid way. I felt very privileged to have witnessed his performance but could not help but wish that he had produced the ballet on a real stage. Just as Balanchine could make a dancer great, he took his genius home with him and trained his cat Mourka to make fantastically high and elegant jumps.

Because of my friendships with people in Balanchine's School of American Ballet and thanks, as well, to Bobby and Arthur and George himself, I was permitted to watch lessons given by the great dancer Alexandra Danilova, who had danced with George at the Mariinsky

Theater in prerevolutionary Russia. The first time I saw Alexandra, she looked at me and said, "How do you like my Oxford accent?" I replied that I thought it was splendid.

Many weekends I would go with Tanny Balanchine and Angelo Torricini to stay with Bobby and Arthur in Watermill just east of Southampton on Long Island. Stella Adler, who lived down the road from Bobby and Arthur, told me that she would like me to play Eugene Marchbanks in George Bernard Shaw's *Candida*. However, she said, "You're going to have to learn to move." So when I was at her house, she would play dance music. We would dance as she explained about rhythm. Although we became fast friends, nothing came of my nascent acting career.

That winter I was hired to translate three French novels for Pantheon Books. I worked with Marian Fenn, John Houseman's secretary, who would type as I translated from French to English. We worked well as a team, and the books were published and got good reviews. One even described the writing as "very poetic."

When Angelo Torricini got a whippet from a litter belonging to Kenneth Coke, a New York poet, I decided that I, too, should have a dog, not realizing that it was cruel to have a dog in a New York apartment, especially a whippet, a breed that needs lots of room to run. I named her Glynis and was soon devoted to her.

One evening I telephoned a brothel keeper who specialized in young men and asked him to send one over to me. I prepared myself by going out to dinner and reading Suzuki Roshi, the monk and teacher who did much to popularize Zen Buddhism in the United States, over a martini and Salisbury steak. I returned to the apartment in a state of anticipation over meeting a stranger. Darling Glynis came and sat next to me, realizing that something important was going on.

The boy, Larry Carrière, arrived, and I was most impressed with his beauty and his masculinity. One evening a few weeks later, Larry telephoned to say that he'd been fishing all day with a friend and his father "and I just had to telephone you because I want to see you so much." I told him to come over, but he said that it would be some time because he was on Long Island. While waiting for him to arrive, I read a Buddhist sutra. I'd become very interested in Buddhist scripture as distinct from the *Upanishads*, scriptures of Hinduism that were taught by Swami Nikilananda. When Larry arrived, I could tell that he was unhappy. He said that being with a father and son had upset him. He explained that his own father had beaten him so often that he had run away from Canada and come to the United States. I felt so sorry for him that I gave him a drink and tried to cheer him up. We made love, and he really seemed to love me. He told me, "You are so beautiful." And I replied, "No, no, you are the beautiful one." And he said, "You are so beautiful that you could get a job with the service I work for." At last someone had told me that I was employable.

At about this time Peter's lease ran out. I found him an apartment that belonged to Stuart Preston, the art critic for the *New York Times* who was one of the "snakes" my mother had to dinner when my father had poker games. Peter gave a lot of parties and dinners there, to one of which he invited Arthur MacArthur, so we had a reunion. After his father's death in 1964, Arthur had moved to the West Side and changed his name to conceal his identity. He had retained a keen interest in music, as well as in literature, arts, and the theater.

When Michael suggested that I get rid of my trustee, Clayton Irwin, because he sometimes prevented me from getting the money I needed, Hugh McNulty, a lawyer friend from Harvard, Dom Aelred, Michael, and I met with Irwin and convinced him to turn my trust over to Michael, who was working at Morgan's Bank.

In 1967, Aelred invited me to go with him to Asia and around the world to meet the heads of non-Christian religions. The plan was for him to meet them while I wrote down their conversations word for word because I wrote in a clear hand. Aelred said, "We are going on an important trip together, and I must know whether you will be able concentrate entirely on the work. You've never worked, so for six months you must have a job." I managed to get a job at Brentano's bookstore working for the buyer, where I did a good job for six months.

That winter Gillian invited me to go with her to the black and white ball that Truman Capote gave for Katharine Graham, the owner of the *Washington Post*, who was a great friend of Gillian's parents, John and Lady Margaret Walker. A few years before my mother had met Capote at a party at the Paleys and invited him to come to the apartment for a drink. When I came into the living room, he was lying on the sofa chatting to my mother, who told me that she had asked Truman to answer any questions I might have about writing. So I said, "Mr. Capote, how do you start a piece of writing?" And he replied, "On my desk I have a mug with a lot of very sharp pencils with the lead facing up. And I take a pencil and a piece of paper and I write."

His party was held in the grand ballroom of the Plaza Hotel and was later referred to in countless magazines and newspapers as "the party of the century." When I picked up Gillian at the Dakota, she had a fit to find that I was wearing white tie when the invitation had said tuxedos. Our friends Carter and Amanda Burden, who also lived at the Dakota, were giving a dinner before the ball that included Andy Warhol but not Gillian and me. So we went to L'Aiglon Restaurant, where we had dinner and one of our typical literary conversations. I said, "My favorite novel by Dostoevsky was *The Possessed*." And Gillian said, "Oh no, no, no. His greatest novel is *The Brothers Karamazov*." So we continued discussing Russian literature, dressed to the nines, waiting to go to the party of Truman Capote for Katharine Graham.

When we arrived, Gillian took me straight up to see Mrs. Longworth, the legendary Washington hostess known for her witty remarks, who was the daughter of President Teddy Roosevelt. Although such parties are often more of a spectacle than enjoyable, Capote's ball was an exception and great fun. Peter Duchin provided the music, and although there was dancing, it was more about seeing people. The Jaipurs were there, and Kenny Lane and Nelson Aldrich, so I saw lots of friends and had a very a good time. I got home at six in the morning after dropping Gillian off at the Dakota, took a bath, slept for a couple of hours, and then got up and went to Brentano's for the day's work. At Brentano's, everybody was talking about the party of the night before, but I said nothing.

PART TWO

In Search of the Nature of the Mind

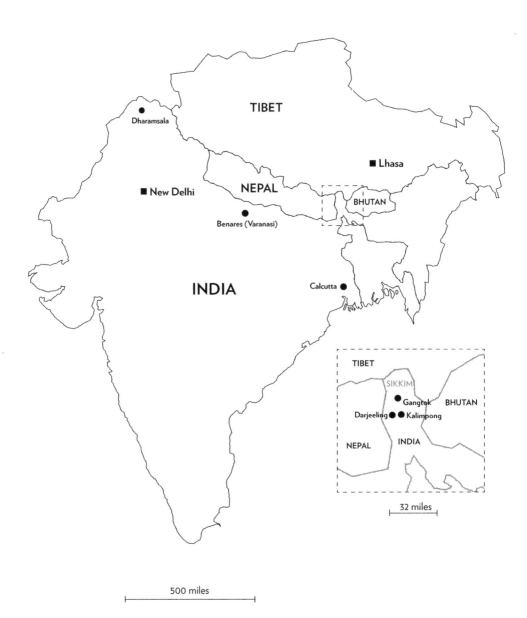

TIBET

● Dharamsala

■ Lhasa

■ New Delhi

NEPAL

BHUTAN

● Benares (Varanasi)

INDIA

Calcutta ●

TIBET

SIKKIM

● Gangtok

BHUTAN

Darjeeling ● ● Kalimpong

NEPAL

INDIA

32 miles

500 miles

CHAPTER ELEVEN

Dom Aelred and I Travel to Asia

After I had worked at Brentano's for six months, Aelred decided that I was capable of holding a responsible job as his secretary during his world tour. My family and friends gave me several farewell parties, I entrusted my beloved whippet, Glynis, to Peter, and we were off.

During a quick stop in California, we stayed at Nell MacVeagh's enormous ranch north of San Francisco, where we had a joyful reunion with Alan Watts, whom we would soon meet again in Kyoto. During our stay, Nell took me riding over the property and told me that she had once owned a ranch in Colorado. One day two air force officers arrived and served her with an eminent domain document stating that the government was confiscating her property. In return, the officers told her, the government would give her a comparable property anywhere she wanted, and Nell settled for the ranch in California.

As it turned out my father, in his search for a suitable location for the new Air Force Academy, chose Nell's ranch in Colorado. Understandably, she deeply resented my father. At one point she called the political columnist Walter Winchell, who, when she told him her story, said that he would use his influence to harm my father. I don't know whether the columnist had any effect on my father's leaving his position as Secretary of the Air Force, but Nell told me that she had felt terribly guilty ever since. In fact, she became quite emotional about it.

After saying good-bye to Nell and Alan, we flew first to Honolulu, where we stayed with an American Zen master, Robert Aitken. From there we flew on to Tokyo to begin a series of dialogues, mostly with Zen masters or senior teachers, called *roshis*, and one with a Pure Land priest. To my surprise and delight, when we arrived in Tokyo, we were met by the celebrated Pure Land Buddhist priest and great scholar Dr. Shojun Bando, an impressive young man whom I had heard a lot about.

He was wearing traditional robes with a bright silk surplice. His long broad sleeves were held open by wicker funnels to let the air in because of the heat.

Dr. Bando took us by subway to Tokyo's Imperial Hotel, built by Frank Lloyd Wright and torn down the following year. Shortly after our arrival, Sumiko Kudo, our interpreter for conversations with Zen masters, came to meet us. She worked for a business company and in her spare time interpreted for her Zen master, Shibayama Roshi of the Nanzen-Ji Temple. Sumiko Kudo took us to lunch at a restaurant with plastic models of the available dishes displayed in the window. Everything we ordered was delicious. Tokyo was very modern, and the streets were as crowded as Fifth Avenue is during Christmas.

At Aelred's first dialogue with a Zen teacher, I was astounded by Sumiko Kudo's brilliant interpretation. It was the first of Aelred's many conversations, Christian and Buddhist, each of which I tape-recorded then wrote out word for word by hand (see appendix 1). Immediately, Aelred sent it off to his publisher in New York, Harcourt Brace Jovanovich, who published it as *Conversations: Christian and Buddhist: Encounters in Japan*. The next day Aelred, Sumiko Kudo, and I took the bullet train to Kyoto. We were astounded by the speed and smoothness of the journey as well as by the sense of order of the countryside. The different shades of green of the rice fields made beautiful patterns and contrasted with the brown farmhouses. At one point in the trip, we saw the sacred Mount Koyasan and felt that we were in the heart of Japan. In Kyoto we stayed at the Miyako, a traditional Japanese hotel. An alcove in the wall of each room held an exotic arrangement of flowers. We slept in duvet-type sleeping bags on mattresses made of straw matting on the floor.

Alan Watts was also staying at the Miyako. He and his wife, Jono, had brought a group of students to see the various temples and to talk to Zen masters. Alan had us to a dinner, where we all sat on cushions. The meal was served on trays with many little bowls full of pickled vegetables and spices along with the main dishes. Alan tended to get a little drunk on sake. Jono was quite accustomed to this, so when he started to fall backward toward a beautiful antique golden screen, she cried out, "Save the *shoji*!"—the Japanese word for "screen"—and everyone rushed to keep it from falling over.

In Kyoto our first meeting was with the Zen roshi Zenkei Shibayama of Nanzen-Ji Temple. It was a most tranquil setting with plantings and paths and rock gardens with raked gravel. The expanses of gravel, which represent bodies of water, were raked into ridges representing ripples of water encircling the rocks. You could sit on the edge of a wooden walkway and dangle your feet over the gravel while contemplating its beauty. We noticed that the relationship between Zen practice and the gardens seemed to make the mind wonderfully calm and free of thoughts.

We met Professor Masao Abe at his house, where we had one of the best conversations of our three-month stay in Japan. Although he was not a Zen master, he was a great practitioner of Zen meditation and a scholar. Among the other Zen masters we met in Tokyo was Kobori San, whose monastery, Daitoku-Ji, was a celebrated temple. He was known to be a traditionalist, and his view of Zen and other schools in Japan was extremely uncompromising.

From Kyoto we took a train through the countryside to a centuries-old temple that had once been the headquarters of a great Zen master, Hakuin Zen-Ji. Nakagawa Soen Roshi welcomed us at the temple and put us up for the night. He invited us to a tea ceremony, over which he presided. Before serving, he stirred the thick green powdered tea with a wooden spoon made of a branch from an olive tree in the Garden of Gethsemane in Jerusalem, which he had once visited. It was a gracious gesture of ecumenism. Nakagawa Soen Roshi invited us to a long Zen meditation that normally lasts for days. Called a *sesshin*, it was beyond our capacity to undertake, although we tried it for part of a day and a night in his temple. I found out how difficult it was to spend that amount of time on a black cushion doing *zazen*, and I thought how incredible it was that people could sit for as long as a week! Something must happen to the mind just by making the effort to meditate at such great length.

The monastery was beautiful, and like all the temples of these Zen masters, it had been built centuries ago without nails. While we were there, it rained so hard that the water came over the extended roof, and as we walked beneath it, it was as if we were walking behind a waterfall. Nakagawa Soen Roshi was most hospitable. Zen masters as a rule are rather forbidding, but once in a while you get the sense that they might not altogether disapprove of someone who doesn't practice Zen, and thus, it's a great pleasure to be accepted by them.

When we returned to Tokyo, we accepted the invitation of Dr. Shojun Bando to stay at his family temple, a large building several centuries old in the very heart of modern Tokyo. It was as remarkable as it would be if there was a family church in the midst of Wall Street. Dr. Bando was a brilliant scholar and the kindest of hosts. His wife drew very hot water in large wooden tubs so that we could experience Japanese baths.

In October we flew to Bangkok, where we had a number of conversations with Buddhist *bhikkus*, or monks of the Theravada tradition, as well as with Western laymen involved in the study of Buddhism. The Theravada, the oldest form of Buddhism, is grounded in the teachings of the Buddha himself in the form of *sutras*, or scriptures, that were written down in Pali about two hundred years after the Buddha's death and preserved. The *theras*, among the original disciples of the Sakyamuni Buddha, had such phenomenal memories that they probably didn't write down everything the Buddha said or taught or recited. Eventually, the sutras were written in the Pali language and are called to this day the Pali Sutras. All the sutras of the Buddha were thus preserved, and they are still recited by Buddhists of all the three branches—Theravada, Mahayana, and Vajrayana.

The eighteen schools of Theravada Buddhism were developed after the death of Sakyamuni Buddha in the fourth century BCE; they comprised an entirely monastic form of Buddhism. The role of the laity was to venerate the *theras* and *bhikkus* and to offer them food and gifts. Every morning to this day in Thailand and Sri Lanka, the bhikkus of a monastery line up and walk through the surrounding villages to receive food in their begging bowls, which they take back to the monastery for their breakfast or lunch. This is their only meal of the day; it is forbidden to eat after twelve o'clock. Theravada is the principal form of Buddhism practiced in Myanmar, Sri Lanka, Thailand, Cambodia, and Laos. For our first conversation we had no need of an interpreter because at a temple we visited in Bangkok, Wat Baworniwe, there was an Englishman with the monastic name of Bhikku Khantipalo. He gave us a very informative introduction to the Theravada Buddhism of Thailand.

The second person we visited was John Blofeld, a professor of English at Chulalongkorn University and the author of a number of excellent books on Buddhism. In India he had been a disciple of lamas of the Nyingmapa school, the oldest of the four major schools of Buddhism in Tibet (see glossary). Later I would myself become a student of Nyingmapa lamas. John Blofeld taught us a lot about Tantra or Vajrayana Buddhism—the third vehicle or approach to Buddhism and the one practiced in Tibet. The Theravada was entirely devoted to the monastic orders. The Mahayana arose in the first century CE as a movement to expand Buddhist teachings to a greater audience that included the laity. It flourishes in Japan in the form of Zen and Pure Land Buddhism today, as well as in China, Korea, Vietnam, Mongolia, and Tibet.

As a practitioner of the Vajrayana or Tantric Buddhism, John Blofeld had a very practical response to it, which he used in his own life and circumstances. He told us that in Tantric meditation you have a *yidam*, or chosen deity, a sublime form of the Buddha such as Avalokiteshvara, the Buddha of compassion, or Manjusri, the Buddha of wisdom. You visualize the Buddha with concentration, and then you recite the mantra or prayer of that particular Buddha. This focuses your mind on the sacred image and frees you from the play of confusing or disjointed thoughts and emotions. Once you are capable in your practice, you regard all your thoughts and emotions as belonging to the mind of the particular Buddha that you're concentrating on; all the phenomena that you're seeing, hearing, or aware of you regard as the body of that Buddha, and all speech and sound as the mantra of that Buddha. John Blofeld told us that his residence in Bangkok adjoined a courtyard where taxi drivers would rev their motors all night long. This kept him from sleeping until he transformed the sound into the mantra of the Buddha whom he was venerating.

John Blofeld, who had the softest most melodious way of speaking, took us to see Abbot Yen Boum, a Chinese Zen monk who some years before had escaped from Mao Tse-tung's China to Thailand. He was a Mahayana monk, not a Theravadin, as most Thais are. He and John Blofeld greeted one another with great affection and esteem. We sat on the floor of his reception room in the same relaxed pose as the *arhats*, or supremely accomplished disciples you see in statues. The abbot was one of the most engaging figures—gentle yet with an inner strength—we encountered in our Buddhist travels. John Blofeld was a real linguist. He taught in Thai, and when he took us to see Yen Boum, they spoke Chinese together, as Blofeld had spent a great deal of his youth in China before the revolution and knew Chinese well. He wrote a book about prerevolutionary China titled *The Wheel of Life*.

One day we ventured from Bangkok to visit a *wat*, or temple, in the jungle where the monks sat beneath the trees, as the original disciples of the Buddha had done. After their morning meditation, they walked to the nearby town and begged for their food. We stayed at the jungle monastery for a couple of days and tried to meditate under the trees ourselves. We ate almost nothing because the food in our begging bowls was so slopped together it was most unappetizing. Before leaving, we went to a tiny restaurant on the beach where we ordered fried eggs. Although the yolks were such a deep orange they were almost red and quite unpalatable, we ate with great gusto.

In October we left Thailand for Sri Lanka. Because of a general strike we could seldom left the hotel to visit people, but the hotel itself was a treat. It was a vast barn of a place that had been built during the British Raj. The beds were surrounded by mosquito nets, there were ceiling fans, and the waiters wore turbans and went about barefoot. It was all very exotic and a good introduction to what we would find in India.

We were able to visit the family of Anagarika Dharmapala, a monk who had been largely instrumental in the revival of Buddhism in India in the late nineteenth century. He had served Buddhism in Sri Lanka but more importantly had helped to restore the Buddhist holy places in India to the Buddhists themselves and establish their communities in India.

One day in Sri Lanka, we took a walk along the beach where an old man stopped us and asked if we'd like to have our palms read. I said sure, so he looked at my palm and said, "In November your life is going to change." I thought nothing more of it, but the next day we left for India, where the following month I would learn that the fortune-teller was right. In November I would meet the Dalai Lama.

From Colombo we flew to New Delhi, where we had been invited to stay with Alvin Moore, an American on the staff of the Library of Congress in India. On our way to his house from the airport, we drove past the Rastrapati Bhavan, Sir Edwin Lutyens's magnificent red sandstone building, formerly the headquarters of the British Raj then housing the offices of the government of India. It is an appealingly fanciful combination of the Neoclassical style and Mogul architecture.

Alvin Moore had a military bearing yet was extremely hospitable. He was a member of the Traditionalist School of world religions, a group of twentieth-century thinkers who deplored what they felt was the decline of traditional forms of knowledge, both aesthetic and spiritual, in the West. They believe primordial and universal religious truths are at the foundations of all major world religions. The Tibetan explorer, Marco Pallis, another member of the Traditionalist School, had given Dom Aelred an introduction to Alvin Moore. Alvin became a friend of mine both during the trip with Dom Aelred as well as during the two years I spent in India afterward and then through written correspondence after I had left India.

Alvin introduced us to Gene Smith, another American who also worked at the Library of Congress in New Delhi. Gene, an eminent scholar of Tibetan Buddhism, ran a program in which he had the Tibetan scriptures printed that were brought to him by Tibetans who had escaped communist-occupied Tibet. Gene published these manuscripts in bound albums, which he sent to a number of American and

European universities that had departments of Tibetan Studies. Later, when he left India, Gene lived in New York City, where he founded the Tibetan Buddhist Resource Center to digitize much of the entire canon of Tibetan Buddhist scriptures. Thanks to Gene's efforts, scholars today can get the scriptures they need from the Internet; and even lamas in Tibet have access to the scriptures from Gene's Tibetan Buddhist Resource Center.

Gene was not only a remarkable linguist but also one of the very few geniuses I've ever met. Like many geniuses, he was very modest and never in any way acted superior to you. Rather, he was incredibly help-ful to many people, including students like myself, as well as scholars in Tibetan Buddhism whom he would advise on their Ph.D. theses. When Gene corrected the scriptures brought to him by Tibetans, he would stand in the middle of his living room in New Delhi and point out the misprints in their texts, telling them to go back and reprint them.

When I returned to India after the trip with Aelred, I came to know Gene very well. He taught me a lot about Tibetan civilization and the society of aristocrats and lamas in Lhasa under the authority of the Dalai Lama before the Chinese invasion. Over drinks at the Oberoi Hotel, where I stayed, or at his apartment, where he sometimes had me to stay, he would unfold the pageant of Tibet, which he knew intimately, as if he'd been there. In fact, he did know many of the aristocrats who had fled and survived in New Delhi and elsewhere, some of them in America.

Later, after I knew some Tibetan and had done meditation practice under a number of different lamas, Gene would help me translate scrip-tures. He was very encouraging and helpful. At one point while I was annotating a scripture, which was a meditation teaching, he told me, "You're going to know more than the scholars."

Aelred and I first met Gene Smith at Al Moore's. Al had also invited Gelek Rinpoche, a lama whom he had asked to tell Aelred and me how we should behave in our forthcoming audience with the Dalai Lama. Gelek Rinpoche showed us *khataks,* or long white silk scarves, and demonstrated how you unfold them before draping them over your

wrists and holding them out to the lama as a form of greeting and reverence. The lama then lifts the khatak, blesses it, and puts it around your
neck. Gelek Rinpoche and I got to know each other when I went back
to India.

To reach Dharamsala, the headquarters in exile of the Dalai Lama, we
took the night train to Pathankot. A most welcome feature of the railway was that you could give your breakfast order to the conductor, who
telegraphed it to the stop up the line so that your breakfast would be
ready when you got there and a bearer would bring it to you on a tray.
It sounds like a system devised under the Raj, and it was very pleasant
indeed. When we reached Pathankot, a young Tibetan driver met us with
a jeep and drove us up into the hills that slowly grew into mountains.

It was the first time I had seen the Himalayas. At one point during
the magnificent journey, the driver took a wrong turn and jammed on
the brakes. Next thing we knew, one of the jeep's wheels was spinning in
thin air over the precipice below! I had been reciting the mantra of the
Buddha of compassion, *om mani padme hum*, and suddenly I realized
that I had reverted to Hail Mary Full of Grace.

When we arrived at Dharamsala, we were met by Rato Rinpoche, the
lama in charge of the Ministry of Religious Affairs. We stayed in a dak
bungalow, or tourist lodge—part of the system the British built during
the Raj for travelers. Along with Simla and Kashmir, Dharamsala was
one of the summer resorts for the British living in New Delhi, whereas
Darjeeling was the main summer hill station or resort for officials who
lived in Calcutta. From Lower Dharamsala, where we were to be based,
we were driven to McCloud Gange in Upper Dharamsala, where the
Dalai Lama had his bungalow, Swarg Ashram, or Dwelling in the
Clouds, which had been given to him by the Indian industrialist Aditya
Vikram Birla. When Aelred and I arrived at the fenced gate of the Dalai
Lama's property, two burly Sikhs with turbans frisked us thoroughly.
We were met by the Dalai Lama's secretary, Tenzin Geyche, who led us
to his office to wait for our audience. When the time came, he took us
to the residence, where we walked through a corridor and into the room
where His Holiness was sitting.

The Dalai Lama got up, shooed a kitten from his chair, and greeted us. We presented our khataks, or white silk scarves, and he put them around our necks after blessing them. We all sat at the same level, which surprised me; all the photographs I had seen of the Dalai Lama while he was still in Tibet showed him seated cross-legged on a high throne with his ministers, chamberlains, and monks standing below him. But he had done away with all that pomp in his exile. Aelred explained that he had come to learn more about Buddhism. The Dalai Lama listened carefully to everything he said. He answered all his questions directly and naturally with great candor and pleasantness. He was a deeply impressive figure, a vigorous and strong young man. You could tell that he was very determined to bear the weight of the responsibility of remaining in India while Tibet was under Chinese occupation, aware that almost all Tibetans were devoted to him as their root lama, or most important spiritual figure. In essence Tibet is the Dalai Lama.

Being with the Dalai Lama felt like being at "the still point in the turning world." I was awed to find myself in the presence of the person to whom I had been devoted since childhood and for whom I felt great sympathy and concern because of the suffering of his people with whom he was so profoundly identified. He was a man first and then a lama and a monk, with utter simplicity and authenticity. Some people, and he is one, are so awe-inspiring that they naturally have a potent charisma. I had not, however, expected him to have a great sense of humor.

After our audience we were driven back to Lower Dharamsala. On the way we stopped at the Upper Tantric College to see some of the novices in training. Paired off, one novice sat cross-legged while the other stood with an outstretched arm, slapping his palm while he asked the seated novice questions about Mahayana Buddhist philosophy. The respondent had to give the proper answer. This was an ancient form of teaching in logic and Buddhist philosophy that has been retained by the Gelukpa order of the Dalai Lama to this day.

As we continued on our way to Lower Dharamsala, a man beside the road stopped our jeep to ask if he might visit us at our dak bungalow. When he arrived, he told us that his name was Sonam Topgay Kazi and that he had been appointed by the foreign office of India as the official interpreter for the Dalai Lama. Having interpreted the talks between Nehru, Chou En-lai, and the Dalai Lama, he was very much on the inside track of both the Indian government and the exiled government of Tibet. He asked about our meeting with the Dalai Lama, and when we told him how wonderful it had been, he started to talk about his own Tibetan Buddhist tradition, which was the Nyingmapa school, which he said practiced the highest form of meditation. He kept looking at me in a searching manner, and I felt drawn to him and also somewhat self-conscious because of his penetrating gaze. This was the first time I had a taste of the style and character of Sonam Topgay Kazi, who became a great friend and adviser when I later lived in India studying with Tibetan Buddhist lamas. After he finished talking to Aelred and me, he turned to me and said, "I think that you and I are interested in the same thing."

Later, we were driven down to Pathankot, where we took the train back to New Delhi. I asked Dom Aelred if I could take a couple of days off to visit the Dalai Lama in private because I wanted to ask him if he would give me teachings when our trip ended. Aelred said that would be fine, so I wrote to Tenzin Geyche, the secretary, and he wrote back with an appointment.

Talking to the Dalai Lama privately with only Tenzin Geyche interpreting gave me a great feeling of liberation. When I asked him if he would be my Buddhist teacher, he asked, "Where is Father Graham?" And I answered, "He's in New Delhi." He asked, "When do you finish your trip with him?" And I said, "In May." And then he asked, "In the work that you have done so far, have you been stable and consistent in it?" I said, "I'm afraid that the opposite is true." He hardly reflected on my answer at all before telling me to "go home and settle your affairs and come back. I will get you a house and appoint a Tibetan teacher for you and a lama to give you instructions as well as myself. I will teach you everything I know. I will make you my monk in America."

During the audience, as is my habit, I used my hands almost as vigorously as an Italian. The Dalai Lama kept shifting his eyes and moving his head from side to side as if he were watching a tennis match. Years

later I was told that one must sit completely still in the presence of the
Dalai Lama.

As the audience was coming to an end, I broke down and wept
because of the misery the Tibetan people were suffering. The Dalai
Lama stood up and, taking my hand, walked me to the open door at the
end of the veranda. There is a detail that I will always remember vividly:
over the doorway from the roof hung enormous icicles that resembled
stalactites. As I went through the doorway and onto the path to Tenzin
Geyche's office, I turned around and saw the Dalai Lama in his robes
with his bare arm waving to me with the icicles around him. And so I
left him, much lightened by his great kindness.

On the way down to Pathankot, I thought about my audience with
the Dalai Lama. It seemed a miracle that a moment after I failed to
give a good answer to his question, he said that he would take me on
as a student of the Gelukpa school, set me up with a place to live, and
provide me with teachers, as well as give me audiences with him as
needed. On the train I was happy, feeling the rattle of the cars on the
tracks and planning my future.

In New Delhi, Dom Aelred had moved to the luxurious Oberoi
Hotel, after thanking Alvin Moore for his hospitality. The Oberoi
became my home during my many trips to India after 1968. It is also one
of Michael's favorite hotels, although the cost of a room today is astro-
nomical. Sonam Topgay Kazi, the official Indian interpreter of the Dalai
Lama, whom we had met in Dharamsala, had invited us to Sikkim to
meet the Gyalwa Karmapa, the head of the Kagyupa school of Tibetan
Buddhism. From New Delhi, I telephoned Mr. T. D. Densapa, the secretary of the *chogyal*, or king of Sikkim, a state in Northern India, to ask
him to get us the necessary permits to enter that country. Mr. Densapa
said the chogyal of Sikkim and his wife were in Calcutta and that he
would arrange for us to meet them while we were there in a few days.

I was shocked by the beggars in Calcutta, some of whom had no
limbs. Little children in rags would poke their spindly arms through the
taxi windows begging for baksheesh in pitiful voices. The buildings of
the city were dilapidated or crumbling, but when you entered the Grand

Hotel, everything was luxurious and comfortable. We went to see the chogyal and his wife, the American-born Hope Cooke, known as the *gyalmo*, or queen of Sikkim, at their apartment in Calcutta. We offered him our white silk scarves, and he offered us a drink. I was amused by the contrast of customs, but women and drink are what maharajas like, and the chogyal was a maharaja, or great king.

From Calcutta, Aelred and I flew to Bagh Dogra, a town in the plains of West Bengal, where you get a jeep for the journey to Darjeeling, the former hill station where officials and officers of the Raj once went to escape from the heat of Calcutta. From the center of town, you have a sublime view of Kanchenjunga floating above endless rows of terraces where Darjeeling tea is grown. In the 1960s, many great lamas who had escaped from Tibet came to live there. We tried to find Chatral Rinpoche, but he was "out of station," as is said in the Indian English of the Raj when someone was away traveling. There were other lamas whom we looked for but failed to find. It wasn't in our karma then. We stayed at the Windamere Hotel, which became my favorite hotel in the world! Later, Thomas Merton and I would stay there while visiting lamas; later still, Tulku Thondup and I would work there translating Tibetan Buddhist scriptures.

The road to Sikkim wound through miles of tea plantations. Giant *deodars*, as cedars are called in Bengali, grew on the mountain slopes. Far below us in the valley we could see the ice blue River Teesta, which wound its way along the border between Sikkim and the adjacent Indian state of West Bengal. In Gangtok, the capital of Sikkim, we stayed at a little hotel that reminded me of the saying of St. Teresa of Avila, *La vida es una noce in una mala posada* (Life is a night in a bad hotel).

In the morning, Sonam Topgay Kazi, with his wife and little daughter, who was a *tulku*, or incarnate lama, took us to meet Dodrup Chen Rinpoche, the dharma master, or lineage holder, of the Longchen Nying Thig tradition of the Nyingmapa school. Dodrup Chen Rinpoche lived at the Chorten Gonpa, a hermitage where the previous chogyal of Sikkim had made retreats. Today it is has become a monastery of more than five hundred monks, because when poor villagers ask Rinpoche to take one of their sons as a monk, out of compassion he never refuses them. When Dodrup Chen Rinpoche met us at the door of his residence, we offered him white silk scarves as we'd been instructed. The lama touched his forehead to Sonam's little daughter's forehead in a charming greeting to the tulku, the reincarnation of the Shugsep Jetsun-ma Rinpoche, a great woman lama who died in 1953 at the age of over a hundred.

Dodrupchen Rinpoche's shrine was housed in a big room with many butter lamps. Beyond the shrine room was Dodrup Chen Rinpoche's own room, where he worked, ate, and slept. We sat down in a row along the wall, and the lama stood leaning against a table piled high with the scriptures he'd been printing when we arrived. He was constantly busy giving teachings, performing *wang* (empowerment), *lung* (reading of sacred texts), and *tri* (instructions for performing rituals), saying prayers for people, including the sick, going to the bedsides of many dying people, and performing their funeral ceremonies. One of his names is Thinley, or Enlightened Activity, and in that he is well named.

I had never seen anyone like him. He wore the skirt of monks and lamas and just a vest without the maroon shawl, even though it was cold. He looked extremely young, perhaps in his twenties, short, slim, and very fit. However, his face was careworn. I was impressed by the deep seriousness of his expression and gaze, yet he had been playful and humorous when he greeted the daughter of Sonam Topgay Kazi. Sonam told us that we could ask him a question about Buddhism, and Aelred told me to do so, as I was so interested in Tibetan Buddhism he wanted to give me a chance to learn about the tradition. When I asked Dodrup Chen Rinpoche for an explanation of the doctrine of the *trikaya*—the three bodies of the Buddha—he replied that he could only talk about the trikaya to someone who was receiving training in meditation under his guidance.

At that time, I knew nothing about the teachings of his tradition, but I thought, "Aha, there must be a secret meditation practice related to the trikaya in this lama's tradition, the Nyingmapa. So there is something you do in order to actually realize the trikaya rather than just studying a doctrine." Dodrup Chen Rinpoche's refusal to talk about the trikaya made me more attracted to that sublime doctrine of the Buddha nature than if he had given verbal teachings. And it gave me a sense that the Nyingmapa emphasized realization through practice.

The *dharmakaya* is the formless body of the Buddha. It is emptiness or openness, without modification and free from conceptualization. The *sambhogakaya* is the first of two form bodies. It is the bliss body from which arise the Buddhas such as Avalokiteshvara, the Buddha of compassion; Manjusri, the Buddha of wisdom; and Tara, the female Buddha. The *nirmanakaya* is the second form body known as the illusory body, because from the standpoint of the dharmakaya phenomena are illusions. From it arise the enlightened human beings, the tulkus, and anything that benefits beings, such as flowers, bridges, medicine, scriptures, even a breeze on a hot day.

The audience didn't last very long, and as we were leaving, Sonam said to me quietly, "Dodrup Chen Rinpoche is your guru," which surprised me because I had already committed myself to study with the Dalai Lama. Dom Aelred said, "He is too young to be your guru." Seven years later I would learn that Sonam had been right.

When we returned to New Delhi, we went to see Dr. Lokesh Chandra, a celebrated Hindu scholar who had just returned from the Soviet Union. He was a stern figure, and there was something about him that was ironic. He told us that the Russians are a spiritual people espousing a materialistic creed, whereas the Americans are a materialistic people espousing a spiritual creed. You could sense that he was very anti-American, as were so many members of the Indian government at the time.

Aelred and I soon left for Benares, the holy city of India where people bathe in the Ganges, whose waters are believed to release them of defilements of the body and mind. Along the shore are the burning *ghats*, where people bring the bodies of their relatives for cremation and throw marigolds into the river for blessings. Shortly before dawn, Aelred and I hired a boat so that we could observe the people at closer range. It was a moving and impressive scene with the palace of the Maharajah of Benares looming high above our heads. I would have liked to have gone inside. In Benares we also went to Hindu University and met Dr. T. R. V. Murti, my favorite writer on Indian philosophy. At Harvard I'd written a paper on his book *The Central Philosophy of Buddhism*, and while we were in Benares, Aelred gave me a copy of the book, which I still treasure.

From Benares we visited Sarnath, where the Buddha gave his first sermon on the four noble truths: the suffering, the causes of suffering, the cessation of suffering (Buddhahood), and the path to the cessation of suffering (Buddhism). From there we went on pilgrimage to Bodh Gaya, where the Buddha attained enlightenment sitting under the bodhi tree. Today, a descendant of that tree spreads out its branches to a great distance. Many Tibetans do prostrations around the very high stupa, or reliquary monument, of the Buddha. Monks come on pilgrimage to Bodh Gaya from India, Sri Lanka, Thailand, and other Southeast Asian countries, as well as from the West.

We returned to New Delhi and regrouped at the beloved Oberoi. From there we flew to Madras, where Aelred interviewed a number of Hindu scholars. At the end of our stay, we went to see Dr. Sarvepalli Radhakrishnan. He became the first vice president and the second president of the Indian Republic after India gained its freedom from Britain. Aelred and he reminisced about their days at Oxford when Radhakrishnan was the Spaulding Chair of Religion there. He had also been India's ambassador to Stalin's Russia. Because he came from a peaceful religion, he was the only man who could enter Stalin's office without Stalin being surrounded by guards.

When I left for our next stop at Tehran, I realized that India would be a major part of my life. Everything, even the Windamere and the Oberoi, seemed pervaded by the presence of the Dalai Lama. I loved everything about the Tibetans—the refugees, the prayer beads, the prayer wheels, and all the ceremony of the religion.

From New Delhi we flew to Tehran, where we met Professor Seyyed Hossein Nasr, a great scholar of Islam and a practitioner of Sufism, the esoteric aspect of Shia Islam. He was the Sufi tutor of Farah Pahvali, the *shahbanu*, or empress of Iran. Among his family were men of letters and religious scholars; in fact, his father had been the only non-French member of the Académie Française. Dr. Nasr arranged for us to meet in a sort of "bull session" with a good many of the ayatollahs, or religious leaders of Shia Islam, who, after the revolution, turned out not to be very spiritual people. Some of them in fact were responsible for the human rights atrocities visited upon the opponents of the Ayatollah Khomeini's regime. The ayatollah himself was not among them because he was in exile in Paris and did not return to Iran until after the revolution.

One night, Dr. Nasr took us to a Sufi gathering held in a large marquee under very bright halogen lighting. The dark figures of the Sufi members under this brilliant light, which for them had spiritual connotations, was an unforgettably dramatic scene. Dr. Nasr was another member of the Traditionalist School that Marco Pallis had given us an introduction to. Dr. Nasr had already written a number of books by the time we met him. When the revolution came, he fled to the United States, where he lives to this day, almost fifty years later. He was professor of Islamic studies at George Washington University and wrote many respected books on Islam and especially Sufism.

From Tehran we took a bus to Isfahan, one of the most enchanting cities I have ever seen, and from Isfahan we went to Shiraz, an even more beautiful city, full of rose gardens. Our hotel window overlooked the roof of the former theological seminary with its enormous turquoise dome, decorated with the calligraphic script of quotations from the Koran.

From Iran we flew to Istanbul. Aelred had hoped to visit Mount Athos in Greece, but as a member of the Roman Catholic Church hierarchy, he needed a permit from the Metropolitan of Constantinople, who was unfortunately away. But we enjoyed Istanbul thanks in large part to Jean-Claude Petit-Pierre, a Swiss who was an expert in Islam. The son of a president of Switzerland, Petit-Pierre was attractive, very slight, and with a small mustache. He was always beautifully dressed, with the manner of a diplomat, and gave us some valuable insights about Islam. From Istanbul, we traveled to the Holy Land, where we stayed in Palestine but did all of our business in Israel. Having been in India for a while, where we experienced the less-than-efficient way things were done, we were impressed by the efficiency of modern Israel, where the hotels were luxurious and the streets and houses modern and impressive. Once you crossed into the Palestinian sector where our hotel was, everything became quite primitive and simple.

In Jerusalem, Aelred had appointments with a number of scholars of the Hebrew scriptures. One of them, Dr. Hugo Bergman, had us to a seder with his family. It was spring, and the fields were bursting with red and purple anemones, which in the Bible are called "lilies of the field." We went to several holy places, including the Garden of Gethsemane and the Via Dolorosa, the road Christ followed carrying his cross to his crucifixion on Golgotha. It was Easter. Aelred thought that it was funny that I was reading a book on Buddhism in the Holy Land during the greatest day of the Christian calendar.

We went on to Greece, where we met another member of the Traditionalist School, Philip Sherrard, an Englishman who wrote about contemporary Greek literature and translated the poems of the Nobel Prize–winning poet Giorgos Seferis. Sherrard had planned to accompany us to Mount Athos, but upon learning that Aelred was not able to get a pass to visit the monastery, he suggested that we go instead to Patmos, the island where St. John the Divine wrote the Gospel of St. John and the Book of Revelation. As we couldn't get on a ferry, we went instead to Paros, where there was a Greek Orthodox monastery where Sherrard had done retreats. We learned about the prayer of the heart, or *hesychasm*, for which one sits on a little stool instead of a cushion and recites the mantra "Jesus Christ, son of God, have mercy upon me, a sinner." We attended the beautiful Byzantine liturgy and monastic hours of the Greek Orthodox Church.

From Greece we flew to London for the last lap of our eleven-month trip. We went to see Aelred's friend Marco Pallis, who had done so much for us on our travels by introducing us to so many people who told us about their religious traditions and showed us their countries. Marco had been on expeditions to Tibet in the 1930s and had written a famous book, *Peaks and Lamas*, about his travels. He was most impressive, and I felt that I had made a friend when I later went to see him and Richard Nicholson, with whom he shared a house near the Brompton Oratory in Knightsbridge. During that private visit after I told Pallis that I wanted to return to India and hoped to study with the Dalai Lama, he gave me an introduction to Lobsang Phuntsok Lhalungpa, who lived in New Delhi, where he was head of the Tibetan broadcasting department of All India Radio. Lobsang would become very important in my life and provide me with a great deal of the knowledge of Tibetan Buddhism and culture that I was able to obtain outside my actual practice with lamas. I became great friends not only with him but also with his family.

While we were in London, Aelred invited his friend the historian Arnold Toynbee to lunch. I was quite impressed that he would agree to have lunch with us. He was most interesting in his observations about the part of the world we had seen and the state of affairs in England and the United States. Aelred had great respect for him, and it was nice to see them talking as old friends.

While we were in England, Alfreda Rushmore, a great friend from New York whom I had met through the composer Chuck Turner, invited us down to stay the weekend at her house in Amberley, West Sussex, which helped us to readjust to Western life. Alfreda, whose grandfather founded Putnam's publishing house in England, later became a close friend. She was stout but unbelievably charming and very intelligent. Unfortunately, she made no use of her exceptional intellect. Her husband, Robert Rushmore, used to deplore her habit of leaving a keen intelligence totally at rest and daily waiting for darkness to fall: a darkness enlivened by a cocktail or two. Sadly, drink eventually ended her life.

Aelred and I later had a wonderful reunion with Alan Watts—in the bar, of course, at the Grosvenor House Hotel. Michael Aris, a Tibetan scholar from Oxford, joined us. I don't think that he felt that Alan and Aelred were properly respectful of the solemnity of the Buddha dharma because they discussed it in such a joyful and light way.

Michael later married Aung San Suu Kyi, winner of the Nobel Peace Prize in 1991, leader of the National League for Democracy, and the first incumbent state counselor, a position akin to prime minister. For many years she was kept under house arrest by the military junta and not allowed to see her husband or children. Michael eventually died of cancer in 1999.

My friend Elsie Mitchell, who had helped fund Aelred's and my trip and had spent several months in Japan in the 1950s becoming a Zen Buddhist, used to say that when a Westerner returns home from several months or more in Asia, "he has cultural whim-whams." That was true to some extent for me, but as I knew that I was going back to Dharamsala to study with the Dalai Lama in India immediately after I settled my affairs at home, I felt as if I was already on my way and that coming home was just a visit.

From London we returned to New York, where I had many friends to see and family to visit. I saw Nanny in her rest home outside the city in Ossining and Vera Somoff in her apartment on 63rd Street. I was happy to return to my own little apartment, which was about to be dismantled because I believed that I would never live in America again.

**Apartment at
450 E. 52nd St.**

Dining Room collection
of 17th and 18th century
porcelain.

Small library — Portrait
of Great Uncle Nathan-
iel Chapman by Sully.

Upstairs living room —
Painting of Venice by
Belotto.

Peggy Thayer Talbott,
portrait by Savely Sorine
(42 sittings!), 1933.

Harold E. Talbott, portrait
by Augustus John.

Harold, HET, John — Beach
Club, Southampton 1946.

John, Nanny, and Harold.

"Bubble Gum John," Lulu Vanderbilt, Harold.

Duchess of Windsor, HET, Nancy Harris, Polly, Duke of Windsor, Roddy Cole, Sharmin Douglas, and PTT.

Harold E. Talbott — Secretary of the Air Force.

HET and Ike playing golf together.

HET with Chinese political and military leader, Chiang Kai-Shek.

The New Y

Copyright, 1955, by Th

VOL. CIV .. No. 35,619.

NEW YORK, TUE

TALBOTT RESIGNS AIR POST; PRESIDENT COMMENDS HIM, CALLS DECISION 'RIGHT ONE'

CONGRESS SPEEDS BILL ON HOUSING; TIED UP ON FUNDS

Adjournment Delayed Agai
—Measure on Legislative Costs a Big Obstacle

TIES UNDER FIRE

Secretary Leaving to Avoid 'Embarrassing' the Administration

Talbott and Eisenhower letters are printed on Page 12.

By RUSSELL BAKER
Special to The New York Times.
WASHINGTON, Aug. 1.—
Harold E. Talbott resigned to-
night as Secretary of the Air
Force.
In a letter to the President he

McGinnis Answers Critics Of His Railroad's Policies

The New Haven's Energetic President Cites Fiscal Progress and Defends Cutbacks in Rebuilding Line

This is the second of two articles on the New York, New Haven and Hartford Railroad.

By CLARENCE DEAN
When Patrick B. McGinnis, president of the New York, New Haven and Hartford Railroad, is in his office at Grand Central Terminal, an electric percolator burbles continuously on a table beside his desk.

station platforms at the head of a retinue carrying briefcases and blueprints.
One thing even his enemies concede: "Pat" McGinnis is a hard worker.
He seldom sees his home on

By WILLIAM S. WHITE
Special to The New York Times
WASHINGTON, Aug. 1—Th
first session of the Eighty-fourt
Congress approached the com
pletion today of its greatest sin
gle remaining task but it agai
postponed final adjournment.
The House of Representative
giving up all hope that the ser
sion could be brought to an en
by early tomorrow morning, qu
for the night at 6:11 o'clock.
will reassemble at 11 A. M. t
morrow.
The Senate carried on long
is circumstances in which noth
ing final could be done in an
case. The Senate gave up for th
night at 11:30 o'clock until
A. M. tomorrow.

Harold Talbott's resignation reported in *The New York Times*, 1955.

TALBOTT, 68, DIES; HEADED AIR FORCE

Resigned Under Fire in 1955 Over Conflict of Interests

Special to The New York Times.

PALM BEACH, Fla., March 2—Harold E. Talbott, former Secretary of the Air Force, died here today of a cerebral hemorrhage at the estate of Mrs. Harry Payne Bingham. His age was 68.

Mr. Talbott was Air Force Secretary from 1953 until August, 1955. His resignation came about when it was discovered that there was a conflict of interest between his private financial holdings and his public office.

His wife, the former Margaret Thayer of Philadelphia, was with him at his death. Surviving also are two daughters, Mrs. Blanche Noyes of Darien, Conn., and Mrs. Owen Toland Jones of Wynnewood, Pa., and twin sons, Harold E. Talbott 3d and John Thayer Talbott. There are four grandchildren.

Mr. Talbott also leaves six sisters. They are Mrs. Duddleson Brown, Mrs. Schuyler Church and Mrs. George H. Mead of Dayton, Ohio, Mrs. Frederick M. Thayer of Philadelphia, Mrs. Charles A. Thomas of St. Louis and Mrs. Alfred W. Jones of Sea Island, Ga.

Mr. Talbott's body was cremated in Miami. A funeral service will be held at 4 P. M., Monday, in St. James Protestant

Continued on Page 84, Column 4

The New York Times reports Harold E. Talbott's death, 1957.

Mrs. H. E. Talbott Dies in Fall; Widow of an Aide to Eisenhower

Note Tells of Grief at Death of Her Husband, Former Air Force Secretary

Mrs. Margaret Talbott, the widow of Harold E. Talbott, Secretary of the Air Force in the Eisenhower Administration, plunged to her death yesterday morning from a rear bedroom window of her twelfth-floor apartment at 1133 Fifth Avenue. She was 62 years old.

The body, clad in a negligee and house coat, was discovered in the rear yard of the adjoining building at 1 East Ninety-fourth Street.

Detectives said later that Mrs. Talbott had left five handwritten notes. Four were addressed to domestic employes. A fifth, addressed to no one, told of her despondency following her husband's death.

Mr. Talbott, who died on March 2, 1957, in Palm Beach, Fla., of a cerebral hemorrhage at the age of 68, had served

Mrs. Harold E. Talbott

The New York Times reports on Peggy Talbott's death, 1962.

John and Anne.

Me, dancing with Anne Kinsolving after wedding to John on June 25, 1965.

Polly and husband Jonesy Toland at their wedding October 3, 1950.

Peggy and husband B. Noyes at their wedding, June 13, 1953.

Dodrup Chen Rinpoche and Semola in Marion, MA.

Dodrup Chen Rinpoche and Harold Talbott at Silver Shell Beach in Marion, MA.

Dodrup Chen Rinpoche giving an initiation at 15 Main Street in Marion, MA, 1978.

Footprint in rock of Lama Gyurda-la in Darjeeling.

Dodrup Chen Rinpoche at Chorten Gompa in Sikkim. (photo by Carola Lott)

Lama Gyurda-la in Darjeeling.

Me and Tulku Thondup translating on the porch of 15 Main Street in Marion, MA.

Tulku Thondup at his home in Cambridge, MA.

Tendzin Parsons, Vivian Kurz, and Harold Talbott in Shelburne Falls, MA.

Harold Talbott with Lobsang and Deki Lhalungpa in New Delhi. (photo by Thomas Merton)

Thomas Merton and Chatral Rinpoche in Darjeeling in 1968

Kanjur Rinpoche in Darjeeling.

Polanarua, Sri Lanka. (Photo by
Thomas Merton)

Thomas Merton and The Dalai Lama in Dharamsala.

Me, His Holiness The Dalai Lama, and Michael Baldwin in Dharamsala.

Dodrup Chen Rinpoche enthroned in The Mahasiddha Temple, Hawley, MA (left) with Tulku Thondup, right.

Lama Gyurda-la and friend in Darjeeling.

Dudjom Rinpoche.

The Maha Siddha Temple in Hawley, MA.

CHAPTER TWELVE

The Dalai Lama

spent a few weeks settling things in New York before returning to New Delhi, where I stayed once again at the Oberoi, which had yet to become prohibitively expensive. I asked if I might have a room overlooking Humayun's Tomb, a marvelous pink monument of the Mughal era, which I went often to visit. In future years I would sit on the parapet on the second story of the tomb and do my meditation practice early in the morning as the sun rose over the city.

As soon as I got to the Oberoi, I wrote Tenzin Geyche, the Dalai Lama's secretary, to say that I was in New Delhi and hoped that I could soon come to Dharamsala. Eventually, Tenzin Geyche wrote to say that they had not yet sent for me because they were having trouble finding a suitable place for me to live. I suspect the real reason was that they were dithering around trying to decide if it was safe for me to stay in Dharamsala because of the delicate situation between India and America. Pakistan and India were currently at odds. Because of India's close alliance with Russia, Nixon had backed Pakistan. As a result, India was against anyone from the United States.

The first thing I did when I reached New Delhi was look up Gene Smith, with whom I would often get together while I waited to be summoned by the Dalai Lama to study with him. Soon after my arrival, I called on Lobsang Lhalungpa, the great Tibetan scholar to whom Marco Pallis had given me an introduction. We quickly made friends. I also became friends with his beautiful wife, Deki, and their three children: Samphe, the oldest and very good looking; Jigme, the middle beautiful son; and Tenzin, charming and humorous. They became like my family and would often invite me to their apartment near the Oberoi for dinners of *momos* (dumplings) and other delicious Tibetan dishes.

Sometimes Gene, who was a great friend of Lobsang's, would join us. I felt very much at home with them all and grateful that I had found such a close circle of friends in New Delhi. The adorable Deki was the daughter of Mrs. Ama-la Dorje, the hostess in Darjeeling of Lama Gyurda-la, who some months later became my *tsawai* lama, or root lama. Lobsang loaned me a copy of *The Path of the Buddha* by Kenneth Morgan in which Lobsang had written the chapter on Tibetan Buddhism. I learned a lot from his account of the Tibetan Buddhist tradition, and over lunch at the Oberoi, I peppered him about different points in the text. He agreed to give me Tibetan lessons and teach me about Tibetan Buddhism while I waited to go up to Dharamsala.

Several months went by while I waited in New Delhi. I continued to study with Lobsang, who had written a Tibetan grammar and who was the best possible teacher of the Tibetan language. He was the head of the Tibetan section of all India Radio as well as a learned scholar about all the four main schools of Tibetan Buddhism. Lobsang came from a noble Tibetan family, and his father was the Nechung Oracle. Tibetan Buddhism has a shamanistic vein, which includes the use of oracles to channel deities or spirits to answer questions about a plan of action or some other inquiry. The Nechung Oracle is the state oracle of Tibet, as well as the Dalai Lama's personal oracle for state matters. He was attached to the Nechung Monastery in the valley of Lhasa, home to a group of monks who say prayers in the Potala for the Dalai Lama. The oracle wears an enormous and extremely heavy mask. Possessed by the deity Pehar, he goes into a trance and dances in circles and, with his body rigid, falls down on the floor in something like a seizure. When the Dalai Lama asks a question about a matter of action or policy, the deity or spirit gives the answer through the oracle. Before fleeing from the Chinese Communists, the Dalai Lama asked for a reading from the Nechung Oracle, who told him that he must leave at once.

Because of the weight of the mask and the effect of the trance and seizure, Lobsang's father, like some of the other preceding Nechung Oracles, developed excruciating migraine headaches. He received the permission of the Thirteenth Dalai Lama to give up the job. While they were still in Tibet, Lobsang's father wanted him to become a monk. Lobsang agreed to do so, but the Dalai Lama of the time—the so-called Great Thirteenth, the predecessor of the present Fourteenth Dalai Lama—refused to allow it. Instead, he wanted Lobsang to become a lay monk or official in the Potala Palace. Lobsang began as a secretary. His handwriting in Tibetan script was beautiful, and he became very good at his job.

When he was a young man, Lobsang belonged to a group of political radicals who called for democratic reforms of Tibet's feudal system. To get rid of him, the government made him the tutor of a group of boys of noble family who were being sent to study in Darjeeling and thence to Rugby in England. As a result Lobsang was safe in India when two years later the Chinese invaded Tibet. The rest of his family, who remained in Tibet, were imprisoned by the Chinese. His father, although an old man, was ordered to work in the fields but refused to do so because he didn't want to kill worms or insects. As a result, he was beaten until his bones broke, and he died from his punishment. All the Tibetans in exile I knew in India had a similar story about their family under the Chinese occupation.

Finally, after two months in New Delhi, I got a call from Tenzin Geyche to say that they had found me a bungalow in Dharamsala and that I could come up and begin my studies with the Dalai Lama. When I arrived in Dharamsala, I was shown my new quarters, a little bungalow with a porch. I was thrilled with my house, which was quite empty and austere. The narrow front room, which I used as a living room, had a couch, a little table smaller than a card table, and two wooden chairs where I took my meals. A door led to the "kitchen," a little room where Pu-chung, a quiet and cheerful young Tibetan, cooked all my meals on a tiny Primus stove and washed the dishes in a plastic basin. Pu-chung had been a monk, and in the 1959 uprising he had fought the Chinese and survived a harrowing escape, but because he had taken up a gun, he had to "give back his robe." He was charming, and I was grateful for his company, and he served me beautifully. Eventually, he got the chance to emigrate to America, and the last I heard he was working as a logger in Maine.

Beyond the sitting room was my bedroom. A *charpoy*—a wooden frame with interwoven thin ropes strung across it like a cat's cradle— served as a bed. There was no mattress because you were expected to bring your own bedding. Fortunately, I'd bought a very thin folding mat in New Delhi that I spread over the cat's cradle as a mattress. It was not long enough, which made sleeping quite uncomfortable. The bedroom had a mantelpiece where I put little photographs in silvery frames that you could buy in the shops in Lower Dharamsala. I had a photo of His Holiness seated on his throne in the Potala when he was seventeen and two smaller snapshots of the senior tutor of His Holiness, Ling Rinpoche, and the junior tutor, Trijang Rinpoche, both of whom I had met with Dom Aelred.

Next to the bedroom was a little study, which I loved. You know how a room, or even a whole house, where you are happy and in which you are doing interesting work can seem like a friend? Perhaps even like a living being, a bodhisattva, if you are studying and practicing dharma? That was the way the study felt. I lined up my books about dharma by Edward Conze, the great German English scholar of Buddhism, on a book shelf, along with books on Tibet, such as the histories by Hugh Richardson and Tsepon Shakabpa. Here in the study I would sit in a chair and read and study Tibetan grammar and phrase books and practice writing the Tibetan alphabet and sentences.

At the end of a sort of cloister at the back of the house, a door led to the bathroom. As the sweeper who cleaned the bathroom was not allowed to come into any other part of the house because he belonged to the caste of untouchables, I had to hand him his salary through the window of the study. After a while I refused this arrangement and told Pu-chung to ask the sweeper to come into the house to receive his pay. "No, no, no, don't do that!" said Pu-chung, looking frantic. "We will be killed." So much for my crusading zeal against the caste system. I surrendered to it.

A Tibetan official, Mr. Ngawang Thondup, strict but patient, was assigned to teach me Tibetan. I learned to read a bit, as well as a smattering of Tibetan grammar, which like Sanskrit is very logical but intricate, although fortunately not quite as intricate. Every afternoon it rained torrentially. The downpour would stop at precisely four o'clock. Shortly before four, I would have tea with a couple of simple English biscuits, which were my treat for the day, and then take a walk in the mountains.

At my first audience with the Dalai Lama, he gave me a meditation and a visualization of the Buddha that was quite complicated. He also gave me a mantra to say on my rosary. When I asked him to bless the rosary, he looked at it with curiosity because it was just a set of orange plastic beads. He laughed, because Tibetans have beautiful rosaries, some of which have bodhi beads, seeds from the same kind of tree as the bodhi tree in Bodhgaya. Attached to their rosaries are little chains of metal rings that can be moved up and down to tally the number of recitations if the practice requires a certain amount, like a hundred thousand. I was doing these meditation practices, which included visualization, so I was used to creating forms in the air, and I would usually visualize the Buddha. But every now and then I would visualize a huge martini glass filled with gin, atop the Himalayan peaks. *Plus ça change, plus c'est la même chose.*

At one point His Holiness asked a scribe to write out the famous brief prayer to Je Tsong Khapa, the founder of the Dalai Lama's own order, the Gelugpa School, and sent me into a shrine room next to his audience chamber and told me to start reciting the prayer, which I liked very much. Today, I have in a frame the piece of paper with the prayer that His Holiness gave me. I did my best to recite it diligently. Some time afterward, His Holiness gave me a *sadhana,* or prayer, of Shakyamuni Buddha. There was no written text; he simply recited it to me, so perhaps he composed it himself. The sadhana involved a rather complicated visualization of the Buddha, and it was quite an interesting exercise to maintain clearly in one's mind the various elements, one inside the other.

One thing that has helped me very much in trying to do any practice of dharma is not to be the least bit daunted if one's practice is not perfect, or even if it's somewhat disgraceful. Of course, one can't be sloppy or give in to distractions. However, the effort to do the practice and to improve one's capacity is what counts, for it is bringing you grace and blessing and power from the lama who gave it to you, as well as from the lineage. I found that if I persevered, little miracles of accomplishment would occur along the way, as slowly the length of time between glimpses of awareness and the ordinary mind grew longer.

I ended up making my own sadhana, its visualization, recitation, and meditation on the nature of the absolute reality. It seems that a practice of meditation can elevate your mind and make it more subtle. I pray that the meager practice I do will eventually make me kind and less attached to my ego. After practicing the teachings the Dalai Lama gave me, I told him of my experience with the prayers and visualization and recitation of the mantra. He then gave me another longer prayer of Tsongkhapa, which I took to my little bungalow, where I recited it many times.

In the autumn, while I continued dharma teachings, I was sent for by the Indian official who dealt with matters related to the Dalai Lama and the members of his court who had escaped with him from Tibet and been granted asylum in India. The official had me to tea on his office veranda in a pleasant clearing in the woods. I was very naive—perhaps you could say even childish or stupid—so I wasn't fully aware how precarious my situation was as an American student of His Holiness.

It was a time of political delicacy for him in relation to the government of India. When the Dalai Lama left Tibet, he had deeply offended the Chinese. As a result, Chou En-lai prevailed upon Nehru, who wanted an alliance with China ("Indians and Chinese are brothers") to see the Chinese leader and the Dalai Lama together with Sonam Kazi as the interpreter. Nehru neglected to tell the Dalai Lama that Chou En-lai would be at the meeting, and as a result His Holiness was unprepared and very shocked. When Chou En-lai demanded that the Dalai Lama return to Tibet, he refused, and from then on he became a thorn in the flesh of the Indians.

Nor did I realize how suspicious the Indians were of an American who was residing in Dharamsala and who was in regular contact with His Holiness. Nevertheless, I got an uncomfortable feeling that I was being questioned in a manner that implied doubt and suspicion. Because I thought that the truth would satisfy the official and whomever he was reporting to, I simply explained that I was in India to study Buddhism with His Holiness the Dalai Lama. Thinking that if I dropped an important Indian name it would make him understand that I was welcome in India, I told him that I had met Dr. Sarvepalli Radhakrishnan. When the official questioned me about that meeting, I said that I'd told Radhakrishnan that I wanted to study Buddhism. I said, "I don't think I can learn much Tibetan; it's quite a struggle." "If you try, you can do anything," the official replied. And suddenly I got the feeling that he was using what appeared to be a simple statement of encouragement in a hostile way. I left the official with a feeling of anxious foreboding.

The summons and the meeting also alarmed the Dalai Lama's staff. A decision was made to send me down to Bombay for a while to get me out of Dharamsala. I was told that Mr. Ngawang Thondup would come down and continue to tutor me in Tibetan. They said that while I was in Bombay, I should ask for my visa extension as it would be much easier to get it there. When I got to Bombay, I stayed in splendor at the Taj Hotel. I'm sure the irony of my living in this grand hotel studying Tibetan with a view to becoming a Buddhist monk was not lost on others. During the years I lived in India, I spent so much time living in various delightful hotels that I became quite used to improvising a shrine table with images and scriptures, flowers and water bowls in each successive room, and doing a lot of prayer and meditation.

Katie Urquhart, the daughter of my friend Alfreda Rushmore, was teaching English to the sons of maharajahs at a school in Hyderabad. As it turned out Katie would be on vacation just when I'd be in Bombay, so I invited her to join me at the Taj. She was rather Bolshie and disapproved of staying at the Taj as she no doubt disapproved of many of her royal students, but I persuaded her to ditch her principles temporarily in favor of our having a good time together far from home. And this we did. Katie had learned to wear saris properly in Hyderabad, and with pale blue or green saris and her blond hair, she looked like a Botticelli. Mr. Ngawang Thondup allowed her to join our Tibetan classes, and she was a much better student than I was.

CHAPTER THIRTEEN

Thomas Merton

While I was still in Bombay, I received a letter in November 1968 from Thomas Merton, whom I had not seen since I visited him ten years before at his monastery in Kentucky. He had asked Dom Aelred Graham to recommend someone who could introduce him to lamas in India, and Dom Aelred recommended me as someone familiar with the Dalai Lama and other Tibetan lamas in both Darjeeling and Dharamsala, whom we had visited on our trip together. I wrote Thomas Merton back saying that I would be delighted to help him out.

I waited for Merton at the International Airport in Palam, when he arrived in New Delhi from Calcutta, where he been attending a conference sponsored by the Indian industrialist Aditya Vikram Birla. Tom (Merton had asked me to call him Tom) had given a speech that so impressed Birla that he sent a car and driver to meet him at the airport. Because I couldn't get rooms at the Oberoi, we stayed at the Jan Path Hotel, a delightful white elephant left over from the Raj with large high-ceilinged rooms. The following morning, we met at the desk. Tom collected his mail and was especially pleased to have received a letter from Octavio Paz, the Mexican poet who had been influenced by Marxism and surrealism. Later, Tom told me that he had corresponded with the Russian poet Boris Pasternak. I was impressed, but at the time I wasn't aware that Tom himself was an extraordinary poet. He had his poems posthumously published by his friend James Laughlin, founder of New Directions Publishing. Merton's complete poems cover more than a thousand pages.

That evening I invited James George, the Canadian high commissioner to India, and his wife, Carol, to dinner along with Gene Smith, Lobsang, Deki, and Tom. Mr. George, whom I later called Jim, said, "No, you all dine with Carol and me at the embassy." It was a splendid occasion, just ourselves with the Georges, so we were able to get to know them. Both the Georges were very interested in religion, particularly Sufism and Buddhism. They had been posted to Sri Lanka, where they had been able to study Buddhism firsthand. They were also teachers in the Gurdjieffian movement.

The following night, I invited them all to the Moti Mahal Restaurant for tandoori cooking. Tom was delighted by the entertainment, which consisted of a singing contest between two singers of *gazals*—songs in Urdu from the Mogul conquest about unrequited love as well as satires on contemporary politics. During the day, we would often take walks around New Delhi, and Tom took some of his wonderful photographs, which appear in his book, published posthumously in 1975, titled *The Asian Journal of Thomas Merton*.

From New Delhi we went to Dharamsala, where we stayed at my bungalow. I gave my room and study to Merton and bedded down on a sort of wooden sofa in the front room. There was hardly any furniture, we were freezing, and Merton was sick with a terrible cold. He had often been ill in later life, no doubt because he kept up the crushing schedule of a working Trappist monk, as well as staying up late to write countless books. He burned the candle at both ends to a frightening degree. At the bungalow I would see his light go on in the bedroom at two in the morning, when he would begin his prayers; then at four in the morning, I would see the light go on in the study. I was delighted when I read his *Asian Journal* to discover that he had been reading some of the books on my shelf, including Edward Conze's *Buddhist Thought in India*.

Soon after we arrived in Dharamsala, Tom went for a walk in the mountains and came upon Sonam Topgay Kazi, whom Aelred and I had met when we were in Dharamsala. Sonam invited Merton to a teahouse and talked to him at length about the Dzogchen meditation of the Nyingmapa school. Tom was fascinated. Sonam can put a person in an altered state of consciousness, and although I was not used to altered states of consciousness, Merton understood it immediately. After Sonam Kazi introduced Merton to Dzogchen, he said, "What you're calling Dzogchen—that's what I want. I came to Asia to study

Zen in Japan, and now I have changed my itinerary and I'm going to study Dzogchen in India with the Tibetans."

When I told him that an audience had been scheduled for him with His Holiness the Dalai Lama, Tom said, "I'm not going." When I asked him why not, he said, "I've seen enough pontiffs." I told him that I thought that if he came to India to study with lamas, he would be making a mistake not to meet the Dalai Lama. "Furthermore," I told him, "the Dalai Lama has heard all about you from the Canadian High Commissioner, James George, and has taken the trouble of having a film screened of Cistercian monks and abbeys in France. He's done his homework, and I think you should show up and meet him." So, Tom said, "OK, we'll see."

Tom didn't trust organized religion, and he didn't come to India to hang around the power elite of an exiled central Asian Vatican. But despite his misgivings, he went to meet His Holiness, wearing his white robe with black scapular. In the jeep, as we were going up the hill to McLeod Ganj, the Dalai Lama's residence, I said that I thought it would be impolitic for Merton to refer to the Dzogchen school because it's an entirely different school from that of His Holiness. However, when at our first audience, His Holiness asked Tom, "What do you want?" Tom replied, "I want to study Dzogchen." The Dalai Lama said, "Well, in order to study Dzogchen, you have to have a thorough grounding in the three vehicles, or *yanas*. I will tell you about them starting with the fundamental teachings of Shakyamuni Buddha." He went on to tell us about the four noble truths and the eightfold noble path and *tendrel*, or interdependent causation, as well as suffering, impermanence, and not-self. That was the first audience.

In the second of our three audiences, to my astonishment, the Dalai Lama got down on the floor and showed Merton the lotus meditation posture and the hand position. He remained on a level lower than ourselves for the rest of the teaching and gave us very, very clear meditation instructions, which would be completely familiar to *vipassana* practitioners. He spoke to us about Mahayana Buddhism, compassion and emptiness, and about Tantra or Vajrayana Buddhism. When he spoke about emptiness, he asked Tom, "Is there a horse on that table?"

And Tom said, "No." And the Dalai Lama said, "The table is empty in respect to a horse, but that is not the meaning of emptiness." And then he gave a deep explanation of emptiness.

In the third audience, when the Dalai Lama asked Tom to tell him about Catholicism, Tom gave an impressive explanation of his religion. I thought the Dalai Lama's robe and Thomas Merton's white Cistercian habit with its black scapular looked almost Giottoesque. It struck me that these two figures deserved to wear their robes, which were part and parcel of the worlds they represented. There was so much good humor, so much laughter and camaraderie, and so much understanding between them that there was no need for any explanation. They had both done their homework. After our three audiences were over, we left the bungalow and went down to the town of Lower Dharamsala, where Tom bought a newspaper with a banner headline that read "Nixon Wins." When Tom said, "It's all over," I didn't understand what he meant. Later I learned that Tom had been a notable figure in both the antiwar movement as well as the civil rights movement. People like Joan Baez who were involved in those causes would visit him at Gethsemane Monastery.

Later, Sonam drove us in a jeep to the Kangra Valley to visit two lamas. The first was Chokling Rinpoche, a way-out yogi, a wild man who was an incredible kick-over-the-traces, irresponsible-type person, a tremendous troublemaker, and extremely rollicking in an unpredictable way but nonetheless a top-flight, wonderful Nyingmapa yogi. "When Sonam Kazi brings someone, I know I'll be able to talk to them and that it'll be OK," Lama Chokling said when we arrived. When he asked Merton, "Do you believe in karma and rebirth?" Merton said, "Well, I think it's a very, very fascinating, persuasive proposition, but I wouldn't say I believe it, no."

Chokling Rinpoche then said, "Let's assume that you believe in karma and rebirth so I can teach you about the yogic meditation practice of *powa*. By practicing powa at the time of one's death, it is possible to transfer the consciousness out the top of the head so that one goes to the Pure Land of Amitabha, the Buddha of Boundless Light." I was surprised that Chokling Rinpoche immediately gave Tom such a very esoteric Tantric teaching. Perhaps Chokling Rinpoche felt Merton did not need teachings of karma and suffering, calming the mind, or insight meditation but rather needed to be taught how to dispose his consciousness at the time of death. Merton scribbled in his journal: "I'm not sure about all this consciousness and shooting out the top of the head. I'm not sure this is going to be very useful to us." However, in ten days Tom was dead, and it occurred to me that perhaps Chokling Rinpoche was clairvoyant, as many lamas are.

A human being has a *srog*, or life force. He has a consciousness, and when he dies, to ensure the proper destination of the consciousness, it's very useful to practice powa. There's a fontanel on top of your head. At birth, it's a soft, big space between the head bones, and as babies grow it closes. Through yogic training, you can reopen it, and then when you die, you can shoot the consciousness out the fontanel and straight to the paradise of Amitabha Buddha. At an enlightened level the universe is viewable as a boundless number of Buddha fields—areas of enlightened consciousness. The field around a Buddha and his enlightened bodhisattvas resonates as what we might call, figuratively, a paradise.

We then drove toward Palampur to see Khamtrul Rinpoche. When a jeep coming from the opposite direction passed us, Sonam waved them down, and they backed up. Khamtrul Rinpoche was in the jeep, so we got out and went to the forest, where we sat and talked. Sonam, of course, wanted to talk about Dzogchen. When we got back to Dharamsala, Sonam took us to a broken-down shack of a bar where he ordered scotch for the three of us. I don't like scotch, so I declined politely, and he looked at me and said, "Are you a *tantrika?*" Unlike the other schools of Buddhism, tantrikas in Vajrayana Buddhism can drink alcohol, so I said yes, even though I was by no means acquainted with the Tantra at that time. Sonam talked to us again about Dzogchen, and in that bar there was no longer Catholicism or Buddhism, only the nature of the mind existed.

The following day Tom and I went to Darjeeling and met several other lamas with whom Tom had some most enlightening conversations. When Tom made a retreat in the house of a Catholic tea planter, we visited the forest hermitage of Thugsey Rinpoche. Only Khenpo Noryang, his *nyerpa*, or steward, was there. So we missed Thugsey Rinpoche and the little lama for whom he was the regent, the Gyalwa Drugchen Tulku.

On the last day we went to see Chatral Rinpoche, who was building a nunnery down the road from Ghoom, near Darjeeling. When we arrived, he put planks on some bricks as a seat, and we sat and talked with the help of an interpreter. Chatral Rinpoche started by saying, "Ah, Jesus Lama, you know I have never been able for the life of me to get a handle on Christianity, so I'm glad you came this morning. I would like to ask you a question about Christianity. At the center of your religion is a man who comes back to life after death, and in Tibetan Buddhism, when you have one of those people, a *rolang*, or a walking corpse, we call our lama to put him down. Why is the Resurrection so important to you?"

Tom answered, "I'll explain it in terms of the Tantra. The Resurrection means the overcoming of the fear of death." Chatral Rinpoche said, "You have made me understand Christianity. You and I are not enlightened. Let's have a contest to see which of us will get enlightened first. I have a hermitage in Bhutan where you could stay and do a retreat on the preliminary practice, and after that I will teach you Dzogchen." "It's a deal," Tom said. In the jeep back to Dharamsala after the meeting with Chatral Rinpoche, Tom said to me, "That is the greatest man I have ever met."

Although Chatral Rinpoche gave the flavor of the Tibetans, I would never have dreamed of studying with him because he was completely unpredictable. He was savage about ego, and he would put you on the spot, and I was not prepared to up the ante to that degree. Nonetheless, I wanted to make sure that Merton met all the outstanding lamas whom I could find to give him the whole spectrum of the force field. And, of course, it was an opportunity for me to hide behind Merton's skirts and meet Chatral Rinpoche, of whom, from his reputation alone, I was terrified.

That evening Tom came to my room at the Windamere with some brandy, and we had a farewell party. He said to me, "I would like to travel with you again." I was sad when he left the following day because I knew that I would miss Tom. But at the same time, I was happy to have my solitude back.

One afternoon soon after I got back to Dharamsala, a worried-looking Pu-chung came to say that some people were at the door of the bungalow asking to see me. I found several policemen standing there in their tarbooshes—cockaded turbans—with rather malicious smirks on their faces. "Come in," I said. "Pu-chung, please bring them tea." I had obviously been reading too many books about grand duchesses confronting the Bolsheviks. Pu-chung shook his head with a warning look, seeming to send a silent message that this was not a moment for aristocratic irony. Whereupon the tarbooshes presented me with a "quit notice," ordering me to leave India within twenty-four hours.

I knew I couldn't get to Delhi in twenty-four hours, let alone out of the country. The best I could do was take a bus to Pathankot and then a train to New Delhi. I ran up to McCloud Ganj, found Tenzin Geyche, and explained my disastrous predicament. I asked him if I could borrow some money as I had very little. He told me to catch the afternoon bus and that he'd meet me with the money. I packed, managed to give Pu-chung some money, and rushed to the bus. I had just enough for a ticket, so I got on. The bus was about to leave and no Tenzin Geyche. Finally, I saw him running out of the bank, his robes flying. As the bus started, he handed me a large bundle of rupees through the window and said good-bye.

The moment I reached New Delhi, I went straight to the Vikram Hotel and I called Anthony Quainton, the American consul. When I told him that I'd been booted out of the country and was now there illegally, he said that I should not leave my room. America's only friend in the Indian government was the interior minister, and Anthony said that he would try to get him to fix it. A short while later, Anthony rang to say the the minister would have the quit notice rescinded after the weekend. He said that I must give him my word, which he would relay to the minister, that I would not go back to Dharamsala. I should remain in New Delhi for six months, and then I would be free to go anywhere in India, although not to see the Dalai Lama. I said, "It's a deal." It wasn't until many years later that I had the joy of again seeing the Dalai Lama and talking with him, when he gave lectures at Harvard and Smith. And finally, I had a private audience with him at the dharma center of the students of the late Geshe Wangyal in New Jersey.

Not long after Tom left India, while I was staying at the Vikram Hotel, I received a cable. I walked up and down the room holding it in my hand, composing a reply. Then I realized that I hadn't opened the telegram. It turned out to be from Michael saying, "Very sorry to inform you that Thomas Merton died yesterday." I had known before opening it that the cable was from Michael and what it would say. Tom had died in Thailand, accidentally electrocuted while stepping out of his bath. I could not help but think of Chokling Rinpoche's decision to teach Tom the practice of powa.

Shortly after Tom died, I met Thugsey Rinpoche at the Lhalungpas's apartment in New Delhi. He asked me to give him a photograph of Tom. I asked him why he wanted it, and he replied that Thomas Merton had liked his forest hermitage so much that he might be reborn in his monastic community. I asked him where Tom was. He replied, "He is here, but I can't say anything more." It was almost as if things had been arranged for me to be with the Dalai Lama for a short while in order to bring him and Tom together. Then, when I was cast out of Dharamsala and separated from the Dalai Lama, I was free to follow Tom's recommendation that I find a Dzogchen lama.

Looking back on my time in India with Tom, I remember the way the Indian people greeted him as a pilgrim, a seeker, as if they realized his spiritual quality. Even people in airplanes knew it. There was no question about it. Thomas Merton was an event. Tom was so kind in insisting that I accompany him to his meetings with the Dalai Lama, which allowed me to be present at the discussions between these two great men. Since then, so many new friends and so many blessings and opportunities have come my way through my brief friendship with Tom. I feel that these are unquestionably expressions of grace through him.

And then there are his writings. When I read them, I hear his voice. They reflect his realizations and are full of wisdom and a passionate sense of justice. Among my favorite theologians and mystics is Fénelon, and Merton's essay on his life and writings, *Reflections on the Character and Genius of Fénelon: An Introduction to Fénelon's Letters*, is the best thing in English that I've read on that seventeenth-century French mystic. Above all, in speech and in writing, Tom was natural. If he tended sometimes to be unnecessarily discursive, it didn't matter because one always heard the charm, sincerity, and intensity of his voice. Another reason why I loved Darjeeling and the Windamere Hotel so much was that I was there with Aelred and later with Tom.

CHAPTER FOURTEEN

Dudjom Rinpoche and Lama Gyurda-la

Entering the Path of Dzogchen

After the visa problem was straightened out, I asked Lobsang Lhalungpa if he would oversee my studies since it was now impossible for me to enter the dharma under the direction of the Dalai Lama as I had hoped to do. Lobsang told me that I should first take the Three Refuges or Three Jewels (Buddha, dharma, *sangha*). He would ask Geshe Tenpa Gyaltsen, a scholar of the Madhyamaka philosophy from Gyalthang Monastery in Kham, to give me this formal commitment to the Buddha, the dharma, and the sangha. Geshe Tenpa Gyaltsen was the tutor and guardian of a tulku who had run afoul of Dharamsala, so that he himself was not in good odor with the powers-that-be in the government in exile.

Lobsang took me through the responses for the ceremony and set up a shrine in his living room with images, water bowls, butter lamps, and offerings of fruit, flowers, rice, and cookies—the whole panoply of offerings Tibetans make from what is at hand in the modern Western world. The shrines in America, for example at our temple at Hawley, Massachusetts ("our" meaning the students of Kyab-Je Dodrup Chen Rinpoche), are laden with the most delightful array of junk food and candy as well as what is available here of the traditional Tibetan Buddhist offerings, all beautifully arranged on the altar. Geshe Tenpa Gyaltsen in his maroon robe said the words of going for refuge to the Buddha, dharma, and sangha, and I repeated them after him, getting some of the Tibetan right and a lot wrong. After the little ceremony, Deki, Lobang's charming wife, gave us a delicious lunch. There was such mutual esteem and affection between the lama and his friend Lobsang, and the atmosphere in the room was filled with radiant kindness.

Geshe Tenpa Gyaltsen gave me a very short prayer of refuge and told me to say it one hundred thousand times. The prayer was simply *Lama-la gyap-su chi-o* (I go for refuge to the lama), *Sangye-la gyap su chi-o* (I go for refuge to the Buddha), *Cho-la gyap-su chi-o* (I go for refuge to the dharma), *Gendun-la gyap-su chi-o* (I go for refuge to the sangha). He neglected to tell me that you say the entire prayer once, then a second time, and so on until you've said it one hundred thousand times. I mistakenly recited the going for refuge to the lama a hundred thousand times and then the Buddha, the dharma, and the sangha separately as well.

Geshe Tenpa Gyaltsen and Lobsang said that there was nothing really wrong with the way I had incorrectly recited the little refuge prayer. They were being kind. But faith, devotion, compassion, and diligence breed confidence so that then one can experience what the Dzogchen masters mean when they tell you to relax the mind. But perhaps recitation is effective even if done wrong, like the story of the old man who recited the mantra of Tara over and over as he made his circumambulations of the holy places in Lhasa, and Tara was seen to be radiantly present above him. Then somebody corrected an error in his recitation of the mantra, and he started saying it correctly. But Tara withdrew her presence. So he went back to saying it wrong, and she reappeared. Anyhow, the presence of Tara must have depended in part on the devotion of the old man and the power accumulated from the many recitations he had done wrong. Devotion doesn't really depend on how perfectly a prayer is uttered. In doing my own simple dharma practice for years and years, I have always relied on the grace of the Buddha nature, rather than struggling to be a hotshot practitioner.

At the same time, Lobsang arranged for Lama Cho-pal to teach me conversational Tibetan. Lama Cho-pal, a monk from Thugsey Rinpoche's monastery in Darjeeling, was in Delhi printing scriptures for his monastery. In return for his instruction, it was arranged that I would teach him some English. Lama Cho-pal was young, shy, and funny, and it was great fun to spend time with him. Sogyal Tulku Rinpoche, a young lama proficient in English who was studying at St. Stephen's College in New Delhi, also gave me lessons in dharma in his free time. His English was perfect, like Lobsang's, so it was easy to communicate with him—too easy for the sake of making progress in Tibetan. He read me the *Bodhicaryavatara*, translating it into English, and I wrote it down and learned a little of the Tibetan text. I loved the ornateness of the chapter "Perfection of Offering," with its descriptions of jeweled canopies and all, and thrilled to the young tulku's warnings about the hard-to-decipher depths in the chapter "Emptiness," expounded from the standpoint of the Madhyamaka philosophy, of which Shantideva was a great master.

Tulku Thondup says that the point of the Madhyamaka texts is nonduality. This is what fascinated me since I had read Alan Watts's book *The Supreme Identity* and had had a discussion with Alan at lunch years before. The following is what Tulku Thondup says about nonduality in his book *Hidden Teachings of Tibet*: "The duality of the objective and subjective is overcome. That is the freedom from dual conceptions and perceptions." He goes on to say that "it is the meditation on the luminescent wisdom of self-discriminating awareness." The realization of that teaching is the reason I came to study with lamas in India.

Among other texts, Sogyal Tulku and I worked on a translation of the *Kunzang Lama'i Zhalung*, but it remained as a handwritten manuscript. Many years later in Marion, Sogyal Rinpoche asked if he might have it back and sent one of his students to pick it up at my house. Eventually, the text came out in two English translations, first Sonam Topgay Kazi's and then one by the Padmakara Translation Committee. To this day I also have a handwritten translation of the *Outer Preliminary Practice of Dzog Chen Longchen Nyingthig* from the commentary by Patrul Rinpoche on that practice, the *Kunzang Lama'i Zhalung*, that Lama Gyurda-la and Lobsang and I did together.

After I had taken refuge, Lobsang said that the next step was to take the bodhisattva vow and arranged for Nechung Rinpoche to confer it. Nechung Rinpoche was the tulku of a monastery that historically was a Nyingma institution. But the Fifth Dalai Lama, who was a Nyingma adept, incorporated it into the Gelugpa monastic establishment in the seventeenth century. Nechung at some point became the college, or *trat-shang*, of monks, which performed the prayers and ceremonies for the

Dalai Lamas in the Potala. The monastery itself was somewhere in the Lhasa Valley. The institution of the state oracle was associated with Nechung Monastery, and as I have said, Lobsang's father had been the Nechung Oracle under the Thirteenth Dalai Lama.

Again, Lobsang created a beautiful shrine in his living room, and Nechung Rinpoche conferred the vow, "the entrance to the Mahayana," with Lobsang interpreting. At the end of the ceremony as we were getting ready to leave, Lobsang said, "Now that you have been given the bodhisattva vow, you should next do practice on your *yidam*"—the expression of the Buddha nature in the form of a particular deity for whom you feel an affinity or to whom you are devoted.

"So who is your yidam?" Lobsang inquired with his warm smile. At first, I said uncertainly that it seemed to me that since Chenrezi, the deity who manifests the compassion of the Buddha, is the patron yidam of Tibet, as an outsider and a beginner trying to become assimilated into Tibetan Buddhism, I should choose Chenrezi as my yidam. But when I told Lobsang that I felt a very strong attraction to Manjusri, the lord of wisdom, he agreed that that particular divine being was indeed my yidam. Handing me a beautiful eighteenth-century Tibetan gilded statue of Manjusri adorned with small jewels, he told me that when he left Tibet for India in 1948, he had carried this favorite image in his saddlebag. I said that I couldn't possibly take it, but he insisted. He said that all his life Manjusri had been his yidam, but now that his yidam was Tara, he wanted me to have this Manjusri image. At all the various hotels where I would stay, I always had in my room this masterpiece of a *lima*, or image made from a number of metals and conforming to the proportions required by the canons of Tibetan images of Buddhas. I would wrap a pile of four or five books in a silk scarf or a piece of brocade and put Lobsang's Manjusri image on top of them, and before it, seven water bowls.

Having identified my yidam, Lobsang said that I should next receive an initiation into Manjusri practice, which would be my introduction to the Vajrayana. Once again Nechung Rinpoche conferred upon me a *je-nang*, or "permission to follow," which Lobsang said was something less than a wang, or empowerment. And I received the lung, or reading that empowers one to recite a particular text, in this case the eulogy of Manjusri, which students recite to sharpen their minds and many people recite to achieve wisdom. With it I received the mantra of Manjusri: *om a ra pa tsa na dhi*. Nechung Rinpoche, Geshe Tenpa Gyaltsen, and Lobsang composed a sadhana incorporating the eulogy and mantra with the parts of a simple meditation liturgy, beginning with going for refuge, followed by the bodhisattva vow, the seven acts of devotion, the visualization of the deity or Buddha, the recitation of the mantra, the dissolution of the Buddha image, the meditation of dwelling in emptiness, and finishing with the dedication of the merits to all sentient beings and the final element of the sadhana, the *monlam*, or prayer of aspiration. And Lobsang instructed me in how to perform the sadhana.

Some time after I had begun to practice the Manjusri sadhana, Sonam Topgay Kazi offered to take me to meet Dudjom Rinpoche, a fully realized Dzogchen yogi and scholar and the supreme figure among all the Nyingmapa lamas of our day as well as the tsawai lama, or root lama, of all the Nyingmapas.

At that time, in the late 1960s and early '70s, it was possible to call on a lama without knowing him or her and be received warmly and with exquisite politeness. And if you asked, you could receive teachings. Thereafter, of course, you made an appointment if you wanted to see the lama again. I think access was often easier for a Westerner than for a Tibetan. *Injee*, or "Englishman," was the Tibetan word for a Westerner, the term having never changed from the time when most Westerners whom the Tibetans came in contact with were British. The term for a non-Buddhist was *chirolpa*, meaning "outsider," in contrast to the synonym for a Buddhist, which is *nangpa*, or "insider." Shamefully, to some extent I took for granted this ease of access and these great lamas' unbelievable generosity with their time and wisdom. Tibetan friends would tell me that they envied the attention Westerners were given. Although I was sorry that Tibetans had a hard time getting the teachings they desired, I was grateful that great Dzogchen yogis would consent to teach me. In my own country, I was a nonentity, and here in India among the Tibetans in exile, I was a somebody.

Such is the danger of setting out to study the religion that teaches how to penetrate through the illusoriness of the ego. One thing that did not escape me was my pride at being accepted as a student by these Dzogchen masters in contrast to their liberation from the Laocoönian coils of grasping. This inestimably precious training freely given made me think from time to time of the difference between the West and the world of the lamas. In the West, one certainly couldn't walk into the office of a university president or a great writer or psychologist or scientist—I'm not sure sages exist in the West—and ask for free "teachings." Perhaps one could have easy access to a great religious scholar or holy person in our culture, but whom among us could one receive training on the true nature of the mind?

Although I was somewhat anxious at the prospect of meeting Dudjom Rinpoche, I was confident that the meeting would go smoothly because Sonam was taking me. He was deeply devoted to Dudjom Rinpoche, and he had a skillful diplomatic touch as well as a sharp sense of humor. There was something mysterious about Sonam and also something sly. He has been deeply helpful to me, and I owe him a great debt of gratitude.

Rinpoche was in a hospital in New Delhi, but Sonam said that it would be all right to visit him. He was sitting in his pajamas, cross-legged on top of the sheets on an iron bedstead, wreathed in smiles and talking to Sonam with great good humor. To me he seemed to transcend the designations he was given, be they yogi or scholar. He was gentle—friendly and encouraging—yet at the same time majestic and authoritative. After Sonam introduced me, I told him that I was doing practice on Manjusri. Rinpoche smiled broadly and inquired, "Who is Manjusri?" Somehow I knew what he meant and immediately put up resistance to the implication. He had taught me a very great lesson by that sudden, unexpected question. Thinking about it now, the answer to the question lay in the sadhana Dudjom Rinpoche composed for me about six years later in 1974. Rinpoche laughed and proceeded to give me teachings on the nature of the mind. Talking to him I felt that I might be capable of making progress in understanding and practicing dharma. Yet it was frightening to feel that he could lead me to an altogether new, simpler, and more immediate understanding of reality. But after all, wasn't that what I was in India to obtain?

There is a Dzogchen saying that the mind of a meditator should be "like an old man watching children playing." Dudjom Rinpoche was that old man, and I was those children playing. I wanted Manjusri to be a deity outside myself whom I could venerate. Dudjom Rinpoche was telling me that Manjusri is not outside yourself but is your own true nature, which you are trying to recognize. I told him that I knew this but wanted to continue to venerate him as a Buddha and was certainly not ready to do away with visualization and recitation and "realize my own true nature." This again was a complete misunderstanding of the Nyingmapa approach: visualization and recitation are practiced in whatever state of realization the mind has attained.

Later, reflecting on the odd sense of fear I had in confronting this radiant being in his pajamas, I realized that I was afraid of losing my narrow concepts about the truth, the mind, and the dharma. However, Dudjom Rinpoche was natural and joyful, without guile or judgment. He smiled and radiated such a sense of pleasure at what was taking place before him, as if enjoyment and kindness were for him one and the same. I was bowled over by his graciousness. Then there was his voice, soft and fairly high-pitched when he was teaching how to be and how to maintain one's consciousness so as to attain awareness of the mind's true nature. He was speaking from the direct experience of an enlightened mind without conceptions and dualities, perfect, pure, and still, like the ocean without waves. And all this outpouring of revelation about the mind was offered in the most open-handed, generous fashion.

Having been taught by him, you were left with no doubt that what you had heard is the natural state of the mind when it is unobscured and that it is available to you if you practice in the way that he instructed you. Meanwhile, he seemed not only present but also dwelling in a realm that one couldn't penetrate. He was simple and sublime. There was nothing about him to be afraid of. I was awed and charmed by him at the same time.

After a long session that I feared might tire him out, we left. Going home in the taxi, Sonam said that because Dudjom Rinpoche had given me these high teachings immediately upon meeting me, it was obvious that I should learn to practice Dzogchen. I listened but remained noncommittal. Sonam had started me on a process that I could not foresee, for Dudjom Rinpoche did indeed become my tsawai or root lama, and he did give me the Dzogchen initiations and teachings without holding anything back. I have Manjusri to thank, and of course Sonam, for that first meeting with the embodiment of Guru Rinpoche. Later on, I would have Lama Gyurda-la to thank for giving me Dzogchen teachings and then taking me to Dudjom Rinpoche for an examination of understanding, after which he conferred the *rigpa'i tsal wang* on Lobsang, who interpreted for me as well as Lama Gyurda-la and Tendzin. Later I had Tulku Thondup Rinpoche to thank for interpreting many of my interviews with Dudjom Rinpoche. And I also had Bakha Tulku and Khenpo Tsewang to thank for interpreting for me at other times.

I would go to see Dudjom Rinpoche in Darjeeling and Kalimpong as well as in New Delhi. And later I went with Tulku Thondup, and once with Khenpo Tsewang, to hear him give public teachings in New York. Some were seminars over two successive days, and one seminar at Yeshe Nyingpo, his students' center in the country, lasted for several days. At that seminar, Tulku Pema Wangyal interpreted with Sangye Khandro, the astonishingly fluent American *dakini* with the flowing blond hair. Never have I heard such a performance of knowledge and wisdom conveyed in a spontaneous, quiet, matter-of-fact flow of eloquence as that of Sangye Khandro interpreting for Kyab-Je Dudjom Rinpoche, and years later for Yangthang Tulku Rinpoche at the Temple of Dodrup Chen Rinpoche.

I think that first meeting with Dudjom Rinpoche finally inspired me to seek out a Dzogchen yogi who would teach me on a regular basis. When Gyurda-la did begin my training, he said that he was going to teach Tendzin Parsons, a young Englishman, and me and then take us to see Dudjom Rinpoche in Calcutta, where he would give us a sort of exam to determine whether we qualified to receive the empowerment from him. In England Tendzin had become a disciple of Trungpa Rinpoche, who had suggested that he become a monk. He was ordained by the Gyalwa Karmapa and remained a monk for some years until he gave back the robe when he decided to get married. Tendzin, his wife, and daughter Amy later moved to Providence, Rhode Island, to be near Dodrup Chen Rinpoche. He then moved to Hawley, Massachusetts, where he became the treasurer of the Mahasiddha Nyingmapa Center.

In Calcutta we went to see Dudjom Rinpoche, who was sitting at the kitchen table of his apartment. We made prostrations to him and sat cross-legged on the floor in front of him. He said that he was going to give us an exam. After he sent Tendzin out of the room, he said to me, "What is it?" And I answered with my understanding of the true nature of the mind. He said nothing, and Lobsang said that I should go outside and send for Tendzin. Tendzin went into the kitchen and in a short time came back out. We then went in together and talked to Dudjom Rinpoche. He gave us the rigpa'i tsal wang, or the introduction to the nature of the mind. Then we made our thanks to him, and after the wang, or initiation, Lama Gyurda-la said to me, "I have more teachings to give you, but first you must do the inner *ngön-dro*, or preliminary practice."

I sent a cable to my friend Betty Duke-Wooley in England, asking if I could do a long retreat in her house. She cabled back, "Come immediately. Everything is prepared for your retreat."

Betty had grown up at Amerdown House. Her father, Lord Hylton, had been the chairman of the Conservative Party. When Betty's eldest brother was killed in the First World War, her other brother inherited the title and family property. One afternoon she went with him to hunt rabbits. He prepared to crawl through a hedge into the next field and handed her his gun to hold, which somehow went off and killed him. Although it was an accident and not her fault, her parents rarely spoke to her again.

I took a plane from New Delhi to London in 1970 and settled down at Betty's house, where I spent the next year and a half doing the inner ngön-dro, or preliminary practice, of Dzogchen Longchen Nyingthig. The practice is in six parts, starting with the refuge taking. The second preliminary practice is developing *bodhichitta*, the compassionate enlightened mind. The third practice is purification by Vajrasattva recitation, and the fourth practice is offering of the mandala. The fifth practice is offering one's body to the Buddhas to eliminate one's attachments to it and ego clinging. The sixth practice is the actual practice, unification with Guru Padmasambhava (see Glossary, Guru Rinpoche). When I returned to India, I went to see Lama Gyurda-la and told him what I had understood as a result of practicing the sadhana, and he said, "Yes, you've had the result."

While I was in England, I met Marilyn Silverstone, whom Gene Smith had told me to look up. One of the first women to become a member of Magnum Photos, she lived in India with Frank Moraes, the editor of the *Times of India*. When he had to leave his country because of a disagreement with Madame Indira Gandhi, Marilyn found them a house in Connaught Square in London, where she began studying with a lama, Khenpo Thubten Rinpoche. Moraes was so jealous of her interest in Buddhism that she would have to hide in the bathroom to do her practice. Three years after Moraes died in 1974, Marilyn took vows as a Buddhist nun and moved to Nepal, where she lived for the rest of her life.

Back in New Delhi, where Lama Gyurda-la was spending the winter, Tulku Thondup would come up from Lucknow University, where he was a professor of Tibetan, to interpret for us. Lama Gyurda-la gave me the two highest practices of Dzogchen, called *thegchod* and *thodgal*. For the thegchod we sat in the hotel room, and for the thodgal Lama Gyurda-la took us out into the garden, where we squatted down and received the supreme revelation from him.

In 1975, I left India for New York and then went to Vancouver, where I stayed with the Lhalungpa family, who had moved there from New Delhi so that Lobsang could take a professorship at the University of British Columbia. From Vancouver, I went for a vacation in Venice with my friends Gold and Fizdale. After that, I finally went back to New York City, where I stayed with Michael in his apartment on East 77th Street.

Later that year, in the spring of 1969, my meditation training began while I was living at the Maiden Hotel in Delhi. With Lobsang interpreting, Geshe Tenpa Gyaltsen gave me teachings on *shiney* and *lhaktong* (*shamata* and *vipassana* in Pali and Sanskrit) from the Lamrim Chenmo of Je Tsongkhapa. The moment the teachings began, I became very sick to my stomach and had to spend some time in the bathroom. The entire time as my teachers waited, talking together quietly, I wished that they would go away. Finally, I emerged, feeling absolutely rotten, and the teachings resumed. The next time they came to continue the shiney and lhaktong teachings, I was very chipper and even had things to report about how I was doing in the meditation practice. After asking for clarification of some of the instructions, I was given a new meditation to do, the original one given by the Buddha in the *Satipathana Sutra*, in addition to the Manjusri sadhana.

Soon after I had received the je-nang of Manjusri, Sogyal Tulku presented me with a khatak and a *pecha*, or Tibetan book, which has oblong rectangular pages or folios, placed one on top of the other. This pecha, a copy of the *Jampel Tsan Jö Tantra*, a miraculous and brief Tantra of Manjusri, had been handwritten in Tibet by the secretary or scribe of Jamyang Khyentse Rinpoche, who gave it to Sogyal Tulku when he was a child. The *Jampel Tsan Jö Tantra* has been translated by Professor Alex Wayman, using a different commentary than Pandit Vimalamitra's, which is the commentary used by Nyingmapa lamas. The many levels of meaning in the lines culminate in a Dzogchen interpretation. A lyrical and noble translation has been done in French, a language particularly suited to translating Mahayana sutras and Vajrayana or Tantra because of its clarity, simplicity, and sweetness and its power and capacity for superb and formal rhetoric. The French translation is by Patrick Carré. Michal Abrams, in whose house in Darjeeling Bakha Tulku had taught me to recite the Tantra, sent me the Carré translation in Marion years later.

Again, I was reluctant to accept such a sacred and precious possession of Sogyal Rinpoche's, but he insisted that this gift would be auspicious, and indeed his copy of the scripture did turn out to be auspicious for me. Sogyal Rinpoche would read it to me from time to time so that I received the lung, or empowerment, to read it until I was finally able to incorporate it into my practice. For a long time, then, I recited the Tantra every day, doing the visualization and meditation that accompany it. If I got to bed late and had not recited it that day, I felt compelled to do so before I went to sleep. Sometimes I would fall asleep over the pages, then wake up and resume where I'd left off, alternating between sleep and recitation until, with a sense of relief for having done my duty, the longed-for last page came in sight.

Tulku Thondup gave me the copy of the Tantra in Tibetan print that I use and treasure to this day. Instead of getting a proper pecha cloth in which books are wrapped according to Tibetan custom, most of my pecha are wrapped in scarves that I have requested from friends. My copy of the Tantra, *The Proper Recitation of the Names of Manjusri*, is wrapped in a blue cotton scarf with white polka dots given to me by my beloved friend Alfreda Rushmore, and when I see it I think of her, and so the pecha itself is a source of happiness because of its association with lamas and friends.

Lobsang translated every line of the Tantra for me, and above the English line I wrote the Tibetan, which made it very easy to read and study. After reading a few lines in English, I would put the translation aside and recite the Tantra, reading from Tulku Thondup's copy. I can recite it with such ease that I am tempted to think that it is the blessing of Manjusri. But it's probably because I've recited it so often. I'm glad to say that in America years later Sogyal Tulku had need of this pecha, and I was able to return it to him. It was written in Tibetan script, which I couldn't read; I could just read Tibetan print in a beginner's sort of way.

While I was beginning my studies, I would have lunch or dinner with Gene, Lobsang, Deki, Sogyal Tulku, and Sonam Topgay Kazi, most often at the Ginza Restaurant in Connaught Square, a Chinese restaurant whose owner had changed its name to Japanese after the Chinese had become unpopular in India for their attempt to encroach on territory belonging to India. Fortunately, he didn't change the menu, so it remained a place where we friends gathered, which made it feel very cozy. However, there was a distressing aspect to the restaurant. In the winter there would be people lying under ragged blankets near the door as we entered. I am a terrible handwringer. I love to hear about bodhisattvic people who help others, whether friends and acquaintances or people in distant parts of the world as well as suffering sentient beings—dogs, cats, horses, monkeys, whatever.

The history of Tibet and the intrigues, worldly as well as sacred, which are as prevalent in exile as in the thirteen centuries of Tibetan culture, were an open book to Lobsang and Gene. I spent countless evenings at dinner with them and Deki, fascinated by the stories of the aristocratic houses of Lhasa, the Dalai Lamas, the powerful monasteries, the cabals and civil wars. The sacred counterpart of this enthralling worldly lore was the outpouring of knowledge of the lamas, their lineages and their works, that both Gene and Lobsang unstintingly shared with their friends. Being in their company day after day in Delhi made me feel close to the realization of my lifelong dream, to be in the Tibet of the days before the Chinese invasion. In Tibetan society, the needs of living and working blend with the Buddhist aspiration to develop the virtues, to make merit for attaining enlightenment for the sake of all sentient beings. Everyone has faith; everyone recites prayers and mantras. Many people receive wang, lung, and tri, and many study the scriptures and practice meditation.

It was while I was studying with Lobsang Lhalungpa in New Delhi that I first heard of Lama Gyurda-la. The year before, Gene used to tell me about this amazingly deep meditative path called Dzogchen, which for very gifted and diligent yogis produced swift results. Sonam Topgay Kazi also used to talk to me about this yogic path in such a compelling and mysterious manner that it was almost hypnotic. Sonam seemed to be an experienced meditator of this tradition, while Gene, who was knowledgeable about the entire scope of Tibetan Buddhist scripture, recommended in a benignly ironic way that I study Dzogchen. And, of course, I remembered Thomas Merton telling me, "If you want to be the equivalent of a Vatican diplomat stay in Dharamsala, but if you want to study Buddhism you should find a Dzogchen lama." Although I had great respect for these friends, I felt that I had a duty to remain loyal to His Holiness and to the Gelugpa path. But I knew that I was definitely missing out on something.

According to the Nyingmapas, Dzogchen is the highest yana, as the methods of spiritual practice of Buddhism are called. At first I thought of it as forbidden because I had been advised by His Holiness the Dalai Lama to follow a gradual path of study and meditation, and Dzogchen was the polar opposite. For example, the Dalai Lama and the monks of the Gelugpa school cannot get married. Having women and wives, however, could be part of the Tantric tradition of the Nyingmapa, which is the oldest of the four schools of Buddhism. For them coition between a yogi and a yogini is one of the avenues to enlightenment.

In the Gelugpa tradition they could say that I have had moral trouble—homosexuality, sensuality, and self-indulgence—but in Nyingmapa Buddhism, you take all those factors of your nature, like arrogance, pride, sensuality, and greed, and use them as your practice. I doubted that the essential meaning of the dharma, the Buddha nature itself, could be communicated by an enlightened lama and that just through practice one could attain this inner realization in one's own life-time. So although I was fascinated by my friends' talk, it had a slightly irritating effect. How could the vast content of the scriptures of all three yanas be "reduced" to something unelaborated? How could one become a Buddha? Wasn't the premise of Dzogchen a form of vaulting ambi-tion? These doubts all stemmed from my ignorance of Dzogchen and its method of training. Far from reducing Buddhism to some concep-tualized essence, Nyingmapa dharma is a summation of Hinayana, Mahayana, and Vajrayana Buddhism culminating in the simplicity and naturalness of the Dzogchen view of meditation and action.

At that point in my life, however, I believed that the dharma was an external pursuit of learning: the *vinaya* monastic rules for pure conduct and the dialectical approach to emptiness for understanding the abso-lute nature of reality. What might happen to these cherished aspects of Buddhism if a realization of absolute simplicity were communicated by an enlightened lama as the basis of a yogic practice? The final push came from my first meeting with Dudjom Rinpoche some time later in 1969. I had asked Lhalungpa if he could find me a Dzogchen lama with whom to study. "I know a real Dzogchen yogi," he said, with his charming, inscrutable laugh. "He lives in my mother-in-law's shrine room in Darjeeling. But he comes down every winter to print *termas* [scriptures or commentaries] and stays here with me in the little room out on the landing where we keep the bicycles. It's a nice little cave, which he prefers. This winter I plan to ask him to help me with some Dzogchen texts I'm going to study. Perhaps I could ask him to teach you as well."

I told Sogyal Tulku that the following winter Lobsang was going to introduce me to a Dzogchen yogi named Lama Gyurda-la, whom I was planning to ask to teach me. "Gyurda-la taught me *ka-kha-ga-nga*," said Sogyal Tulku, meaning his abc's. "Dzongsar Jamyang Khyentse Rinpoche asked him to teach me reading and writing. Gyurda-la used to beat me, and I would run and hide in Khyentse Rinpoche's robes. And Khyentse Rinpoche would laugh and push me back to Gyurda-la." Sogyal Tulku offered to take me to meet him. So we traveled to Darjeeling and out to Aloobari, where Lama Gyurda-la lived at Ama-la Dorje's house. Ama-la, a tiny, wrinkled woman wreathed in smiles, was warmly hospitable. She was wearing a *chuba*, the traditional Tibetan dress with a colorful striped apron. During that visit I met for the first time Ama-la's beautiful daughter Sangye Drolma, who was studying at a college in Darjeeling. I also met both her husband, Tashi Trogawa, who was working for the Jesuits at a social service center, and his elder brother, the great doctor, Lama Trogawa Rinpoche.

We went through the cottage to the shrine room, which looked out on a beautiful garden with a small tree whose spreading branches resembled trees in Chinese Buddhist or Taoist paintings. Lama Gyurda-la was seated on his cushion, wearing a ragged robe of burgundy red that had faded to pink, his hair parted in the middle and pulled back in a knot. He and Sogyal Tulku greeted each other warmly. One could say that Lama Gyurda-la had a beautiful face but that would not convey its Buddha-like quality. I felt that my future was tied to this person, but first he would have to agree to teach me. He and Sogyal Tulku talked together for a very long time, speaking in low voices that underscored the gravity of what they were discussing, especially the situation of the Tibetans in exile in India.

At one point, Sogyal Tulku told Lama Gyuda-la that I was in India hoping to study Buddhism with lamas. As she always did when visitors came to Aloobari, Ama-la prepared a wonderful lunch for Sogyal Tulku and me. After we returned to the shrine room, I asked Lama Gyurda-la for Dzogchen teachings. He replied that he would teach me provided that I learned Tibetan. This struck me as a triumph but also as a huge challenge. However, I said that I would learn Tibetan.

Lama Gyurda-la had been the student of some of the great lamas of Dzogchen Longchen Nyingthig. While he was teaching, Lama Gyurda-la would talk about the Gyalrong Khadroma, Jamyang Khyentse Rinpoche, and Dudjom Rinpoche—great lamas who confer wangs to help you realize the nature of the mind. Lama Gyurda-la had studied at Yag-Dze, a monastery in Kham named for the hair on a yak's back because of the way the buildings are spread out on a mountain-top (the English word *yak* is derived from the Tibetan word *yag*). In his teens he had served and studied with the Gyalrong Khadroma, a woman who was very tall and awe-inspiring, even perhaps fierce. Lama Gyurda-la had lived for some time with the Gyalrong Khadroma at her mountain hermitage. She was clairvoyant, and some days she would tell him to cook a certain dish for lunch, saying that it was so-and-so's favorite food. A few hours later that person would come into view riding toward the hermitage.

In the region there was a chieftan's son who was brutal and out of control. He got in a lot of brawls and "every day he raped a girl." One day he came to Lama Gyurda-la and asked him for the lung, or ritual read-ing, of the Seven-Line Prayer of Guru Rinpoche. Lama Gyurda-la had no intention of fulfilling any request for dharma by this evildoer, and he told him to get out. But the unruly fellow came back several times to request the prayer, only to be told each time to leave. Finally, one day when Lama Gyurda-la was meditating and reciting his book of daily prayers, the chief's son came up and stood behind Lama Gyurda-la until he reached the page on which was written the Seven-Line Prayer. The young man snatched the page and held it in the air. "Now I've got it," he said, "so you may as well give me the lung." "What do you want it for?" Lama Gyurda-la asked him. The young man replied, "I'm going to go up to a cave in the mountains and recite the prayer and stay there until I have achieved realization. My wife will bring up food and water from time to time and leave it at the mouth of the cave." Lama Gyurda-la told him to go and practice in the cave but not to have his wife bring up food and water. "Nobody ever starved practicing dharma," he said. Then he gave the young man the lung.

The chieftain's son went to a cave in the mountains and recited the Seven-Line Prayer of Guru Rinpoche. Days and nights passed, and he became famished. He decided that he had to go and get food and water. He managed to stagger to the cliff's edge, from where he saw that some travelers had pitched a tent in the valley. He tottered down the hill and reached the tent, where he begged for food and water. The travelers fed him and gave him some provisions. Then he climbed back up to the cave and resumed his prayers. Again, days passed. Suddenly, the Gyalrong Khadroma appeared before him in the cave, and with her *dorje* (a metal ritual object representing a thunderbolt), she struck him on the forehead. At that moment he attained realization. He left his mountain retreat and wandered far and wide and became a respected teacher.

Lama Gyurda-la did indeed come down to Delhi that winter. He was printing various texts, including the life of Khadro Yeshe Tshogyal, the consort of Guru Rinpoche. He said that if Westerners liked *The Life of Milarepa*, they would love *The Life of Yeshe Tshogyal*. He was always very partisan. Somehow, I loved that about him. But first Lama Gyurda-la gave me the preliminary teachings, or outer ngondro, by reading from the *Kunzang Lama'i Zhalung* while I took verbatim notes. Lobsang translated, and we worked for several hours each day in my little room at the Lodi Hotel. At the end of the session, Lama Gyurda-la would ask me to ponder on the teaching that had been given that day. The sessions lasted a week, and I stayed in retreat until they were finished.

The outer ngön-dro, or preliminary practice of the Dzogchen Longchen Nyinghtig tradition, consists of the following four meditations: (1) fortunate human birth, difficult to obtain, (2) the impermanence of life, (3) karma: cause and result, (4) the suffering of *samsara* (cycle of death and rebirth). For each of these four practices, Lama Gyurda-la asked me to ponder on the teaching given that day.

From the teachings of the Buddha there is a poem that teaches the impermanence of life.

> The three worlds are impermanent as the clouds of Autumn.
> The births and deaths of beings are like watching a dance.
> The speed of human lives is like lightening in the sky,
> It passes swiftly as a stream down a steep mountain.

I think it was the Georges' spiritual gifts that convinced Lama Gyurda-la that they were qualified to receive training in Dzogchen, and that made him include the rest of us on their coattails. I am deeply grateful to the Georges for that.

The circumstances for receiving the training and doing the practice were perfect, in fact almost magical. Lobsang was a consummate interpreter, and he, too, greatly desired to receive these teachings from a realized Dzogchen yogi. We would meet at the Canadian High Commission at 7:00 a.m. and sit on the floor to receive a meditation training from the text *Tri Yig Yeshe Lama* by Rig-dzin Jigme Lingpa (see Glossary).

The practices Lama Gyurda-la taught us usually come after a student has performed the outer and inner ngön-dros. However, he was teaching us at this level without our having done those essential preliminary practices. This was his decision, and I don't know why he made it. Later, he told me that he had further teachings to give me, but that I must first do the ngön-dro. I was surprised because I thought that he had waived the preliminaries in our case. But I was delighted with the assignment because it came from him.

When the weather grew warmer we would go up onto the flat roof, with its splendid view of the sky and the huge garden of the embassy, and sit cross-legged together, doing the practice that Lama Gyurda-la had given us the day before. Then we would go back downstairs, and the lama would see each of us separately in the little study, where we told him our meditation experience. He would question us and then give us the next meditation, adding it to the ones we were already practicing.

After the session, the Georges would have us to breakfast. We could talk to Lama Gyurda-la with Lobsang interpreting, and the combination of splendid surroundings, the Georges' hospitality, and the presence of this Tibetan yogi in his faded, tattered robe created an atmosphere of peace and joy. After breakfast Mr. George would repair to his office at the other end of the white Neoclassical building, which was a beautiful treasure from the Raj. Years later I learned of the plans for projects he was overseeing between the governments of Canada and India. I thought back on the spiritual training he made possible for us at the same time that he was working as Canada's representative to India.

CHAPTER FIFTEEN

Darjeeling

In the coming years I would often go to Darjeeling to receive teachings from Lama Gyurda-la at Ama-la's. On the way up, one passed monkeys who lounged along the low wall by the side of the road, unaffected by the drop. Families sat together, babies clinging to their mothers. Grooming went on along with all the other monkey pastimes. Of course, they were there at the cliff's edge seeking food from the passing vehicles. After you reach a certain altitude, there were no more monkeys. But you could look forward to seeing them again on the way down.

Trips up the mountains implied trips back down. It might be nice to spend one's life in the presence of Kangchenjunga in Darjeeling, Kalimpong, or Sikkim, but it's always been an up and down thing for me. There was the problem of visas, and such exotic requirements as "inner line permits," which remind me of the Raj and make the places where one is allowed to stay for just a few days seem cloak-and-daggerish. The permit is an outward sign of how precious one's time is. Each time one went "down to the Plains," as Kipling called it, it felt as if one were being expelled from Eden.

There are fanciful sides to traveling in the Himalayas, but they're not an obstacle to the seriousness of a Buddhist pilgrimage. I've always gone to Darjeeling and Sikkim to see a lama to request teachings on the nature of the mind, to learn the meditation, and to achieve the result— the realization of the true nature of the mind. When in my late twenties I began to ask lamas for Buddhist teachings, I found a sort of vocation. The dharma transcends words; yet our feelings when we come in contact with its embodiments do not. Whenever I visit a lama to receive teachings, I have a sense of calm urgency. I feel that I am being allowed to engage in something far beyond my present ken, which I understand is the lama's gift. Moreover, the anticipation of meeting a great meditation master flavors everything I see around me. I am confident that I am capable of responding to the lama's instruction that he conveys with the power of his blessings.

Because we all have the Buddha nature within us, we need never feel that ignorance or wrongdoing will prevent us from experiencing a revelation of something that has so far been hidden. Something will lead us from nonawareness or ignorance to an experience of awareness, which will become the basis of future meditation.

During a meeting with a lama, I almost feel that I am at the center of the universe. I sense the perfection of things. Then I wonder: Where is compassion? How can I be blissfully happy while so many others are suffering? How can I have the leisure to do something "magical" when so many people are crushed by their work? I have no responsibilities, no ties. I do not helplessly witness the agony and hunger of loved ones. And I can't attribute my favorable circumstances to "good karma" and be done with it. This twinge of conscience that I used to feel while leading a happy, free, and exalted life studying with great yogis was the product of divorcing compassion from mind training.

I was confused and ignorant about many aspects of the wisdom of Nga-Gyur Nying-M'ai Chos, the Old Translation School of Tibetan Buddhism. And this lack of understanding of the paramount place of compassion in this, as in all forms of Mahayana Buddhism, was part of the problem. I could only make out fragments of the scope of Nyingmapa Buddhist teaching, like the oft-told story of the blind men, each of whom mistook a part of the elephant for the whole animal. And those fragments I had learned something about, from Gene Smith as much as from lamas, seemed ill assorted. How could the Nyingmapa interpretation of the *tathagatagarbha*, or Buddha nature, coexist with such high, elaborate ceremonies from termas as Long Chen Nying Thig or Lama Gong-Du? What place did divinations have, or the many different kinds of siddhis, some of which Lama Gyurda-la practiced?

When you first get a view of Darjeeling, perched on its mountainside, it doesn't look especially distinguished. The only thing that stands out is an odd white building with a blue dome toward the lower edge of town built on different levels down the mountainside that had been the palace of the Maharajah of Bardwan. There are several monasteries in the town including the long house perched on the cliff's edge where the Thirteenth Dalai Lama had his residence after fleeing the Chinese invasion of Tibet in the early 1900s. Everywhere one sees majestic cryptomerias, which are the sentinels of Darjeeling.

Someone who gets his bearings easily could learn the layout of Darjeeling in only one walk. As I have no sense of location and am rather oblivious to my surroundings, Darjeeling remains in my mind as discrete parts on my own map, on which everything that counted, apart from the joy of the old-fashioned cozy simplicity of the Windamere Hotel, was related to "my" lamas and monasteries.

Darjeeling looks out upon Kangchenjunga, which stops the mind with its white majesty. The whole mountain range moves in stillness like music. The mountain and the deodars make Darjeeling a noble place, just as the presence of the great lamas made it a holy one. Even its name evokes Nyingmapa dharma, for it is the Anglicization of the name of a major *terton*, Dorje Lingpa. (A terton is someone who discovers ancient hidden texts, or termas.) There was also a Catholic presence, the Canadian Jesuits were in the part of town named West Point, and there was also the Convent of Loretto, where Mother Teresa taught history and coached basketball. And then of course there is the other emblem of Darjeeling, the glorious, eponymous tea, which is raised on plantations out of town. On the main street of Darjeeling was the Planters' Club, an intriguing institution because of its Rajness. When I walked by the club I would think of how remote the world of planters and tea pickers was from my way of life. Yet lamas and tea planters were both an integral aspect of that celestial town.

As I say, I would always stay at the Windamere Hotel, a marvelous leftover from the Raj with its chintz and fireplaces, servants in smart livery, down comforters, hot-water bottles, dog-eared copies of books about adventure in Tibet, desks supplied with Windamere writing paper, wrinkled old servants who would tuck the rupees I lavished on them into their turbans. I loved the "bed tea"—picked in Darjeeling, of course—with which the servant would wake you in the morning with the words, "Salaam, Sahib." What could be more Raj than that?

The Windamere was near the Chowrasta, the mall in the center of Darjeeling where both tourists and locals would come to sit on one of the benches and savor the view of the mountain peaks and valleys all around. One day I was walking through the square with Yudron-la, a wonderful woman devoted to dharma who became a great friend and helped me a great deal, as she did so many people studying dharma. A beautiful woman was sitting on a park bench, and Yudron-la introduced me to her. Her name was Semo-la. Afterward, Yudron explained to me that she was the daughter of the king of Ling Tshang and that her mother was the daughter of the king of Derge. Years later Semo-la and I became dharma friends when she would accompany Dodrup Chen Rinpoche on his trips to the States and stay with me in Marion. The word *chow* means "a road crossing," so the mall is where four roads meet.

If you took the road on the left-hand side of the Chowrasta, you would be on your way out to Aloobari, where Lama Gyurda-la lived at Ama-la's. On the far side of the square was the musty old Oxford Bookstore, narrow and ill-lit, where I would browse and buy books about Tibet or on Buddhism. It was also where I would buy schoolchildren's notebooks, which I used for taking down teachings or prayer in Tibetan with English translations by Tulku Thondup. If you crossed the square, you could walk through the town to Gandhi Road, where Kanjur Rinpoche lived with his family, including his wife, Sang-yum, their son, Tulku Pema Wangyal, and their daughter, Rigdzin-la. After passing the train station of the famous Toy Trains of Darjeeling Himalayan Railway, the road becomes Hill Cart Road and takes you to the monastery of Thugsey Rinpoche and the child for whom he was guardian and regent, the Gyalwa Drugchen Tulku.

Trayab Ani Sherab and her son, Dorje Tshering, lived in a tiny, flimsy wooden cabin. The lower Chowrasta was where I went when I needed a jeep taxi to visit a lama or, with regret, to go down to Bagdogra Airport in Siliguri, where, when my Darjeeling permit had run out, I would take a plane to Calcutta and then on to New Delhi.

Sometimes I went for teachings to Dudjom Rinpoche in his house behind the police station in Darjeeling. At first, I would sneak by warily as a foreign permit holder until my friend Michal Abrams gave me an introduction to the chief of police and his charming family; thereafter I felt safe from expulsion.

Michal's father was an accountant, and her mother was an opera singer. She was precise and intelligent yet at the same time volcanic and temperamental, rather like the mad queen in *Alice in Wonderland*. I had known Michal in New York through Peter Prestcott. After she graduated from Wellesley, she went on to Berkeley to study with Edward Conze. At one point she told me that she wanted a rich husband and asked if I could find one for her. She had gone to Darjeeling to study Dzogchen with Dudjom Rinpoche.

Although Dudjom Rinpoche suffered from asthma, he ignored his poor health and gave me an outpouring of teachings. Finally, at the end of one much-too-long session, he leaned back and relaxed and said, "I've been sitting here giving wangs [initiations] and teachings for nine hours, and every bone in my body aches. Don't ever become a lama." And he laughed and smiled his radiant smile.

When I went out to Ama-la's, I would usually find Lama Gyurda-la in the shrine room. On one of my first visits, he was sitting there with another lama, Tulku Thondup, who agreed to interpret Lama Gyurda-la's teachings for me. Tulku Thondup is a most remarkable man who has done as much as anyone to make possible my Buddhist training. Nowadays, he lives in Cambridge, Massachusetts, where he has many students. He was born in Tibet to a nomad family who, as he has described it, lived in tents on "the wild, green grassy tablelands of Eastern Tibet, among the world's highest mountains and rivers." Many times during the year, they would move their camp to different valleys in search of fresh grass for their animals. When he was five, Tulku Thondup was recognized as a reincarnation of a religious master of Dodrup Chen monastery, an important learning institution in Eastern Tibet. Tibetan Buddhists believe that when a great master dies, he or she will be reborn as someone who will be able to benefit other people.

Although his parents were sad to give up their only child, they did not hesitate to offer him to the monastery, where his life changed completely. Rather than having other children to play with as a normal boy would have, dignified tutors were his companions and teachers. Although he missed his family, he adapted quickly to this new life, which many took as a sign that he had lived in the monastery in a previous lifetime.

In 1957 one of his teachers, Dodrup Chen Rinpoche, whom Aelred and I had met in Sikkim, had such clairvoyance that he knew it was time to leave Tibet in the face of the Chinese invasion. Tulku Thondup, who was then eighteen, left his country with his two teachers and a small cohort of lamas and monks. For months they trekked more than a thousand miles across Tibet to the Sikkimese border. As he has written, "Halfway, at a holy cave in an empty valley, where high gray mountains stood watch in every direction, Kyala Khenpo, my teacher who had looked after me like my sole parent since I was five, breathed his last."

When they were stopped at a Chinese customs house at the Sikkimese border, they said that they were going to visit Sikkim. As they couldn't enter Sikkim directly, they hid in the forest while one of the monks in their party went ahead to inform the chogyal of their arrival. The chogyal, knowing of Dodrup Chen's reputation, sent visas for them to the border, and they were able to get across. After they arrived in Sikkim, Tulku Thondup studied with an Englishman, John Driver, from whom he learned English remarkably quickly.

In his early twenties, he was offered a research scholarship by the Universities Grants Commission of India at Visva-Bharati University, founded by Rabindranath Tagore. It is about four hours by train from Calcutta. He learned English, Hindi, and some Bengali. Later as a professor he taught at Lucknow University for nine years and then again at Visva-Bharati University for five years, finally emigrating to the United States in 1980.

When it was good weather in Darjeeling, Lama Gyurda-la might be on the terrace adding to his prayer wheels, which were credited with saving the family when an avalanche came crashing down on either side of the house, leaving the building untouched. But it was not always good weather, and there were often long periods of rain. At Ama-la's little house, the rain clattered so loudly on the tin roof that you had to raise your voice to be heard. Once when I arrived, Lama Gyurda-la greeted me, saying, "ren, ren," meaning rain, rain. And these, I think, were the only English words I ever heard him speak. For a long time, I spoke almost as few Tibetan words as "ren, ren" myself. And one day when I managed to say one, Lama Gyurda-la remarked, "Harold has had the blessing of Manjusri." Mostly I was entirely dependent on Tulku Thondup to communicate with Lama Gyurda-la. And I always relied on him to interpret for me for *sem-tri*, or interviews on the nature of the mind, with Dudjom Rinpoche and Lama Gyurda-la, and later with Dodrup Chen Rinpoche.

On days of heavy rain, I'd wait for a break in the downpour before setting off on the forty-minute walk back to Darjeeling. Sometimes the rain didn't stop, and on those days, it would be dark in the shrine room. Often the conversation between Lama Gyurda-la and Dr. Trogawa Rinpoche, who also lived in the shrine room and had a place for making up his herbal medicines, and Tulku Thondup, if he were there, would go on for a long time. It was soothing and intimate. Their voices are very much softer than ours.

I was frequently invaded by a meditation student's "attention deficit." Not that my mind would wander during the training sessions, for they were too fascinating; it was more a matter of not being able to sustain the necessary mental energy for very long. And if Lama Gyurda-la had a lot to teach, the session could go on for much of the day. I would be aware that Tulku Thondup, who was fully versed in this view and meditation, was so kindly giving me all this time, with no sign of wishing the session would end. Although Tulku Thondup acted as interpreter of the teachings out of his kindness and self-effacement, I could see that Lama Gyurda-la revered him as a great tulku and a highly accomplished yogi. Still there were times when I felt that I had had enough teaching for that day, and I would look forward to the comfort and familiarity of my life at the Windamere. I would go back and have a bath before dinner. The short Bhutia waiter who shuffled about carrying the trays would take my order in a state of earnest confusion over my English, and I would think how lucky I was to have received the day's teachings from Lama Gyurda-la through Tulku Thondup, rather than having to be a waiter carrying heavy trays. While I was having my dinner, the room boy would light a fire in my bedroom, and a maid would slip a hot-water bottle in my bed. I would fall asleep with the flames dancing across the ceiling and hours later awake to the distant chiming of Tibetan prayer wheels.

Studying with Lama Gyurda-la brought me closely in touch with the great Nyingmapa tradition. The greatest miracle Lama Gyurda-la told me about was the story of the end of his father's life. Sonam Namgyal lived what appeared to be an ordinary life, but he actually lived two lives at the same time. He worked all day, and at night he stayed in a hut and meditated. Lama Gyurda-la told me that there were no images in the hut, but he saw the words *ma yeng*, meaning "do not waver," written on the wall. In later life Sonam Namgyal devoted himself to building mani-walls made of flat stones with the mantra of Chenrezi—*om ma ni pe me hung*—carved on them. He would go around singing prayers he'd made up, and people would tell him that he ought to be chanting traditional prayers like everyone else. At night he meditated. At the end of his life, he attained the highest result of Dzogchen meditation—namely *ja-lü*, or the rainbow body, in which the body dissolves into light, leaving nothing behind but its hair and fingernails.

Every day of my life, Lama Gyurda-la has been very frequently in my mind.

CHAPTER SIXTEEN

Dodrup Chen Rinpoche

Dzogchen in Marion, Massachusetts

In September 1975, Lama Gyurda-la rented a room in Old Delhi and hired six Tibetan monks and laypeople to help him with the publication of a scripture. He had chosen as his subject the biography of Khadro Yeshe Tsogyal, the consort of Guru Rinpoche, who founded Nyingma Buddhism in Tibet. Because Lama Gyurda-la was very careful with money, he rented a small room in a slum called Teliwara, and it was a very small room indeed. As I was sponsoring the publication of the scripture, Lama Gyurda-la invited me to stay with him. With eleven of us occupying the room—ten Tibetans and myself—there was so little space that we had to step over each other to get to the bathroom. Visitors who came to see Lama Gyurda-la had to stand outside and poke their heads around the door to speak to him.

I usually sat next to Lama Gyurda-la, often softly chanting the *Jampal Tsan Jot*, the Tantra of Manjusri, doing its visualization and practicing the meditations I had been taught by Lama Gyurda-la, Dudjom Rinpoche, and Tulku Thondup. There was no interpreter except when Tulku Thondup would come up from Lucknow University to see us, and so I had a chance to really practice my Tibetan. It was very easy for me to understand Lama Gyurda-la because he spoke so clearly and simply.

He was sick by that time, and Tulku Thondup and I took him to All India Medical Institute in New Delhi. I had been to that hospital once before with Thomas Merton when Jim George was a patient there. He had asked Tom to say Mass for him, and I served as his acolyte while Tom gave him and his wife Communion before barreling across the room with a big grin on his face to give me Communion. I was very surprised, because by that time I thought of myself as a Buddhist;

however, Tom had nothing to do with that kind of sectarianism between two world religions. In fact, at another time I also served as his acolyte in Darjeeling in a tiny chapel straight out of Hansel and Gretel.

Eventually, I realized that Lama Gyurda-la was extremely ill. Dr. Ahuja, who had been referred to us by Gene Smith, told me that the lama, although he didn't drink, had cirrhosis of the liver, which I knew was a mortal disease. One night I heard groans coming from Lama Gyurda-la, who put out his hand to me. For some reason, I knew that he meant I should take him to the hospital. He said, "Do not call a taxi. Get a scooter." Scooters were cheaper than the Ambassador Taxis; even to go to the hospital he wouldn't spend the money.

One of the young monks on his staff went with me, and in the scooter taxi, Lama Gyurda-la looked up in the air and said to me, "*Thigle mangbo mangbo du*" (There are many *thigles*). Thigles are visible spheres of light that move in various patterns unless the meditator has achieved a high state of Dzogchen accomplishment, in which case they remain in place. Sometimes in the thigle appears the head of a Buddha or a crown or lotus or another symbol of the presence of the Buddha. This is the highest form of meditation, called *thodgal*, and in that scooter taxi on his way to the hospital, Lama Gyurda-la seemed to have reached the summit of attainment as a Dzogchen practitioner.

I stayed in the hospital next to Lama Gyurda-la's bed along with two of his monks, whom I would leave in charge while I had a little respite at Gene Smith's apartment for lunch. On the tenth of February as he was reciting the mantra *om ah hung*, Lama Gyurda-la went into a hepatic coma. Clearly, he was at death's door. After he died, the three of us went down to the hospital office to pay the bill for his medical treatment, his stay, and the cost of his medicines. Tulku Thondup came to be with us and take over the proceedings for Lama Gyurda-la's cremation and funeral. The two monks and I took his body to the morgue, and because Tulku Thondup hadn't yet arrived, we had to find another lama to perform the powa ceremony. This enables the consciousness principle of the deceased to shoot out from the top of his head and go to the Pure Land of Amitabha Buddha, the Buddha of Boundless Light, the same ceremony or practice that Chokling Rinpoche had given Thomas Merton ten days before his death.

Leaving Lama Gyurda-la at the morgue, one of the monks and I took a real taxi, not a scooter, to find someone to perform the powa. Gene had told us that one of the Khyentse Tulkus, the incarnations of Dzongsar Jamyang Khyentse Rinpoche, who had been the main tsawai lama of Lama Gyurda-la, was living in one of the refugee settlements around New Delhi. We found him in his tent, bundled him into the taxi, and brought him to the morgue, where he stood in the refrigeration room and performed the powa for Lama Gyurda-la to allow the soul or consciouness principle to escape from the top of his head.

In the dawn Tulku Thondup led us all to the cremation grounds where Lama Gyurda-la's body was placed on a pyre. We all sat around the pit and participated in a funeral ceremony as the pyre was lit and the body consumed by the flames. The next day we returned to the pit to sift through the ashes to find relics of Lama Gyurda-la's bones. Called *ringsel*, they are tiny spheres of a material unknown to me; they can be white or else in all the primary colors, as were the ringsels of Lushul Khenpo, the past life of Tulku Thondup. They indicate the high meditative attainment of the deceased and are placed on shrines or put in *gaos*, little reliquaries worn around the neck. It is said that if a person breaks *samaya*, or the vow of obligation linking one to a lama or to one's dharma friends, the ringsels disappear. I would think that one would have to check the reliquary from time to time to make sure the ringsels are still there. Lama Gyurda-la once took Michael and me to see the ringsels in the house of a deceased lama, where the family kept them under a glass globe. They were constantly reproducing themselves so that there were lots of them that you could see through the glass.

After the funeral Tulku Thondup had to return immediately to Lucknow University. We all went to see him off at the fanciful pseudo-Gothic train station built years before by the British. After that I stayed with Gene at his apartment and telephoned Michael, who by this time was living in Marion, Massachusetts, with his wife, Margie, and their firstborn baby. Michael told me, "You have to come home sometime, and this is the best time to come, so I will rent you a house in Marion and expect you soon." In March 1975, I went home to America and stayed with Michael and Margie while my house was being readied for me. They were the most generous hosts. During that time, I went down to see Nanny, who was living in an old folks home in Ossining, New York. I also went to see Vera Somoff and renewed my acquaintance with New York.

The house Michael rented for me on Main Street in Marion was directly across the street from his house. It seemed like a palace, everything was so up-to-date and efficient. When I got to the kitchen, I saw on the counter a toaster, and I thought to myself with such ecstasy, "I've come back because of a toaster." In April 1975, Tulku Thondup came to spend his three-month summer vacation from Lucknow University with me. Michael and I drove up to Boston to meet him, and on our way back to Marion, we gave him a little tour of Boston. As we were walking across the Common, an Asian man came up to him and bowed his head to receive Tulku Thondup's hand blessing. He was one of the few Tibetans who had managed to escape to the United States and the only one living in Boston. It was the most amazing instance of tendrel, or the connection between a disciple and a lama, that I could possibly imagine.

I talked to Tulku Thondup about being with Lama Gyurda-la when he died, and he said to me, "Lama Gyurda-la's death was the greatest teaching he ever gave you." Tulku Thondup and I got started at once on the translations of Tibetan Buddhist scriptures. Helping him with his English translations and writings helped me to learn dharma. Our partnership has continued until today. He has written countless books, and a complete list of them is included in the bibliography of this book.

Through the most auspicious interconnection of circumstances, the summer after I returned to America, Dodrup Chen Rinpoche came to visit his students in western Massachusetts. Tulku Thondup and I went to see him at the farmhouse in Conway, where he was staying. Tulku Thondup went upstairs to see Rinpoche, and eventually, I was sent for to have an interview. When I came into the room, there sat the lama whom I had met seven years before and had always wanted to see again. I said that my teacher, Lama Gyurda-la, had died. I told him about the Dzogchen training he had given me, and asked Dodrup Chen Rinpoche to become my teacher.

Before interpreting what I had said, Tulku Thondup asked, "Do you want to say that you have done the ngön-dro?" I said that I had. Then Dodrup Chen Rinpoche said, "Everybody knows what you did for Lama Gyurda-la. There are very few disciples like you today." I was amazed, because all I had done was, with Tulku Thondup, to see to it that he had medical treatment when he was very ill and then to serve him as best I could when he was dying.

Dodrup Chen Rinpoche didn't answer my request that he be my teacher. He told me to meditate on the inseparability (*yer-med*) of the nature of one's own mind, the enlightened mind of the tsawai lama, and the primordial wisdom of all the Buddhas. Then he said, "There are a lot of empty corners in this farmhouse. Go and sit in one of them and meditate on that, and then come back and give me the result." So I went and did the meditation for a half an hour or so, and then went to see him again. He said nothing, and his expression didn't change, but Tulku Thondup said, "Rinpoche says OK."

Sonam Paljor Denjongpa, Dodrup Chen Rinpoche's chief Sikkimese disciple who served him at his monastery, was also there at the farmhouse. Hope Cooke, the gyalmo of Sikkim, had gotten Sonam a scholarship to Brown University, and he was living in Providence with his heavenly girlfriend, Maria Lauenstein, who became his wife. They have two splendid sons. As we were leaving to go back to Marion, Sonam said, "Rinpoche is going to visit you and Michael." I replied, "Oh, wonderful. I'll tell Michael that he's coming for the weekend." Then Sonam said that he didn't think it was going to be just for the weekend. I looked up and saw that Dodrup Chen Rinpoche was standing at the screen door waving good-bye to me.

Ever since Sonam Topgay Kazi had taken Aelred and me to visit Dodrup Chen Rinpoche in Sikkim, I had wanted to see him again. Unfortunately, the few times I obtained the necessary permit and went to Gangtok, it was never possible to see him. At one point, Sogyal Tulku invited me to accompany him to Sikkim, where his family lived, to see Rinpoche, but once again fate was against me. I was housed in a go-down (Raj English for a warehouse) that belonged to the Queen Mother of Sikkim. She, along with other people, advised Sogyal Tulku that, given the political climate, it would be unwise for Rinpoche to see an American. I was bitterly disappointed.

However, Rinpoche would occasionally appear in my life in small ways. When we'd met him, he had given us each a booklet on Vimalamitra's life that revealed how the Nyingthig teachings of Garab Dorje and other Nyingthig lineage masters came to Vamilamitra. Years later in 1969 when I met Tulku Thondup, I learned that he had edited and published that booklet for Rinpoche in the 1960s. Although he had not yet learned much English, he had done the editing with help of others because there was no one else around then who knew English.

I read the little book many times and learned the names and stories of some of the lineage holders. Later, when I was with Lama Gyurda-la in Darjeeling, he showed me a greeting card with a bunny on it and on the inside some beautiful Tibetan handwriting. Lama Gyurda-la said softly that the card was from Dodrup Chen Rinpoche, and I could tell that he was thrilled to have heard from him.

Soon after our visit to Conway, Dodrup Chen Rinpoche came to stay. He was waiting for his permanent residence visa or green card, which took a long time to obtain. His Tibetan and Sikkimese monks and disciples, as well as Tulku Thondup, were amazed because Dodrup Chen Rinpoche was not in the habit of staying with people for a long time. Every morning at eleven, I would bring Rinpoche a cup of tea. He would either be in his chair or else in a large closet with a window, where he liked to sit cross-legged on the floor and draw exquisite and complex mandalas. These were filled with images of Buddhas and bodhisattvas, which gave them their living quality and blessing power. He intended to make a lot of xerox copies to take back to his monastery in Gangtok. I think perhaps he liked to spend the day in the closet because he had often done his meditation in a cave in Golok, Tibet.

Nancy Mitton, whom Michael had engaged to do the cooking for Rinpoche and myself, would come every morning and leave us lunch and dinner—delicious casseroles and other dishes, which we thought Rinpoche would like. Nancy and Dodrup Chen Rinpoche got on very well, and Rinpoche gave her a turquoise, which she often wears around her neck. Twelve years later, Nancy took refuge with Rinpoche and became his student. Since then she has received numerous wangs from Dodrup Chen Rinpoche at the temple in Hawley, Massachusetts, that was built by his students. And whenever Rinpoche comes to stay, Nancy comes to dinner with him and Tulku Thondup, and friends and students.

Lama Jigtse, a yogi, and Dzogchen-pa, who was devoted to Rinpoche, came quite often to visit. Lama Jigtse was wonderful company for Rinpoche. Rinpoche would be sitting in a chair, and Lama Jigtse would curl himself around it on the floor. With his shovel-shaped *nyi zhva* (a hat that protects the wearer from the sun) and his canny but friendly eyes, he made me think, curled up that way, of the fox furs that women wore around their necks in my childhood. He was a fearless yogi and a man who went entirely his own way. He had owned a lot of land back in Golok, where he had been imprisoned by the forces of the warlord Ma Pu Feng. He escaped but later was imprisoned by the Maoist Chinese and treated badly. He escaped from that prison, too. In this country, although by no means young, he worked painting houses. None of this "oh, if only I could be a yogi and just do practice" for him. He was a yogi, and he also worked long hours.

Occasionally I attended *nyung-ne*, or sessions of prayer and fasting led by Lama Jigtse in a storefront in Providence that Sonam Paljor rented for us. Tulku Thondup told me not to participate in any more of them for they were too rigorous for a tenderfoot. Lama Jigtse became an important teacher to Rinpoche's student group, the Mahasiddha. David Dvore, the head of Mahasiddha, was devoted to him. And when Lama Jigtse died, all the students were grief-stricken.

Once Lama Jigtse framed a page of Tibetan print and gave it to me as a present. Tulku Thondup told me that it was a scriptural text and that its purpose was to give one a good reputation. I have it on the bureau in my bedroom. I wrote to thank him on the back of a postcard reproduction of François Boucher's portrait of Madame de Pompadour, which still hangs in the Fogg Museum at Harvard. Lama Jigtse stuck it on his refrigerator.

Sometimes people whom Dodrup Chen Rinpoche didn't know would want to see him, and I'd ask him if they could. The first time he inquired, "Do they have faith or do they have interest?" But he never refused to see anyone, although he preferred not to see anyone who didn't have faith in dharma. He would receive people in the little shrine room next to his bedroom. His visitors would sit in a row on cushions against the wall, and he would sit at the end of the room near the door to his room. I stayed if he needed me to use my little bit of Tibetan to interpret; otherwise I'd bring them tea and leave. Once two students of a lama who had many followers in America asked him to come and give teachings to their sangha. While they were upstairs, I wondered what they were talking about with Rinpoche, and afterward, they told me that he had declined their invitation.

Rinpoche's own students would come from time to time, and often his devoted Sikkimese student Sonam Paljor Denjenjongpa would come to Marion from Providence. Sonam's friend from their Brown University student days, David Devore, would also visit. He had traveled to Sikkim with Sonam Paljor and met Rinpoche and become his devoted disciple. Today, in addition to his own work, he runs the organization of Rinpoche's students in America, the Maha Siddha Nyingmapa Center. When Rinpoche comes every two years to visit his students, he stays at the temple in Hawley, Massachusetts, which was originally built in 1970. After it burned down in 1975, the disciples built a larger one.

Tulku Thinley Norbu Rinpoche, Dudjom Rinpoche's son, came to New York on his first visit to the States. When he came up to Marion to see Dodrup Chen Rinpoche, I went to the airport to meet him with a friend, Terry Clifford. And so through Rinpoche, I met the great lama, son of Dudjom Rinpoche, who became a teacher to me and deepened what understanding I have. I showed him the *Dorje Trollo Sadhana* that Dudjom Rinpoche had composed for me and the teaching on Manjusri that he wrote for me in his own hand. Tulku Thinley Norbu read them but didn't say anything.

One night after dinner when I assumed that Tulku Thinley Norbu Rinpoche was upstairs with Dodrup Chen Rinpoche, I was watching a detective story on television, and he came into the room and sat down. After a while he asked if it was interesting. I said that it was just entertainment but sort of fun. "I don't understand it," he said, and walked out of the room as softly as he had come in.

Tulku Thondup had been a disciple of Dodrup Chen Rinpoche since he was a small child when he was identified as the rebirth of a great scholar of his generation named Konme Khenpo. Once at the breakfast table in Marion, Dodrup Chen Rinpoche was telling me about the qualities of each of the great Nyingmapa lamas that made them special. I asked him what was Tulku Thondup's special quality. He replied that Tulku Thondup had the blessing of Manjusri. If I'm not mistaken it came to Tulku Thondup by means of an initiation he received from the grandson of Dudjom Lingpa, the first Dudjom Rinpoche, who was his guru's guru. Tulku Thondup went into retreat afterward and received a *rig-se,* or opening of the mind, and from then on he excelled in knowledge and wisdom.

Michael and I and the two lamas formed a unit that was very clearly the product of tendrel, or the relationship between a lama and his disciple that endures throughout successive lifetimes. Rinpoche stayed for nine months. I was so happy for I could never have been with him for a fraction of that length of time in Sikkim. It turned out that America was now the place where I would study dharma with sublime beings. While Dodrup Chen Rinpoche was staying with me, two students of Dudjom Rinpoche and of Kanjur Rinpoche, another lama from whom Michael and I had taken teachings in Darjeeling, came up from New York to see Dodrup Chen Rinpoche. One student was the poet John Giorno, and the other was Vivian Kurz. Together, they ran the Yeshe Nyingpo Center of Dudjom Rinpoche at 19 West 16th Street, New York. Vivian became one of a handful of my closest *chos-dro,* or dharma friends. The only dharma friend I had at that point in Marion was

Michael. My friend from India, Tendzin Parsons, had just come to live in Providence to study with Dodrup Chen Rinpoche. Although Vivian was the disciple of Dilgo Khyentse Rinpoche, a great lama, she was also devoted to Dodrup Chen Rinpoche. It was a great pleasure to make the acquaintance of someone who would become a lifelong dharma friend.

While Rinpoche was staying in Marion in 1975, I didn't have much of a chance to ask him for meditation training because no one was there to interpret. Tulku Thondup didn't come back from Lucknow until the following May, and Rinpoche had already left by then. But I had already been given so much practice to do by Lama Gyurda-la and Dudjom Rinpoche that I was not frustrated by not being able to take meditation teachings from Dodrup Chen Rinpoche at that time. I didn't know what I was missing. We were able to converse about ordinary things, however. Now it seems magical to have sat at the table with him for breakfast, lunch, and dinner. Michael, who lived across the street from the house he had rented for me, would come after breakfast, and Rinpoche would give us a Tibetan writing lesson. Looking back, it seems funny that one of the great siddhas of Tibet was teaching us to write the Tibetan alphabet. His writing is beautiful. Michael learned to write much more correctly than I, and he made our tutorials lots of fun.

Once I served Rinpoche his afternoon tea as usual. He was sitting cross-legged on the bed. I stayed and had tea with him, and then he started to teach. What he told me was way over my head. He talked for hours, and when night fell and we were in the dark, he didn't stop teaching. I think a lot got communicated or just seeped into me. For some reason he wanted to teach even without an interpreter just at that time. I think of the saying of Meister Eckhart that if there were no one in the church, he would have to preach to the poor box.

One day Michael told me that if I wanted to go on living in Marion after my rent was up, I had better buy a house; if I didn't buy one then, I'd never be able to afford one because the price of real estate was going to go up. I decided to take Michael's advice. I wanted to be where he was. And his invitation to come and stay in Marion after Lama Gyurda-la's death had led to Tulku Thondup's summer visit, and then to Rinpoche's long stay. Michael and I looked at a few houses. I picked number 15 Main Street, catty-corner to the house I was renting where Rinpoche was staying. Although he hadn't gone out for a while—it was as if he were doing a retreat—I asked him to look at the house I was proposing to buy. After walking slowly through the rooms observing everything, he said, "If you buy this house, good will come of it." Over the years, Rinpoche and Tulku Thondup have often stayed in that house and blessed it with their presence. Now it seems like a person to me, a companion, cozy and eccentrically elegant. It is impossible in this house to feel lonely. I used to listen to Tchaikovsky's song "None but the Lonely Heart" to remember what loneliness feels like.

Kunkhyen Longchen Rabjam wrote:

> The "Various *Nirmanakayas*" such as forms of art, birth (as beings), ponds, bridges, lotuses, wish-fulfilling trees,
> Medicine, jewels, and lamps
> Provide the source of happiness and joy for beings and
> Bring about the ultimate good (enlightenment) as the final result.

I feel that this house, too, is one of those "Various *Nirmanakayas*." I believe that it has brought me many blessings, beginning with the fact that there is room to welcome Rinpoche and Tulku Thondup along with several friends.

When his three months in America ended, Tulku Thondup agreed to return the following summer so we could work together again. Thereafter, Tulku Thondup would have me stay for three months in the winter at Santi Niketan, where he was teaching at Visva-Bharati University, a few hours by train from Calcutta. This schedule went on until Tulku Thondup came to Harvard on a fellowship in 1980. So during those four years I was able to see him and work with him on his books for about six months of the year. Perhaps I would not have had nearly as much time with him if I'd stayed in India, so that was another blessing of Michael's having created a place for me in Marion.

In 1977, Dodrup Chen Rinpoche conferred the Nying Thig Ya Zhi wangs here. Michael said that the way Rinpoche arranged the schedule was typically practical because he conferred the wangs of the four cycles of Nying Thig over two successive weekends, to allow people to get back to their jobs on Mondays. Michael found houses in Marion and the next town, Wareham, for the people who could stay the week between the two sets of wangs, and the other people drove back to New York, Boston, or western Massachusetts and returned the following weekend. Lama Jigtse, who was the *chopon*, or master of ceremonies for the wangs, gave everyone blessed water at the door leading to the indoor porch, and once they were in that room, they were in the mandala, as the house of Buddha is called, and no one was admitted after the door was closed. Rinpoche and Lama Jigtse and Dechen Dorje worked hard to make every detail perfect for these very elaborate wangs.

A throne was erected on my indoor porch for Rinpoche. Lama Jigtse used a long table that Michael had had made for the occasion and placed it in a hallway off the porch for the mandala, which involved many ritual objects to be handed to Rinpoche as required in the ceremony, as well as many offerings, and candles in place of butter lamps. When Rinpoche completed the preparations for the wangs, he said, "Harold's house is *phunsum tsokpa* [complete]," meaning that everything needed for the wangs was in it. If he said that he needed something, for example, above the throne, I would rummage through drawers and, voilà, a canopy. A lot of the things made of silk, like the *baldachino* over the throne on the porch, had to be sewn, which required a number of late nights of work done in the living room with great concentration. John Driver, a scholar of Tibetan Buddhism and a devotee of some of the great lamas of the Nyingmapa, came over from London to do the interpreting. Sonam Paljor, who is close to Rinpoche and understands him perfectly, could have done all the interpreting, but with Sonam's help, John did very well. Vivian was in charge of the practical arrangements and did the cooking. Occasionally, Rinpoche would say that he needed something, for example, saffron for the water used in the rituals. I would hold my breath, fearing that the whole thing would come to a halt and prove impossible to perform, all because of a small item like saffron. But Vivian would manage to find it.

The porch was transformed into a shrine room where Rinpoche performed the wangs with Lama Jigtse and Dechen Dorje assisting. Twenty-five people sat on the floor of the porch and another twenty-five on the deck. Across the street from the back of the house was Steve Sperry's workshop where he made sails. While the preparations were going on, Steve came over and asked if there was anything that he could provide. Rinpoche said that we needed an awning to put over the deck. So Steve made one, which he gave us, and he helped us to put it up. It was September, and the weather during both those weekends was warm and sunny; things would have been difficult if it had rained.

Nothing went wrong. Two of Rinpoche's students got lost on the way to the first session, and they had an automobile accident. But they just made it while Lama Jigtse was still pouring the water from a vase before we entered the mandala. Afterward, Rinpoche said that sometimes accidents can happen before a wang and that they can actually be helpful, dispelling obstacles or purifying karma. At the wangs, Lama Jigtse would pass rice on a silver dish for us to throw in the air at certain points for offering and rejoicing. He put the dish down between Marilyn Silverstone, who by this time had become a nun, and me. Without looking, I reached down to take a handful of rice. I felt a small object on the edge of the dish and picked it up. It was a turquoise with what looked like a crystal inlaid in the stone. During an intermission, I showed Marilyn the turpuoise and asked if she had seen it on the edge of the plate. "No," she said. "That looks *rang jung gyepa*, self-arisen. Go and show it to Rinpoche." When I went up to the throne and showed it to him, he said, "That is Harold's terma. Always wear it next to your heart." I count that as one of the three miracles of Rinpoche that I have witnessed.

Soon after the wangs ended, the telephone rang, and it was my sister Peggy to say that her husband B had just died. I was able to ask Rinpoche for prayers at once. It seemed that Rinpoche had exerted some power over the telephone, because it never rang during the wangs, only just when they ended. But maybe it was simply that Vivian had stuck a pencil in one of the telephones.

Another thing happened that I thought was mysterious. At one point in the ceremonies, Rinpoche sent us all out to a cemetery. Walking around and seeing the gravestones, I experienced the awareness that we are all going to die. I got back to the house before the others and went upstairs to see Rinpoche, and when I saw him, I started to laugh for no reason and couldn't stop. Rinpoche began to laugh, and we both laughed and laughed for a long time. I was laughing at some sense I got by recognizing that death must come to us all. Not a word was exchanged. At the time that he conferred the Nying Thig Ya Zhi, it seemed an extraordinary good fortune that he was giving us the wangs of this collection of Dzogchen teachings from Guru Rinpoche, Khadro Yeshe Tshogyal, and Vimalamitra and assembled by Kunkhyen Longchen Rabjam (1308–1363). But now looking back, it seems like a miracle engendered by Rinpoche's compassion. And to me compassion seems like the highest miracle.

When Michael asked Dodrup Chen Rinpoche if there was something we could do for him, he said that he would like his nephew, Dechen Dorje, who was in Taiwan, to come and live in America. When Dechen Dorje arrived, we set about getting him a green card. Michael was a master at getting things done in samsara. Once the process had begun, I found it rather fun, and I liked the woman lawyer who worked on the case. Dechen Dorje seemed quite unfazed by the suspense, which can be unnerving. Perhaps Dodrup Chen with his foreknowledge assured Dechen Dorje that he was going to get his permanent residence visa. And sure enough, it came through without a hitch. It was strange that Dechen Dorje got his green card quite quickly, while Dodrup Chen Rinpoche had to wait so long for his. It was very nice having Dechen Dorje staying with his uncle, and we were grateful that he was able to interpret for us.

When Michael learned that Rinpoche was having teeth trouble, he insisted that he see a dentist. The problem was much more serious than we had thought, and Michael had to persuade him to get Rinpoche to undergo the necessary work. Finally, he agreed to have half of it done and the rest later. When later came, Michael reminded Rinpoche that he needed to have the rest of the work done. But this time Rinpoche refused to do it.

In 1980, Michael persuaded Tulku Thondup to give up his position as chairman of the Department of Indo-Tibetan Studies at Visvra-Bharati University in Shantiniketan, West Bengal, in order to try for an academic position in the States, which would make it possible for him to get a leave of absence from his university and also to settle here permanently. I took him to see Professor Masatoshi Nagatomi at Harvard, with whom I had studied Sanskrit and Buddhism. At first, he was skeptical about Tulku Thondup being accepted by the department of Sanskrit and Indian Studies to work at the Center for the Study of World Religions at Harvard because a Thai monk had come the year before but had not been able to adjust to conditions in the States. However, Professor Nagatomi said that Tulku Thondup's curriculum vitae was so extraordinarily impressive that he would take a chance on him. So that is how it happened that Tulku Thondup settled permanently in Cambridge, Massachusetts.

CHAPTER SEVENTEEN

Dodrup Chen Rinpoche

More Teachings and Miracles

In some strange way I am moved whenever I come into the presence of one of my Nyingmapa lamas. It is a scent like incense or a flavor, and it is always the same. I believe it's the essence of Dzogchen meditation or perhaps the whole Nyingmapa tradition. I have never felt that with the Dalai Lama nor with Gelugpa, Kagyupa, or Sakyapa lamas.

One day as I was sitting at the breakfast table across from Lama Gyurda-la, he tapped softly on his water glass and looked straight at me. Some sort of a revolution took place in my mind—a glimpse of awareness that I can't quite describe but that left me feeling very blissful. I was in awe of the lama because of his power to induce some kind of an awareness of the union of clarity and emptiness by using a simple means, in this case tapping softly on a glass and looking directly at me. Another time this kind of thing happened in Darjeeling. Lama Gyurda-la was in his usual seat, and I was sitting on the floor in front of him, when he simply tapped on his table with a pen and looked at me. I experienced a breakthrough or a clearing of the mind, a moment when my consciousness ceased to function, and something luminous, subtle, vast, and empty took its place for a moment.

It seems that each Nyingmapa lama I've known has a remarkably gentle, selfless, and kind personality with a distinct "flavor." When I am in their presence, my mind seems to stop generating thoughts and emotions at its normal rate. There is effortlessness and a relaxation of seeking. I live and absorb and feel as if I'm where I belong and that there is no other place to be. Tulku Thondup, Dodrup Chen Rinpoche, and Lama Gyurda-la all had their own way of teaching and blessing with the impact of their presence. Yet I'm sure they all share many of the same enlightened qualities. You could tell one of these great lamas what you were practicing under the direction of another lama, and he would pick up the thread of your meditation training with total understanding and teach you accordingly.

Even at the subtle level of how they teach meditation, each lama will have his own distinctive method. I think that for them, perception is meditation, or that very freedom from meditation itself, spoken of in Dzogchen teachings. So that what they communicate to you is their own enlightened nature. How you are able to recognize and be affected by this unmediated communication depends on your own capacity. No matter how little headway you make after a particular meditation interview, if you have a good memory, or if, like me, you write down everything that was said, years later you can continue to draw new understanding from what was taught you long ago. Often one way or another the meaning of teachings reveals itself to us at different stages of practice, especially if you have the good fortune to be able to clarify points with a lama such as Tulku Thondup, possessed of vast learning, sharp intellect, and wisdom.

Teachings are the whole spectrum of Buddhism. The Buddha first gave teachings on the four noble truths: suffering, the cause of suffering, the cessation of suffering, and the way to extinguish suffering and attain nirvana, which is the Noble Eightfold Path. Impermanence, suffering, and not-self are also teachings of the Buddha, which a lama will recite. So you meditate on what all this means until you are not thinking at all, and that is the state the lama is guiding you toward. It's called the pointing out of the nature of your mind.

Our minds have a stream of thoughts and emotions, and you learn not to pay attention to any of them. Especially in Dzogchen, there are no rules to obey; you don't think of good and bad. You get to the point (after endless recitations of a teaching) where you don't recite anymore or read the scripture anymore. You read it like using a diving board, and then you plunge into the water and you don't need the diving board anymore. When you have had some experience practicing, there comes a gap between thoughts and emotions in which you recognize the true nature of your mind. For a great lama in the Dzogchen tradition, there is no difference between the everyday life of work and responsibility and meditation. In the kind of practice I do, you don't think of anything—you just dwell in the true nature of the mind, and you're absorbed in clarity and emptiness. Another side of my practice that I also do every day is akin to Pure Land Buddhism—Tantric meditations in which I recite and visualize the mantra.

This very brief teaching that Tulku Thondup read at a memorial service for Gene Smith at the Cathedral of St. John the Divine is the essence of Dzogchen.

> The nature of the mind is Buddha, enlightened from the beginning. Mind has no birth nor cessation. It is like space. All phenomenal existences are peaceful and pure. Rest in this realization as it is, without seeking. That is the meditation.
>
> There is nothing to identify. Nothing to say on this, but if you could remain in the state of knowingness or awareness of clarity and emptiness without losing it, then you are fine. Also aside from merely knowing your own nature by yourself, there is no duality of who and whom.

The year before he died, Lama Gyurda-la composed a prayer to Manjusri while in the state known as *nyam tang milam*, a combination of dream state and meditative experience. The prayer is an aspiration to attain complete realization and to attain the highest result of Dzogchen practice, ja-lü, in which the body of the yogi dissolves into light. His father attained ja-lü in 1954, and Lama Gyurda-la was praying for the same attainment. It is a Dzogchen prayer to Manjusri, and reciting it opens me to the blessing of my yidam and of my teacher, Lama Gyurda-la. After Lama Gyurda-la's death, Tulku Thondup gave me the *zhal-don*, or book of daily prayers, that Lama Gyurda-la had accumulated or written during a lifetime of practicing day and night. In it Tulku Thondup found the prayer to Manjusri "in dream and meditation," and he translated it for me.

Among the other texts of Manjusri that I try to study or practice is an explanation of the mantra of Manjusri by the Third Dodrup Chen Rinpoche. Tulku Thondup read it to me over the telephone, translating as he went along. He told me it is from an explanation of the *Eulogy of Manjusri* that is so deep that very few people have the wisdom to understand it. But a tiny understanding of deep teachings can come through after much pondering and recitation. It put the meaning of the seven syllables of the mantra in a whole new context for me. I try to think of it when I recite the mantra because it reflects the Dzogchen realization of the Third Dodrup Chen Rinpoche on emptiness, the unborn and undying true nature of the mind.

My lama, Dodrup Chen Rinpoche, is awe-inspiring, of course. In later years people would say, "Did you see how awesome and serious Rinpoche looked while he was conferring the wang?" A number of students would agree that Rinpoche is so simple in the way he does things that you can lose sight of his majestic spiritual identity. He has his ordinary side and his tulku side. One evening as night was slowly falling and he was talking softly, I could see the awe-inspiring quality of the tulku. According to the perspective of identifiable rebirths that the Tibetans take for granted, Rinpoche, like the many enlightened ones who have preceded him in his incarnational line, is a siddha, or sage, and a person who has performed miraculous deeds. As a child he was famous for miracles—too famous as far as he was concerned. He attracted great crowds, and that became an obstacle.

There were two incarnations of the Third Dodrup Chen at the monastery in Golok, where he grew up. When he was twelve, "our" Dodrup Chen Rinpoche passed his powers on to the other one, Tulku Riglo (who was Tulku Thondup's guru), saying that in this age miracles were not helpful to people. Yet despite the transference of powers, Rinpoche is still known to perform miracles. I expect most people will be skeptical about the claim that someone can perform miracles, but that doesn't bother me. I saw them.

Dodrup Chen Rinpoche is close to animals, and they seem to seek him out. At his monastery in Sikkim there is a huge *chorten*, or reliquary monument, on one side of which there was once a lawn. So many monks have come for training in the past decades that much of the land around the chorten has been given over to dormitories, and now a temple has replaced the lawn. One moonlit night I saw Rinpoche standing on the lawn as a herd of little deer came up to him, and he patted them and rubbed them behind their ears. When he comes to Marion, squirrels come up to the sliding-glass window to see him when he is sitting on the porch. I have the feeling that he likes squirrels, so I was not surprised when one of the mysterious things I have seen him do involved a squirrel.

Tulku Thondup and he were stretched out on chaise lounges in the backyard of a house in Providence that had been rented for him by his students. Vivian and I were with him. A cat that was prowling around the garden took a squirrel by surprise as it was foraging on the ground and held it in its teeth. Suddenly, Rinpoche leapt from his chair, sped across the lawn, extracted the squirrel from the cat's mouth, and sent it running up a tree. Vivian said, "Did you see that?" We both agreed that Rinpoche had run across the lawn and separated the squirrel from the cat so swiftly that he was almost invisible. I call it the miracle of the squirrel, and it was certainly a manifestation of some kind of a siddhi of speed and skill.

There are other instances of a power over nature that Rinpoche has. For example, while his students were building the temple in western Massachusetts, he conferred wangs, or empowerments, in a big tent. At a certain point in the ritual common to each wang, the wind would become so strong it threatened to blow the tent down. When David Dvore realized at what point the wind would rise, he would get up and secure the ropes holding the tent. Sure enough, along would come a powerful gust, right on schedule. What was the wind doing? Perhaps it got excited because of all the bells and drums and the sound of Rinpoche's voice.

The final incident of a miraculous nature that I witnessed happened one summer at my house in Marion when I had a terrible gash on the sole of my right foot. When Rinpoche's companion, Semo-la, whom I had first met years ago in Darjeeling, found out about it, she told me to show it to Rinpoche. I refused, thinking that it was disrespectful to show him my foot. "You have to!" Semo-la insisted. "Rinpoche is a doctor." I found him sitting in a chair in the living room and told him that I had a gaping wound on my foot. He got down on the floor, took my foot, and spat on the wound. Then he asked if I had some ointment, and I brought him some. He spat into the jar, stirred up the ointment, and told me to put some on from time to time and to keep the foot uncovered. His visit ended later that day. The next morning, I looked at my foot, and it had healed. Over the weekend, Rinpoche's students had arranged a picnic so we could all say good-bye to him before he returned to Sikkim. When I told him that my foot had healed the same day he had treated it, he said, "Thank you"—the last response I would have expected. I could only imagine that he meant, "Thank you for your faith."

If he is a miracle-working siddha, he is also the most practical person imaginable. Michael, who is very good at dealing with the necessities of life for both friends and clients, appreciates his ability to get things done in a way that is not elaborate and doesn't create a fuss. Michael often says of what Rinpoche does, "He is sooo practical." Humble, modest, friendly, and polite—intensely considerate—Rinpoche also has total integrity in all his dealings. It is easy for people to miss his greatness and power; he is what is called a *be-pe pal-jor-pa*, or hidden yogi. Some great lamas are majestic. Dodrup Chen Rinpoche, on the other hand, can make himself invisible to avoid any hubbub that would prevent him from, as he says, "doing my work" or make him inaccessible to anyone who seeks his help or blessing. In Sikkim he is known as the lama of the poor.

Rinpoche is famous for his clairvoyance. People come from near his monastery in Gangtok, from remote parts of Sikkim, Tibet, and Bhutan, as well as from the West, to ask him for divinations. As I am interested in learning meditation from him, I haven't asked him for many divinations except for the time I recounted earlier when Peter Prestcott almost died. Sometimes I asked Rinpoche for advice, which is perhaps the same thing, for Rinpoche seems naturally to be omniscient.

He is matter-of-fact in giving advice and will take responsibility for life-and-death matters. Someone who is ill might ask him whether to have an operation or will give him a list of doctors and treatments and ask which one would be best. And he'll tell them. Once when it seemed that the Chinese were about to invade India through Sikkim, people rushed to him and asked if they should flee. He said that there would not be an invasion. He was right. Often when he was at my house, the telephone would ring, and I would hear the urgent voice of a Tibetan refugee calling from somewhere in the United States or Canada to ask Rinpoche for a divination about a problem. Of course, he never told me about these divinations, but sometimes I overheard. Although most were serious questions about illness or crisis, there were others I rather unkindly thought of as "shall I buy a used car or a new car?" calls.

Once I asked his advice on a serious matter, and he gave me a completely reassuring answer, which fortunately turned out to be true. When he does a divination, Rinpoche takes his rosary and with his thumbs and index fingers holds two beads that are about thirty beads apart. Then he holds two beads within the first set, narrowing down the number between his fingers, sometimes doing that two or three times. Then he looks up and gives an answer to the question. This mysteriously arrived-at set of calculations is made with Rinpoche's beautiful and precise hand movements. Tulku Thondup thinks that Rinpoche doesn't really need to count beads on his rosary to arrive at the answer, but he does it because that is how people expect divinations to be performed. His incarnational predecessor, the Third Dodrup Chen Rinpoche, wrote a book about divination, and his successor is a master at it. His words are *den-tsik*, words of absolute truth. By his saying that something will happen, it does.

I suppose many lamas have *ngon-she*—foreknowledge or clairvoyance—to one degree or another. Tulku Thondup says that he doesn't like to do divinations, but clearly he has powerful mystical vision. And like Rinpoche, he is very down to earth. Whatever you ask him, he gets to the root of the matter and puts it in the most practical perspective. He seems to know how to handle everything. For example, I have often heard from his students that they have consulted him about something related to their job or career, and he gives them perfect advice. I asked him for advice about my job once, and he solved the problem so simply that I didn't see why I hadn't thought of it myself. As for me, I'm still waiting for my foreknowledge to increase. But I have perfect faith that it will happen some day.

A lot of people ask Rinpoche for prayers when they or a relative or friend is sick or dying as well as prayers for the dead. Often people are cured or survive life-threatening illnesses. His followers ascribe these recoveries to Rinpoche's grace or the power of his prayer. The same is true of Tulku Thondup, who was already known as a healer when he was a young boy in Tibet. Here in America he receives endless requests for prayers for the sick. And quite frequently I hear someone say that they believe he has cured them or someone close to them. So he is always hearing about people who are ill and suffering. "So many people are sick," he once said over the telephone in a voice full of sorrow.

I was reminded that my dealings with him have mostly been related to his writings or his generous interpreting for sessions with Dodrup Chen Rinpoche and other lamas, while he has so many sick and dying people on his mind. Once when I was ill, it was reassuring to hear his voice over the telephone, and I felt relaxed and unafraid because I had him to depend on. From what people tell me, it seems that both these lamas have reversed the course of illnesses and extended people's lives. I spoke to someone the other day who had been very ill and after a serious operation made a remarkably swift recovery. I wasn't surprised to hear her say, matter-of-factly, "I guess it was Rinpoche's blessing."

Just being in touch with these holy persons makes illness lighter. I have been bipolar since I was eighteen. I never took anything for the condition until a few years ago when a friend persuaded me to see a brilliant doctor who prescribed just the right psychotropic medicine, and I have been well ever since. But while I was in the depths of despair, I could feel that deep down my mind was free of these wild states of happiness and suffering. This lack of despair about despair was due to a little dharma practice and devotion to my lamas. Once, before the psychic Red Sea parted and I was freed from the most severe symptoms of bipolar disorder, a friend asked, "If you have been practicing for so many decades and you're still a mess, why should I be interested in Buddhism?" But who is to say how I would have been without teachers of dharma? Perhaps much worse.

Much of the time it is impossible to say what has caused someone to have a "miraculous recovery." One of Tulku Thondup's students, about whom he writes in his book *The Healing Power of Mind*, was very ill with cancer. In the hospital he spent all his time doing the visualization and recitation of Vajrasattva. He made a complete recovery and lived a number of years longer. The doctors told him that they did not know what had happened but that he had had "an extramedical cure." As I've recounted, my twin brother was healed of the serious effects of an accident when his horse fell on him. His father-in-law, Dr. Kinsolving, and another minister visited him in hospital and prayed for my brother. Michael sent me a cable about the accident, and I immediately went to Dudjom Rinpoche and asked for prayers. Who is to say what caused my brother's "miraculous recovery"? From the Buddhist standpoint, it would be perfectly possible that the Christian ministers' prayers and those of Dudjom Rinpoche were both part of the interdependent causation that produced such a remarkable cure.

In addition to miracles there is the fascinating subject of siddhis, or special powers that some lamas possess. Alexandra David-Neel made a living telling stories of the exercise of these powers. Although you might think the whole subject is a bit dubious, I am fascinated by miraculous happenings, especially ones attributed to people I know. My favorite is an incident that took place at Ama-la's house in Aloobari. The beautiful Sangye Drolma came into the shrine room one day and said to Lama Gyurda-la, "All you lamas do is meditate and say prayers. Why don't you perform miracles like Sai Baba?" A little later Sangye-la was standing on the terrace looking at the mountains and below her she could see Lama Gyurda-la going down the path to the outhouse. But he stopped halfway there and jumped up and down. When Sangye-la went down to see what he was doing, she found the footprints of Lama Gyurda-la's rubber sandals imprinted in a rock. Some time later when our friend Sybil Weil was visiting the house, she took photographs of the footprints in the rock. I have one of those photographs on my shrine.

Tendzin Parsons tells a story about a *mo*, or divination, that Lama Gyurda-la did. The two of them were on their way from New Delhi to Darjeeling with two large packing cases of books that Kalu Rinpoche had brought with him out of Tibet. Tendzin had made xerox copies of the books, at the behest of the Georges, and was now returning them to Kalu Rinpoche. Between Calcutta and Siliguri the train stopped at the Ganges, which they had to cross on a flimsy barge. Tendzin could see the books loaded onto another ferry that crossed the river with their own. At the other side they took another train to Siliguri, where they would take a car for the trip up to Darjeeling. But the books were not on the train. Tendzin settled Lama Gyurda-la on a park bench on the train platform while he ran up and down trying to find the books. He returned to Lama Gyurda-la and said that the books were lost. Lama Gyurda-la, who was sitting there peacefully, took out his rosary and did a divination. "They'll be here at 8:30," he said and continued to sit imperturbably. At 8:30 a train rolled in, and the books were on it.

There was another incident in Darjeeling when something had been stolen and Lama Gyurda-la did a mirror divination. It requires the power to look into a mirror and see a scene that solves the person's inquiry, and by this method Lama Gyurda-la identified the thief. The recitation of prayers and mantras can help you overcome obstacles and accomplish pure wishes. Lama Gyurda-la, being a *ngagpa*, or Tantric yogi, helped me with a mantra of Shakyamuni Buddha when I was staying with him in Old Delhi not long before his death. My visa was running out, and I was very worried that the foreigners' registration office might not renew it again because I'd had so many extensions. And I was always afraid that my disagreement with the government of India, the old quit notice, would somehow come back to haunt me. I told Lama Gyurda-la of my fears about the forthcoming visa application, and he said that he would give me "a mantra which makes people like you and want to help you." Because it was new for me, he asked me to say it a lot, and he would also recite it so that I'd get a visa extension. A few days later I went to the foreign office in the wonderful Lutyens red sandstone Greco-Indian Raj palace and sat in the waiting room silently reciting Lama Gyurda-la's mantra. On every other occasion when I'd gone to renew my visa, the matter was dealt with by a clerk. However, this time a turbaned attendant came up to me and said, "The minister will see you now." I followed him upstairs, and at the end of a long corridor, he showed me into the biggest office I'd ever seen.

A man sitting behind a desk—I never learned whether he was an assistant, a deputy minister, or the secretary of the ministry—asked me to sit down. He was handsome and civilized, with a pleasant and cheerful voice. "What are you doing in India?" he asked. My fellow dharma students always said that it was better to say that you're studying Hinduism rather than Buddhism. However, I said, "I'm studying Buddhism with Tibetan Buddhist lamas." He asked me how much time I wanted in India, and instead of the normal three months I asked for six. He told me that he would give me a year. Then he wished me well in my studies and got up to show me out. Crossing the vast room, he put his arm around my shoulders. How much love for India welled up in me as I walked down the red stone staircase and out into the winter sun of New Delhi. When I got back to the room in Old Delhi, I told Lama Gyurda-la what had happened, and he smiled and gave a little nod. I think he was pleased that my continued stay in India had been secured, and the power of the mantra had been demonstrated.

When Sonam Namgyal, Lama Gyurda-la's father, was dying, his sons sent for the lama at the nearest monastery, but he did not come. I think the lama knew that ja-lü would happen. When the lama heard of the ja-lü, he said that Sonam Namgyal was the first of nine people who would attain ja-lü, beginning with the lama himself. Sonam Namgyal's ja-lü produced so much radiance that people came and basked in the rays of light. It was 1953, and the Chinese authorities henceforth forbade people to congregate on the pretext of a ja-lü.

There are so many elements of Tibetan Buddhism that seem to be magical but that are just part of the fabric of dharmic life. For example, in the Nyingmapa tradition, there are termas, or treasures—scriptures, images, and ritual objects that were hidden by Guru Rinpoche to be discovered by the rebirths of his principal disciples and from them to successive generations of disciples for the benefit of future generations. A terma comes directly from Guru Rinpoche; *kama*, or scriptures, on the other hand, are transmitted from one lama of the lineage to the next. The whole terma tradition is steeped in the supernatural, and it all follows from one source of power, the "mind mandate," by which Guru Rinpoche concealed a terma in the mind of one of his disciples to be discovered there by one of his future rebirths. In other cases, termas can be concealed in rocks or water or in an object such as a pillar in a temple for the terton to discover when the time is right. This is how one of the two important elements of the tradition is communicated. The way the terton discovers the terma is by an awakening of the memory of the mind mandate communicated to his or her predecessor by Guru Rinpoche. With this source of revelation as a centrally important aspect of Nyingmapa tradition, it seems natural that the whole process of spiritual training and its context, the religious society of Nyingmapa people, will be open to many expressions of the supernatural and many "skillful means" of a mystical nature.

CHAPTER EIGHTEEN

Christianity and Buddhism

Not being a scholar, I like to talk about my own very simple contact with these two religions and the impact they've had on my life. I never thought my way from the Christian faith of my childhood and youth to the adoption of Buddhism. Once talking to Tulku Thondup, I began a sentence with the phrase, "When I left the church . . ." He smiled and said, "You never left the church." I once told the Sixteenth Karmapa that I was a *ge-nyen*, a Buddhist layman who has taken the refuges. "No, no," he said, "you are a Yeshu Lama," Yeshu, meaning Jesus. And he, with his ngon-she, may have seen how much I love Christianity. As for Dom Aelred, he once said to me, "You have had a neurotic adolescent conversion to the church."

I'm not someone who feels something lacking in Christianity and who feels impelled to look elsewhere for what's missing. The older I get, the more I see the transcendent value of Christianity, and I hope that Christians won't lose the power of their own deep skillful means, to use the Buddhist term, for ways of realizing wisdom. I became a Buddhist in the way one leaves one's parents and makes a new life for oneself, although they still remain one's parents. I became attracted to Tibetan Buddhism as a child, and the fascination was rekindled in my early teens. For ten years I was preoccupied with Catholicism, and then in India, when I finally saw a community of Tibetans and met the Dalai Lama, I set out on the path of dharma.

At that time in November 1967, I thought that I had said farewell to Christianity. The following spring when I traveled with the Benedictine monk and theologian Dom Aelred Graham to Jerusalem for Holy Week, I was moved by places in the life of Jesus, especially the Garden of Gethsemane. However, at the same time I was reading Bhikku Sangharakshita's book *A Survey of Buddhism* and doing as much

Buddhist meditation as I could in our room at the King David Hotel. Dom Aelred thought that these Buddhist preoccupations in Jerusalem during Holy Week were funny. But his breadth of mind was a great blessing to me.

And his own deep interest in Buddhism had been the cause of our friendship. The following year, when Dom Aelred had returned to live for the remainder of his life at Ampleforth Abbey in Yorkshire and I was in New Delhi, I wrote and told him that I wanted to take the refuges and become a Buddhist. He wrote back, saying, "Provided you live up to the light that has been given you during the past year, you will be doing the right thing." A month or so before that, Merton had said to me, "If I were your age, I would be doing what you are doing, studying with Tibetan Buddhist lamas in India." These two great men gave me full confidence in the rightness of my decision. However, I remain a person who owes a deep debt to Christianity, both the Protestantism of my childhood and the Catholicism of my teens and twenties.

While Aelred Graham and Thomas Merton were living spiritual teachers to me, a great seventeenth-century French Catholic contemplative master has also been like a spiritual teacher to me. He is François de Salignac de la Mothe Fénelon, a towering figure in the history of religion, as well as the history of humanity. Merton wrote an introduction to a collection of his writings titled *Letters of Love and Counsel*. I was amazed when I read it nearly thirty years after Merton's death. I consider it the best thing in English about this great man's life and teachings. Merton wrote it shortly before he left for India, where he met lamas of the four major lineages of Tibetan Buddhism and became enthralled with the Dzogchen yogi Chatral Rinpoche. Fénelon has an amazing way of teaching Christian contemplation that is very appealing to me because there is something in it that makes me think of Dzogchen meditation. Merton, too, loved Fénelon's spiritual method in addition to what he learned about Dzogchen in India. So I feel that we are akin in the spiritual approaches that appeal to us.

Dom Aelred was different. He once wrote and said that he would like to study with my own Dzogchen guru, Lama Gyurda-la. He asked me to inquire why Lama Gyurda-la's tradition maintained that mind was the basis of all things, whereas Dom Aelred thought that the position of Buddhism is that emptiness is the basis of all things. Lama Gyurda-la replied, "Who is it who is saying that emptiness is the basis of all things?" I relayed the message to Dom Aelred, and he wrote back, "I'm too old for these games." Lama Gyurda-la remarked, "He has a Madhyamaka mind."

Yet Aelred also loved Fénelon. One of the first principles of Dzogchen is "Let the mind relax." Fénelon also wrote of relaxing the mind as the key to meditation. He spoke of *le pûr amour* where you don't do anything in order to be near God. You simply love and that's all. Louis XIV hated that teaching, and so did Bishop Bossuet, the most powerful man in the French Catholic Church. Louis was furious. What would happen to secular authority and ecclesiastical control if all people had to do to fulfill their Christian duty to God was to relax the mind and then meditate on love of God alone? Louis said, "*Fénelon est le plus éphémère de tous les beaux ésprits de mon royaume*" (Fénelon is the most ephemeral of all the beautiful spirits in my kingdom). He and Bossuet forced the pope, who had just conferred a cardinal's hat on Fénelon, to deprive him of that honor and to condemn a certain number of Fénelon's spiritual teachings. Fénelon was absolutely fearless in speaking out against the terrible consequences to the people of France of the war perpetuated by Louis XIV. He wrote to the king that as the Lord's Annointed he was there to serve the people, not destroy them. It's not certain that Louis ever saw the letter, but he stripped Fénelon of his rank and his appointment as the preceptor to the Crown Prince. He banished Fénelon from Versailles and sentenced him to live under house arrest in Cambrai, where he was archbishop, for the rest of his life. Fénelon took his exile and disgrace with the utmost patience, imperturbability, and courage. So, as far as recommending relaxation of mind as the basis for spiritual progress and pure love alone as the way to reach God, Fénelon lived what he taught.

At school in Sacred Studies, we learned about the Old and New Testaments and Christian doctrine. We did not read from the King

James Version, and that was probably sensible because it is easier to understand contemporary translations, and they may be more accurate. However, I thought it wasn't really the Bible unless the wording was the same as what was read in church. I was a purist or traditionalist who did not realize that there was nothing final about the King James Version, any more than the ones that had preceded it. I still do love it for its beauty, as I do the language of the Book of Common Prayer in the version we had been brought up hearing. The Gospel stories of Jesus's ministry and his parables, and of course the terrible events of the Passion and the supreme miracle of the Resurrection, made a deep impression on me. We didn't have to read or study the scriptures very much to know them well: the church services we attended made them part of our minds. Once as a child at Sunday school, I saw a film about Jesus and his disciples. I thought that it was the events themselves and the actual Lord and his followers whom I was seeing, and it was enormously inspiring to me, like the next best thing to having been there myself.

It wasn't until boarding school that I heard of form criticism and the analytical way in which the scriptures had been studied for a long time. I had the unquestioning attitude of a person in the Middle Ages. Even today, although I don't practice Christianity, I find it jarring to read New Testament criticism. What exactly is left? It sometimes seems that the authenticity of the words of Christ is questioned. The Gospels become like novels. But why should this ingenious inquiry affect me? It must be that there is a residue of the old faith in someone who converts to another religion. Christianity, particularly Catholicism, means a great deal to me. When I was very troubled in my teens and twenties in New York, I would go to Mass and then walk all over the city, going into churches and hearing Mass again and again if it was being performed.

As I have mentioned, shortly after my father's death I decided to become a Catholic. The *Apologia Pro Vita Sua* of Cardinal Newman had influenced me strongly. During the Communion services at school, I would have doubts about "the validity of the Anglican sacraments." I was living my own private Oxford Movement. When I worked for a newspaper in Memphis, Tennessee, in the summer of my eighteenth year, I lived in a room at the YMCA that was like a monk's cell and prayed a lot. On Sundays, I would get on my knees and recite the Psalms for my father's soul. I derived a certain satisfaction from my knees becoming a little scraped and painful. I read a lot as well, for example, the autobiography of Saint Teresa of Lisieux and Dr. Suzuki's essays on Zen. Then there was *The Sign of Jonas* by Thomas Merton. Of course, I'd been impressed by his *The Seven Storey Mountain*, but this book had even more appeal for me.

As I mentioned earlier, I decided at the end of my job to take a bus and go to meet Merton at the monastery near Louisville, Kentucky. I went but was not able to see him. However, the abbot invited me to come back in the autumn when I was going to make my first Communion in the Catholic Church and promised me that I could see Merton then. And saw him I did. He was on his way from giving a lecture to the novices to one of the services of the monastic day, and he passed through the guesthouse where I was staying. He invited me into a little room with him. He was too pressed for time to sit down, but he said two things: "I am always happy to meet someone who has just come into the church, because they are full of grace; and the grace rubs off on me," and "the church is a very big place; always remember to go your own way in it." And then he walked off swiftly to the abbey church. Ten years later in the bungalow in Dharamsala, I told Merton that he had given me this advice when we met at Gethsemani. He replied, "Did I say that? That's pretty good! And look at where we've both gone!"

When I was walking around New York visiting many churches, I continued to read Catholic theological works and also books about Buddhism. One day I was sitting on a bench in Central Park, looking at the reflection of the Plaza Hotel in a pond. A sea gull flew back and forth over the pond, and it struck me that the flight of the bird was like a haiku. Then I thought of it as a koan. What was I really seeing, I wondered. It wasn't just the bird flying over the pond; it seemed to point to a mystery, and I thought that if I could understand the "meaning" of the bird's flight, it would convey the meaning of everything. But the meaning was a mystery that the bird in flight over the pond seemed to conceal as well as reveal. Seeing the sea gull and sensing a mystery, tantalizing and incon-clusive as it was, made me feel directly connected to something absolute that inhered within perception, connecting everything in a kind of union. It struck me that God remained inaccessible, and I certainly was not given to mystical visions or the experience of Christ's presence. Yet the flight of a sea gull had awakened something inexpressible in my mind. When I got up from the bench and left the park to wander again through the streets, I still had a feeling of unity that lasted for some time. If things were random, they seemed to have some significance beyond what could be merely defined, such as "sea gull flying over a pond." I didn't see that it was not some secret concealed in the things that unfolded before one. The mystery was in the mind's perception of those things. Nowadays, I think I would describe it with the Tibetan expression *nang-tong*—the unity/union of phenomena and emptiness.

In Dzogchen, after you have concluded your preliminary prayers and meditation, your Nyingma lama confers on you an empowerment that introduces you to the true nature of the mind and enables you to prac-tice meditation that penetrates through the defilements—the thoughts and emotions covering the mind—and enables you to have a sudden deep vision of the union of clarity and emptiness, like the vastness and luminosity and purity of the sky, which is its true nature. It is an aston-ishing discovery, which is the Holy Grail of Nyingmapa Buddhism. The experience to begin with is a glimpse of the true nature of the mind, the beginning of awareness and knowingness, which extends through prac-tice. Your lama dwells at all times in this awareness so that his percep-tions are all enlightened. In the case of some tulkus, they are born with that knowingness.

Tulku Thondup enjoyed learning and sharing ideas at Harvard's Center for the Study of World Religions. He accepted a second year of his fellowship and obtained the agreement of Visva-Bharati University to take another year's leave of absence from his post as chairman of the Department of Indo-Tibetan Studies. Again, he took another year's leave of absence and continued to give lectures at the center and in the department of Sanskrit and Indian studies and in supervising

Ph.D. theses. As Visva-Bharati would not grant him another year's leave of absence, he had to decide whether to stay at Harvard or return to his Indian university. Michael persuaded him to burn his bridges and remain in the United States. When he decided to stay and devote himself to writing translations of Tibetan Buddhist scriptures and original works of meditation teachings with me as his editor, Michael and I founded the Buddhayana Foundation to support his writings. Tulku Thondup and I both receive a salary from the foundation. The foundation was funded by Elsie Mitchell, the founder of the Cambridge Buddhist Association, and by friends of Michael's and my two sisters. Elsie died in 2011. The head of the Cambridge Buddhist Association, Elizabeth ten Grotenhuis, has continued Elsie's grant.

In 1993, Michael founded the Marion Institute. He gave me a job photocopying and performing other clerical tasks, which I did for ten years before I retired in 2003. With this job, I had plenty of time to recite mantras, say prayers, and do meditation. Michael, with whom I have supreme tendrel, and I have plenty of Buddhist practices to do after receiving so many Dzogchen teachings from Dudjom Rinpoche, Dodrup Chen Rinpoche, Lama Gyurda-la, and Tulku Thondup. I maintain my tendrel with our lamas and many dharma friends, including the disciples of Dodrup Chen Rinpoche and Tulku Thondup. Years ago, Ian Baldwin, my beloved friend from Saint Paul's school days, and I received a series of Dzogchen initiations from Dudjom Rinpoche, and so we have the deepest tendrel. So we all have tendrel, as I do with Michael's and my beloved friends, Sonam Paljor and Maria Denjongpa and their sons, Pintso and Aka. They founded the Taktse International School in Gangtok, Sikkim, of which Michael is a founding patron.

Dodrup Chen Rinpoche's monastery outside Tibet, the Chorten Gonpa, is in Gangtok, and Michael and I have gone over several times to visit him there and to see the school with the Denjongpas. Other people with whom I have tendrel are my twin brother, John, and his daughters. Every Saturday after Thanksgiving, John and his daughters, Thayer and Polly, come for lunch. My friend Urszula Solokowska comes and helps out.

In 2013, I was diagnosed with Parkinson's disease. Today I mostly stay in my charming, cozy house where Dodrup Chen Rinpoche and Tulku Thondup Rinpoche have so often come to visit and where Tulku Thondup and I have worked together on his books at a card table on the porch and where the two lamas have given Michael and me teachings. With two dharma friends, Nancy Mitton and Sheila McBroom, I recite, do the visualization, and meditate on *The Ritual Practice of the Blissful Pure Land of Amitabha Buddha* by Jigme Tenpe Nyima, the Third Dodrup Chen Rinpoche. Its purpose is to enable one at death to be reborn in the Pure Land of Amitabha, the Buddha of Boundless Light. May the tendrel of all of us be strong.

I cannot say that my life has been a search for some mystical truth. As Tom Merton wrote at Polonnaruwa, "It is all Dharmakaya without any mystery." In Tulku Thondup's book *Masters of Meditation and Miracle*, he tells the story of the enlightenment of Nyoshul Lungtok Tenpe Nyima, brought about by his guru Patrul Rinpoche.

> Then Lungtok stayed with Patrul at Nakchung hermitage near Dzogchen Monastery. Every day at dusk, Patrul would do a meditation session on the training of Namkha Sumtruk, stretched out on his back on the new woolen carpet on a piece of grassy field the size of himself. One evening, while Patrul was lying there as usual, he asked Lungtok, "Lungche (Dear Lung)! Did you say that you did not know the true nature of the mind?" Lungtok answered, "Yes, sir, I don't." Patrul said, "Oh, there is nothing not to know. Come here." So Lungtok went to him. Patrul said, "Lie down as I am lying. And look at the sky." As Lungtok did so, the conversation went on as follows:
>
> "Do you see the stars in the sky?"
> "Yes."
> "Do you hear the dogs barking in Dzogchen Monastery (At a far distance)?"
> "Yes."

"Well, that is the meditation."

At that moment, Lungtok attained confidence in the realization in itself. He had been liberated from the conceptual fetters of "it is" or "it is not." He had realized the primordial wisdom, the naked union of emptiness and intrinsic awareness, the Buddha Mind.

In 2004, I made a trip to Sikkim with my friends Michael, Maria Lauenstein, and Sally Hunsdorfer. During our five-day pilgrimage, we had the fun and coziness of being together, as Sikkim poured out its beauty and we received the blessings of places sacred to Guru Rinpoche. I learned that the nine yanas, the kama, and the terma are seamless. They include every religious expression from the intellectual analysis of the Prasangika Madhyamaka view of emptiness by Nagarjuna, commented on by Kunkhyen Longchen Rabjam and Mipham Namgyal and the Third Dodrup Chen Rinpoche, for example, to their teachings on Dzogchen and the deep devotion to Guru Rinpoche. By the performance of Tantric ceremonies from the termas, the karma of whole regions, including Sikkim and Tibet, can be improved by raising the merit, or *sonam*, of the country. The names of these great figures of Nyingmapa history may not mean much to some of my readers, but I believe that just seeing their names is a blessing.

After going to Madras, Tom Merton went to Sri Lanka where he stood barefoot on the grass and beheld the monumental stone statues of the Buddha and his cousin Ananda in the ancient city of Polonnaruwa. As he was looking he had the culminating mystical experience of his journey to Asia. In *The Asian Journal of Thomas Merton*, published posthumously by his friend, James Laughlin of New Directions Publishing, Tom writes:

> Looking at these figures I was suddenly, almost forcibly, jerked clean out of the habitual, half-tied vision of things, and an inner clearness, clarity, as if exploding from the rocks themselves, became evident and obvious. The queer *evidence* of the

reclining figure, the smile, the sad smile of Ananda standing with arms folded (much more "imperative" than Da Vinci's Mona Lisa because completely simple and straightforward). The thing about all this is that there is no puzzle, no problem, and really no "mystery." All problems are resolved, and everything is clear, simply because what matters is clear. The rock, the matter, all life, is charged with Dharmakaya … everything is emptiness and everything is compassion. I don't know when in my life I have ever had such a sense of beauty and spiritual validity running together in one aesthetic illumination.

Surely, with Mahabalipuram and Polonnaruwa, my Asian pilgrimage has come clear and purified itself—I mean I know and have seen what I was obscurely looking for. I don't know what else remains but I have now seen and have pierced through the surface and have got beyond the shadow and the disguise.

Today I relax and enjoy, without seeking, the simplicity that Tom experienced at Polonnaruwa, the awareness of the union of clarity and emptiness. I am, as Patrul Rinpoche said, "like an old man watching children playing."

Dom Aelred Graham's Conversations

*with Professor Masao Abe, Reverend
Shojun Bando, and Professor T. R. V. Murti*

What follows are two excerpts from *Conversations: Christian and Buddhist; Encounters in Japan* (New York: Harcourt, Brace & World, 1968) and one from *The End of Religion: Autobiographical Explorations* (New York: Harcourt, 1973), both by Dom Aelred Graham.

Zazen and Related Topics

Conversation between Professor Masao Abe and Dom Aelred Graham in Kyoto, August 26, 1967.

I showed Professor Abe the two fans on which Alan Watts had drawn designs: on one the characters for "form is emptiness" and on the other a circle representing Sunyata, or "Ku." Of the latter Abe asked, "What is this?" Emptiness I replied.

M.A. [Masao Abe]: "Emptiness" is not emptiness itself.
A.G. [Aelred Graham]: No.
M.A.: So what is emptiness itself? Not in words.
A.G.: It is only to be experienced—it cannot be described.
M.A.: But you describe it in the terms of "indescribability."
A.G.: Ineffability. Yes. It cannot be spoken.
M.A.: But . . . you are still speaking.
A.G.: Therefore . . . silence.
M.A.: You said "silence." That's not silence; it's not actual silence . . .
   What is the true silence, or true emptiness?

There was a long pause.

M.A.: Thank you very much.

A.G.: Thank you.

M.A.: On the meaning of the phrase "ultimate truth," the question is: What is the ground for speaking of ultimate truth? If there is no basis for ultimate truth, then it appears to be a concept based on our uncritical assumption. So it cannot be said to be ultimate truth or ultimate reality, for you must try to go behind any kind of assumption before we can reach ultimate reality. That is why Buddhism does not admit the one God as creator.

A.G.: That is very impressive and hard to refute. The theologians say that there are certain things *per se nota,* self-evident; they maintain, many of them, that all gain knowledge through the senses, that all our ideas come from the senses. They would say that that is a fact of experience; it is not an assumption, they would say. This is self-evident.

M.A.: Yes. The question is: Who takes it as self-evident when you say that some final statement is self-evident?

A.G.: Not the final statement, but the initial statement. Thomas would say that there is movement. That is self-evident. If people deny that, well, you can't get any further.

M.A.: But who does recognize that everything is moving? Whether you deny or affirm that everything is moving—who does so affirm or so negate that everything is moving?

H.T. [Harold Talbott]: Professor Abe, when you asked, "What leads you to deny or affirm anything?" were you asking about some particular thinkers?

M.A.: No. I'm asking: When you say there is movement or everything is the creation of God, what is the relation between the speaker and the very statement? Where do you find yourself in such a statement? Do you find yourself in every created thing? Or in God as creator? Or somewhere else? That is the point of Suzuki's question to his guest about Genesis. Who was the witness when God said, "Let there be light," and there was light?

A.G.: I think when one is pressed—and it is a very important question —one is obliged to say: It seems to me, or it seems, that there is a creator God.

M.A.: What are you talking about when you say "God"?

A.G.: We are using the word "God" because it seems to the observer to apply to a reality more fundamental than any other object of experience. I think one would say that you do not find yourself in that statement at all—except indirectly.

M.A.: You do not find yourself in that statement?

A.G.: No.

M.A.: But who is saying, "You do not find yourself in the statement"? What of you says so when you say so?

A.G.: What of you? That statement could be asked of any statement, it seems to me.

M.A.: Surely.

A.G.: If you say, "Form is emptiness, emptiness is form," you could ask the same question about anybody who says that, couldn't you? Why do you? What leads any individual to make that statement? You challenge me to say what of you is in the statement "There is a creator God." Cannot I say, "What of you is in the statement that form is precisely emptiness, emptiness is form"? If you agree to that statement.

M.A.: It's Emptiness. It's Nothing, and neither God nor everything, but Nothing.

H.T.: And that's the answer to "What of you is in that statement?"

M.A.: Yes.

A.G.: Very thought-provoking.

The following is from the glossary in Aelred Graham's book.

Koan: An existential problem, often translated into a verbal puzzle, the solution of which is intended to lead the Zen disciple to *satori* (enlightenment). The Gen-jo koan arises from a living situation. Kosoku koan is one recorded in writing.

Nembutsu: Pure Land sect: The Jodo sect of Japanese Buddhism, founded by Honen in the thirteenth century. It was in part a reaction against the metaphysical and scholastic teaching that permeated contemporary Buddhism, and it focused attention on devotion to Amitabha (Amida) Buddha, as expressed in the Nembutsu (Namu Amida Butsu, Praise to Amida Buddha).

In the Pure Land

Conversation between the Reverend Shojun Bando and Dom Aelred Graham at Ho-on-ji, Higashi Ueno, Tokyo, October 14, 1967.

S.B. [Shojun Bando]: Your recitation of the Nembutsu is nothing but proof of the realization of the Buddha's will in you. So Buddha's vow is moving in you.

A.G. [Aelred Graham]: And what is the Buddha's vow? Is it one vow or many?

S.B.: Buddha's vow is usually expressed in 48 vows, but the fundamental spirit is one. That spirit is expressed: "Unless you attain Buddhahood, I will not attain Buddhahood. If there is anyone in illusion or suffering, then I cannot become enlightened in the true sense of the term."

A.G.: Unless everybody else does?

S.B.: Unless everybody else attains enlightenment, I cannot truly attain enlightenment, so my destiny and everybody's destiny are one. That is Amida's vow. Amida's vow is the fundamental vow, the basic vow of every one of us. We have many wishes, desires, wills; they are particular wishes and wills. But what is it we really wish to do? What is our fundamental will? It was pointed out by the Buddha, the Enlightened One, that our fundamental will is expressed in this vow. It was pointed out by the Buddha and expressed in terms of 48 vows.

A.G.: What is the literal translation of Nembutsu in English?

S.B.: There is no fixed term for it. No English is suitable, because for the term "nen" there are many meanings: to think of the Buddha, to remember the Buddha's vow, to recite the name of the Buddha—all these meanings are contained in the term "Nembutsu." So it can vary according to the occasion.

A.G.: And is it part of the doctrine that saying Nembutsu once brings Enlightenment?

S.B.: Yes. To say Nembutsu once in sincerity is enough. The merit of reciting Nembutsu once and the merit of reciting Nembutsu many times are not different, it is stated in the sutra. According to the human mind, the more the better, but in the eyes of the Buddha the merit is equal in both cases.

A.G.: Before concluding this most valuable discussion, there are two further points that I'd like to raise with you, Reverend Bando. In our encounters with Zen roshis and authorities on Zen in Kyoto and elsewhere, there has been unanimity on one matter: that the roshi knows when the disciple or student has reached Enlightenment and he is in a position to certify that. From any Western background that is very difficult for me to understand. I wonder if from your tradition of Buddhism you could comment on that.

S.B.: I think Enlightenment can be judged only by the Buddhas, and it is one of the wonders for us Pure Land Buddhists to see some Zen monks highly confident of their qualifications to judge the disciple's Enlightenment. I think it can be done, to some extent, even by the beginners of faiths. Some intuitive understanding may be had by ordinary believers, but how far that judgment is accurate is open to question, I think. Insofar as even Zen roshis are human beings, I don't think their judgment can be one hundred precent correct.

Nonduality in Hinduism

The spiritual principle that has been very important to me is nonduality. In Nyingma Buddhism it is the word *yer-met*, or inseparability. In Hinduism it is described as *tat tvam asi*—that thou art.

Aelred asked Dr. T. R. V. Murti, the Indian academic, philosopher, and writer, about nonduality in Hinduism. He recorded Murti's answer in the chapter "Promptings from India" in *The End of Religion: Autobiographical Explorations*. Dr. Murti replied, "Look, the world itself is false appearance. And what the Veda [the ancient Hindu scriptures] says is: 'Behind the world is Brahman [absolute reality].'"

So the Veda is a revelation in the sense that it removes the veil of appearance and asks you to see through, see beyond appearances, and see Brahman behind the things that form the world. And tat tvam asi, that thou art, is the last word of the Vedas, as of the Vedanta. The word *vedanta* means the "end of the Vedas." The principle of nonduality is what has interested me the most in Hinduism and especially Buddhism.

Dudjom Rinpoche Teachings

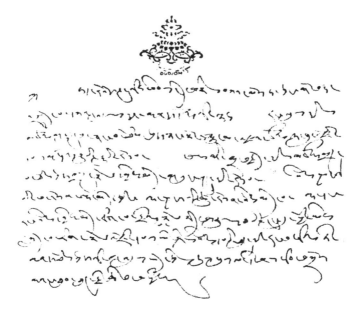

Dudjom Rinpoche sent this letter in his own hand to Lama Gyurdala after I visited him in Darjeeling in 1969. Tulku Thondup translated it into English and Lama Gyurdala transcribed it into clearly legible Tibetan. His transcription follows the English text. The teaching is on the youthful Manjusri.[1]

> Harold came here to see me. Because of language it is hard for us to have a good communication. Nevertheless the important points are:
>
> 1) To see all the appearing forms, such as one's own body, as the Displays of the Body of the Youthful Manjusri; the inseparability of appearances and emptiness is like a rainbow and Maya, illusion;

---

1 The Buddha of Widsom.

2) To hear all sounds, such as one's own speech, and the display of the Speech Mantras,[2] as the inseparability of sound and emptiness;

3) To relax evenly in the innate nature, which is emptiness, naked awareness, and in the inseparability of one's own mind and the Mind of the deity. Besides mind there is no deity and besides deity there is no mind.[3] And that is the nature of the Mind of the Youthful Manjusri.

All the important points are condensed in this. Thus I have offered Harold.

ༀ ༈ འཛམ་དཀར་སྒོམ་དུམ། རང་ལུས་ཀྱི་མཚན་
གཟུགས་སྣང་ཆད་འཛམ་དཀར་སྐུ་སྣང་སྟོང་སྤྲུལ་འཛར་
ཆེན་ལྟ་ར་བསྒོམ། དག་གི་སྐུ་བརྗོད་ཀྱིས་མཚན་
སྐུ་གོ་རྣམས་ཅུ་ལ་ར་པ་ཙ་ནཱི༔ གྲགས་སྟོང་སྔགས་
ཀྱི་རོལ་བ་བསྒོམ། སེམས་སས་རིག་བ་འཛམ་དཀར་
དགས་ དགས་དང་རང་སེམས་དོ་ནེ་གཉིག་ལས་ཁྲོད་
མེད་ལ་ ལྷ་དང་རང་སེམས་རིག་པ་ཏེན་པ་དབྱེར་མེད་
པ་ལ་ རིག་སྟོང་འཛམ་དཀལ་གཞོན་ནུའི་རང་ཞལ་
འཛམ་གསུངས་བ་འདི་ཡིན་ནོ།

2 The Speech Mantras are the sound essence of the deities. The Mantra of Manjusri is *Om, Arapatsana Dhi.*

3 Tulku Thondup: Literally, "On the other side of abandonment of mind there is no deity and this side of the abandonment of the deity there is no mind."

June 17, 1976, New York

Interpreted by Tulku Thondup

"When you recognize the arising of thoughts, do they automatically dissolve like writing on water?

"Whenever thoughts arise, don't try to stop the thoughts with the view that thoughts are something unfavorable.

"Do not run after the thoughts. Do not follow thoughts by thoughts.

"Whenever thoughts arise, without feelings of happiness or unhappiness, just look at the thought itself.

"When you watch thought itself, it will dissolve automatically; that is its nature.

"When dwelling in the state of voidness, it is called "dwelling." When thoughts arise, as the projection, it is "movement." When projections of movement is watched, it will be dissolved or it will vanish automatically. That is liberation.

"When you meditate, after some time there will certainly be different projections, such as a feeling of very blissful ease, physically or mentally. And sometimes it will feel very clear. And even in the night it will feel like day—very bright. And sometimes, even in the day, you will feel darkness or sleepiness or unclear mind. But do not feel happy or unhappy on account of the projections. Be like an old man watching children playing. Only try to watch the nature of the mind itself.

"But if you feel darkness or unclarity, sometimes it is necessary to take off some clothes or to go and sit somewhere in a bright place or with a nice view. Sit up and shrug the upper part of your body.

"Whatever forms, good or bad, that you see, whatever voices that you hear, good or bad, do not feel happy or unhappy, but follow them and just watch your mind itself.

"Different appearances always will be there, and you cannot stop these appearances. But do not have grasping or attachment to them.

"Sit at a place where you can watch blue sky. Concentrate very strongly on the blue sky. The interdependence, the union or touching, meeting of the outer voidness of the sky and the inner voidness of the mind, the unborn awareness will arise automatically. And relax in that state.

"When you go to sleep visualize a shining white 'AH' in your heart, suffusing and clarifying or illuminating the whole body like light. And go to sleep concentrating on the 'AH.' And when you wake up in the night, again while you are going back to sleep, concentrate on the 'AH.'

"In the daytime it is easy to spend time in meditation, but at night it is difficult to stay in meditation. And so one is wasting time. And so concentration on the AH, the letter signifying the Unborn, will help to mix the true nature of the mind with luminescence.

"Dzogchen meditation is very easy. The difficulty is not that it is difficult, but that it is too easy."

Tulku Thondup's Summary of the Interview

"Just watch where thoughts will arise.

"Don't feel happy or unhappy.

"Just watch the mind itself.

"And try to extend the state of emptiness or awareness.

"And do it again and again.

"So Dudjom Rinpoche and Lama Gyurdala are making the same point."

February 11, 1983, New York, NY
Interpreted by Khenpo Tséwang

Dzogchen meditation: "We need to practice there is no difference between meditation and post-meditation. Always, whatever you are doing, keep your mind in its naturally aware state, the natural level. Remain always in meditation. However, at the beginning, do practice *Rang Sem Yer-med* (inseparability of your own mind and awareness of emptiness). Do guru yoga practice, receive initiations. Then do meditation. Always keep in your own natural open awareness. That is *Lam'ai Thug Tang Yid Yer-med* (the inseparability of the lama's enlightened mind and the disciples's ordinary mind). Your awareness will increase.

"Then, whatever we do, walking, etc., remain all the time in the natural level. Effort is the artificial way.

"Don't judge good or bad. Such phenomena and conceptions do not enter from outside. It is we ourselves who judge and decide these things. So also, we don't have to stop making such judgments. Don't check yourself. Just relax in the natural level. Whatever we perceive, just relax without attachment. Then everything—thoughts, judgments etc.—will dissolve. Whatever we heard don't judge. So you don't have to run away from noise or the city: *trak-tong*.

"As for thoughts: whatever arises in the mind, don't judge past or future, just rest in the natural level. That is dissolving thought in dharmakaya. That is the great, easy technique."

Dodrup Chen Rinpoche Teachings

May 9, 1977, Marion

Tulku Thondup's advice on practice

"You should take things very peacefully without any excitement or hope or fear. Doing this you will be very happy, but you should not be excited or else like a rocket exploding, your meditation will reach the moon but you will be here.

"You should try to control excitement and your emotion and you should keep your experience to yourself for the time being, not tell your friends to practice saying, 'There is something.' That is not the way. For the time being you have to keep it to yourself. Of course, if there is a very good friend you can discuss your experience, but otherwise it is not wise to do so."

May 23, 1977, Marion

Dodrup Chen Rinpoche, interpreted by Tulku Thondup

"When you concentrate in meditation all the appearances of phenomena, such as persons and objects, will be there but with no grasping and no effects from them, like calm water without any movement. At that time, if you look at the observer of the Emptiness state you will find continuity of understanding.

"*Ha ko-wa zhin-pa de'i nang ma-shor-war dad-na ré yöd* (It is okay if you dwell in the emptiness state without losing the understanding of that state, **Third Dodrup Chen Rinpoche**). You will find a 'sense.' If you look at that, which is to say, if you look inside at the observer of the Emptiness, then all the appearances will be weakened and there will be some sort of a turning outside to inside. Sometimes you may feel unconsciousness with the stopping of all thoughts, but it is not necessary to worry. In that state there is no mind or object or subject. But we have to use these words to explain. See and practice this and we will discuss more.

"When you concentrate on this state, whether you feel happiness, suffering, or pain, because our mind is only one, it is always the same. As when the clouds are dispersed, it is always the blue sky. Because of that state, it is said that we should 'take defilements as the path without rejecting them.' *Nyon-mong ma-pang lam-khyer gyi man-ngag gom-bya gom-byed med.*" [The foremost instruction of taking afflictive emotions as the path without rejecting them, with no action or object of meditation.]

June 3, 1977, Marion
Dodrup Chen Rinpoche, interpreted by Tulku Thondup

"All the attachments and thoughts come like waves from the ocean. But they will disappear in the ocean, the *rig-pa'i long*, nowhere else. They come because of the wind. Likewise, clouds appear in the sky, but they dissolve in the sky, nowhere else.

"If you cannot concentrate, and then get worried, that is not the way—the thoughts increase. When your mind is calm, then you should concentrate. And when you gain experience, you will be able to concentrate whatever happens. If you gain strong experience, whatever happens will not affect you. But you haven't much experience, you will be affected by things. The important thing is that you should concentrate on meditation when you are in the right frame of mind.

"If you use this practice for controlling very strong desire, it is not a matter of stopping it, but that the desire will automatically disappear.

"Do not follow past thoughts. And if you do not follow the previous thoughts, then the thoughts automatically will cease. If you just look at the thoughts, the thoughts will automatically disappear. They will be in the Emptiness. You may not be in the actual state of meditation, but your thoughts will disappear in the Emptiness. This practice will help to make the distracting thoughts and attachment to them cease.

"Everybody has very good experiences sometimes, sometimes because of vissisitudes, not good. But the important thing is not to worry. The important thing is not to practice by force. This sort of thing also happens to lamas. So, the most important thing is not to worry.

When your mind is distracted by this kind of happiness, you should think of the sufferings of samsara—the four thoughts: suffering, sickness, old age, and death. When people are happy they forget practice, but when unhappy, they do not have favorable circumstances for meditation. Don't do the practice by force."

June 7, 1977, Marion
Dodrup Chen Rinpoche, interpreted by Tulku Thondup
Rig-pa'i Long
"Defilements (negative emotions)are not to be rejected by the antidotes (abstention and denial).

"We are still on the path, have not reached the final result. So, we cannot control everything at the present moment. The most important point is that you realize you can automatically stop your thoughts. With practice it gets stronger, but at the beginning it is difficult.

Rig-pa'i rang-rtsal.
bDag-dzin.

"The most important thing is to get experience from what happens to you, to practice with one's own life. The fear of losing an opportunity is not a fear—the real fear will come in the Bardo when you see those forms and most fearful appearances, and an unrealized person flees from them as bad and frightening. Then you will get bad unfortunate rebirths.

"The 84 Siddhas and Kunkhyen Longchen Rabjam (1308–1363), the greatest teacher and writer of Dzogchen, were ordinary persons but they practiced and realized the nature of the mind. So the most important thing is to practice. In Tibet there were many persons who practiced and attained *ja-lü*, or rainbow body.

June 13, 1977, New York, Orgyen Chö Dzong
Dodrup Chen Rinpoche, interpreted by Tulku Thondup
"It will be difficult to realize the phenomena arising as *rig-rtsal* after meditation. Perhaps you'll feel something like, "How funny, how like a dream these phenomena are." That will be a good study.

"Generally the teacher can understand the mind of his disciple. But a teacher like me has to examine each disciple's mind. Rinpoche thinks Harold's nature is air, "like Rinpoche's." If you practice when you are not calm, you may get some mental trouble and you won't want to practice more. But it is important to make the effort and to do practice no matter what.

"About *rig-rtsal*, it's a good study, and you will understand, but not now. "Oh, it's like a dream," you feel, and are convinced that's an indication of the path. Mostly it depends on people's natures—some get strange *nyams*, some not, some get realization soon, some not.

"Of course we will continue to have attachment to samsara, because we have experienced it from time, immemorial. Buddha accumulated merit for three *kalpas*."

June 16, 1977, Marion
Dodrup Chen Rinpoche, interpreted by Tulku Thondup
For Depression
"Try to meditate that a bone springs from your forehead like a spark from the fire. Touched by that bone, the land and everything else becomes made up of various kinds of bones. Try to concentrate on that scene. See if it will benefit you or not.

"In our meditation there is only one purpose. But in this meditation you visualize various kinds of bones—long, short, animal, human, white, black. Involve your mind in it and keep it busy. This is a test to make your mind keep busy and not depressed."

June 22, 1977, Marion
Dodrup Chen Rinpoche, interpreted by Tulku Thondup
"Generally you are doing the main practice well. If you feel normal, do the main practice. But if you have any difficulties you can do the "bone practice" again. If you have any different experiences, we can discuss them and you can do a different practice. Otherwise, if you're feeling normal, do the main practice. If you can be diligent, it is very good.

"If one can have diligence then he will gain positive experiences and confidence. But without *tsondrü* it just remains as a traditional system. That's why Buddha said, 'I showed you the path of liberation. Now liberation depends on you—you should realize it.'"

July 1, 1977, Marion
Dodrup Chen Rinpoche, interpreted by Tulku Thondup

"When you feel laziness or want to sleep or to have entertainments, think about how difficult it is to get human life, and even if you get it, how impermanent it is, and how difficult it is to get a good teacher and teaching. That will help awaken your mind from sleepiness and reverse your mind from craving entertainments. You should think of impermanence; people young and old dying of different diseases; why shouldn't I die today? And if you think of the *dal-jor nyed-ka* and *tshé mi-tak-pa*, it will help awaken your mind from sleeping.

"About extreme feelings: it will be difficult to meditate when you have feelings of extreme happiness or unhappiness. But you should try even in those conditions. For example, when someone is sailing on the sea, when the waves are very high, the sailor has to exert more effort. You know the areas of difficulty and danger for yourself and you should try to work it out through practice.

"You have been doing this practice for only a few weeks and yet, with just a few periods a day, you have made good progress. Typically it can take months and years. So, you should be diligent in doing it.

"It is good that you have faith and devotion. I am not such a good lama. But if you have faith in someone, it will benefit you. All lamas are the same, and all Buddhas, so if you have faith in one, you will get the benefits of all of them for realization.

"It is said that *dewa, daknang,* and *damtshig* are like the entrance to obtaining blessing or attainments. I am very happy to give you whatever teachings I can because I have faith that you will have very good *damtshig* with your lama and teachings. No other student here has as much understanding of the general ground.

"In Tantra the main thing is the mind. When I came to India from Tibet, first I wanted to spend my remaining life practicing in retreat so that the benefits would accrue to my people in the homeland, Tibet, who respected me as a Buddha. And if I got some attainment, I would be able to help them. Then, later in Sikkim, I went to the hermitage at Menam and practiced. But I was always thinking how will I get food? And always my mind was in the towns and markets. So as the early teachers said, there is not much benefit keeping the body in retreat if the mind is not in solitude.

"One of my students in Gangtok wanted to do a retreat in a solitary place. I told him maybe it is not proper to go to such a place—you will face difficulties and be unable to do practice. But he went, and he came back with an illness.

"In Tantra one should realize one's body and mind as pure, and one's body should be recognized as consisting of the mandalas of different kinds of divinities. And you should enjoy all the objects of senses as offerings to those divinities. As in King Indrabodhi's story, the Tantra depends mainly on realization of the mind, not on physical practices. So there is not much difference in devotional or meditative behaviors if they do not have much effect on your mind. But you should keep your mind in the practice."

July 2, 1977, Marion
Dodrup Chen Rinpoche, interpreted by Tulku Thondup
Two Things:
"First, it will be very beneficial to practice the 'human-life-difficult-to-obtain' and 'impermanence' meditations. At the end of all getting together is separation. The end of birth is death. Then end of happiness is unhappiness. There is no essence or truth in the worldly things or happiness. If you meditate about impermanence again and again, then the lure of worldly affairs will decrease.

"Second, when one has strong lust or anger, any kind of defilement or passion, one will have very strong *rigpa* at the same time. When this happens you should dwell in the state of *rigpa,* and all the defilements will automatically transform into *rigpa.* The same is true of fear.

"Last time you said it was very difficult for you to concentrate on your practice, so I told you about the bone practice. Otherwise you have to concentrate on the *rigpa* whenever you have a defiling emotion. And that will be more beneficial.

"In Tantra it is said that practice is like a peacock eating poison—the defilements are transformed by the practice. It is not necessary to reject them. *Nyonmong lam-khyer-pa'i thab.*

"If you can't do this practice, then concentrate on the difficulty of getting human life, impermanence, and the 'bone practice.' The most important thing is impermanence. If you think from the heart that the end of all getting together is separation, and the end of birth is death, and the end of accumulation is dispersion, then you will attain a very repentant mind and you will forget all worldly pleasures.

"Concerning the *rigpa'i rtsal:* taking the defilements as the path means realizing the *rigpa'i rtsal* (see Glossary). At the beginning one should think that all appearances and phenomena are *rigpa'i rtsal* and by realizing that, one should concentrate on the practice. But afterwards, when one has fully perfected the meditation, then there is no need of thinking or meditating that all phenomena are *rigpa'i rtsal.* Then there will be only one state. And there will not be any non-*rigpa.* For example, light and darkness will never be present together. And if you are in the state of *rigpa* there will be no non-*rigpa.* And you will not need to practice according to 'it is *rigtsal* or it is not *rigtsal.*'

"There will be no doubt that you can succeed. But for success it is necessary to do hard practice with *tsondrü* (diligence). There is a saying: "Even if one realizes *rigpa,* if he could not maintain it by hard practice, then like a baby taken by enemies in a war, it will be lost." And so it depends on hard practice, and then there is no doubt of being successful. But hard work is necessary. Your nature is stable."

July 16, 1977, Providence

Dodrup Chen Rinpoche, interpreted by Tulku Thondup

Practice as follows:

"When you see the objects or appearances in daytime, determine or think with confidence that all these things are dreams. Then concentrate in meditation. Do it again and again. Afterward it will help in taking the dreams into the path of attaining enlightenment. Try to do this and see what happens, and we will see how to apply it to your dreams.

"This practice will be beneficial in reducing grasping. It will make the appearances of daytime seem as dreams and these dreams will be made into meditation. But it will depend on your diligence."

July 25, 1977, Providence

Dodrup Chen Rinpoche, interpreted by Tulku Thondup

"This meditation is not, 'Everything is *like* a dream.' Rather: 'It *is* a dream.' So, when you have a dream, like turning on a light, you will be in meditation.

"If in daytime you have the experience that everything happening is a dream and you go into meditation, then at night when you dream, you will recognize it as a dream and you will be in meditation.

"Generally prayers and sadhanas are good for you to continue if you like. But main thing is your meditation. Now you know what it is. And what is necessary for you to practice. You should not be satisfied only by knowing it, but you should practice until all the day and all the night have become one continuous circle of practical experience. In a day there are 21,000 *namtoks* (thoughts), roughly. If you practice, first you should reduce the number, and afterward all *namtoks* should be transmuted into the practice.

"In the daytime, and especially at night when we are sleeping and there is no practice at all, we should try to transmute sleeping into practice.

"You got teachings from Lama Gyurda-la and many other teachers. And you know now what the *rigpa* (awareness) is. So now it only depends on you to practice and get the result.

"I am very happy to meet some people who are doing well like you. I am very busy in Sikkim but I came here to help people like you who are doing well, so it is a very happy thing for me. If you learn, I feel happy.

"You now know, but if you feel satisfied just by understanding it, that is called one of the four demons of satisfaction or happiness. And if you say, 'Okay, I know now', that is an obstruction. You should not be content just to know what it is."

October 9, 1977, Providence
Dodrup Chen Rinpoche, interpreted by Sonam Paljor

"Clinging to the doubts which make you deviate from seeing the dream-states of all phenomena is the imperfection of your practice. Your practice is in process. How is it that all phenomenal existents are no more than a dream? Well, for example, a Sikkimese shaman pierces his own body with a sword. When you hold on to the sword, you can see and feel it splitting his chest. When he withdraws it, it has blood all over it. He spits on the wound, and it's healed. If he leaves the trance, or the *Lha* leaves him, he could die. But in the trance, he is immune from being wounded. This is proof of the dream state. If you proceed further with your practice, you will have proof of the dream state, of what appears to you is nothing more than a dream.

"Now you are given this as your *nyamlen* and you *must* make this the salient feature of your meditation and not seek other paths. Meditation must end in *Dzogrim*. Without it, *Kyedrim* causes a lot of trouble. It is safe to tell you what to do because you won't expose it. Now the *Dzogrim* is the important part of your meditation. It is very important to remain in the *same practice*. If one's mind, like a string made up of many strands being cut, is dispersed, it's bad. You have come to a point of understanding the thought processes; it is very important.

"This is *Min-thrid (khrid)*, not *Shad-thrid* which you get from teachings that say, "Let that be the state of mind"—you won't be able to understand from such other teachings. But from *Min-thrid* you can see it. So, it is good that you understand that these teachings are *Min-thrid*.

"*Nyamlen* is important because as the Third Dodrup Chen Jigmed Tenpa'i Nyima said, 'It is all right to visualize and chant; and it is also all right *not* to visualize and chant'."

October 1977 Providence
Dodrup Chen Rinpoche, interpreted by Sonam Paljor
Harold: "Is *réwa* about turning about?"

"No. But could become *tetsom*. When the time comes that there is *tetsom*, you should loosen the reins.

"It seems like the mind is turning inside. But if you hold on to it and clutch, then it will become something that is not turning inside. So, relax your grip."

November 8, 1987, Providence
Dodrup Chen Rinpoche, interpreted by Sonam Paljor
"That is the experience. But there are two paths. The first was to realize all phenomena as a dream. For that you have to practice more. The sign of realization is that you have a frightening dream and you see that it is a dream while you are dreaming. For instance, I had a dream of Dorje Phagmo [the wrathful Tibetan deity] scooping a man's brains out of his skull and thought, 'This is a dream.' If you practice realization within the dream, you will come to have peaceful dreams and you will realize they are dreams, as you are dreaming."

April 12, 1991, New York
Tulku Thondup to Helena Hughes, a poet and disciple of Dodrup Rinpoche
When Helena told Tulku Thondup that Jimmy Schuyler, an American poet, died at 6:00 a.m. this morning, and she was upset and wanted him to tell her how to view the death, he said: "One by one."

July 19, 1991, Marion
Dodrup Chen Rinpoche, interpreted by Tulku Thondup
I said that I had not lost an understanding of the teaching I received through his (Dodrup Chen's) blessing, despite many problems with my

mind and my defiled emotions, and I described the result of a couple of the *ngöndros* at the *Nyingthig Yabzhi wangs*.

Dodrup Chen Rinpoche: "It is very good. There is a proverb: When very bad circumstances come, people become ordinary. When you're happy, you feel like you're a great meditator."

Rinpoche knows I'm not feeling well sometimes. He has heard about it in India. But still I keep my meditation as the most important part of my daily life.

Rinpoche responds: "That's very good. Sentient beings have only one mind. When you feel unhappy, instead of thinking about problems, try to concentrate on practice, divert to meditation, and feelings of sadness will cease, because there's only one mind.

"Mind moves with air, like energy. If you could cease thinking about problems and concentrate on meditation, the air and energy will be harmonized and so your mind will become calm. That could be called esoterically a *rushan*. It is very important to keep that in mind."

Rinpoche then said a long prayer over me and blessed me on the top of my head with his rosary, or maybe Tulku Thondup's.

April 6, 1992, 9 Chauncey Street, Cambridge
Tulku Thondup on how to deal with people being tiresome

(1) "The first thing is to be realistic, to look at it, to know the truth why the problem is happening and is there participation on my part, instead of just watching the person ironically and with distaste.

(2) "But if you don't want to or can't bear to look at it, if the problem is too strong, you should be realistic and avoid it."

Then for the healing:

(3) "Appreciate the person, be compassionate and feel sorry for them, as this person is saying and doing negative things to me and bringing unfortunate habits and karma for himself. And be thankful to him for providing me with a chance to practice tolerance and

equanimity and for teaching me the nature of samsara and real life: suffering.

(4) "Or be like a log. Don't say, don't do anything when you are under emotional pressure unless it will be helpful to say something to this person and you are talking honestly and not out of the heat of your emotions.

(5) "Then another thing is to pray and bring blessings and compassion lights from Guru Rinpoche or Amitabha and touch you and him with the lights of compassion and feel that the problems are dispelled and both of you become one in compassion and love, instead of being part of a harmful environment. Lights or nectar of Ödpagmed (Amitabha).

(6) "Or, instead of obsessing over the reasons for it, or over the source of the problem, meaning that person, and instead of being overwhelmed by emotions and feelings, either with relaxed mind or when you are having strong emotions such as anger about it, suddenly look at the face of the feeling of anger, or the mind of anger—or fear, or anything else—and let the dissolve spontaneously."

June 24, 1997, Marion shrine room
Dodrup Chen Rinpoche, interpreted by Tulku Thondup
"There's no need of another technique. Using the same technique, trying to get stability through diligence is the most important thing now.

"Try to get back that feeling of vast expanse and expanding the dimensions of the room during the *bLadrup Thiglé Gyachan* wang of Rinpoche at the Mahasiddha Temple earlier in 1997 and maintain and strengthen it. Try to go back into it. If you maintain that experience through mindfulness, then when you fall into laziness be mindful of the laziness. Then you bring yourself back to the meditation again and again and it will deepen your meditation and help to heal your mental and physical health too."

July 6, 1999, the Temple, Hawley, MA
Dodrup Chen Rinpoche, interpreted by Tulku Thondup, after a lunch for
Michael Baldwin. Harold presenting, Tulku Thondup interpreting

Tulku Thondup read the 1977 advice of Dodrup Chen Rinpoche and his last teaching of two years ago. The experience of *rigpa*, or awareness which he gave me to practice is now more familiar and natural, and its effect lasts longer and I feel confident of it. I do a mechanical job of xeroxing, so I do the practice when I work. I still have strong *nyon-mongs*, or negative emotions, like anger. But when I practice this state of *rigpa* or say prayers, eventually the anger dissolves. (Rinpoche gives his wonderful little smiling laugh after I relate this.)

When Rinpoche reminded me to practice the unification of my mind with the guru's mind, I said I do that and will continue to do it, and I recognize that that is where the capacity to do guru yoga comes from.

Dodrup Chen Rinpoche: "You should maintain that meditation just as you are doing and rely on the unification of one's own mind with the guru's mind. It brings blessings and increases the meditation. Because of the power of blessing, the experience will grow like a child grows. Yes, you are doing well."

Remarks on Dzogchen by Harold Talbott

with quotations by Dzogchen Masters

Dzogchen is the practice that produces in the mind an awareness of its own true nature. For the practice to achieve its purpose, it is necessary to receive an initiation from one's guru. The lama performs a "pointing out," which empowers the disciple to undertake a rigorous meditative process, preceded by an outer and an inner preliminary practice (ngön-dro). Eventually, either quickly or after a long time, the meditator achieves the awareness of the true nature of his or her own mind. The primordial purity of the mind, unmodified and free from conceptualizations and the duality of subject-object thinking, is uncovered. The constant chain of thoughts and emotions disappears like clouds dissolving in the sky.

Kyab-je Dudjom Rinpoche told Tulku Thondup Rinpoche, "Dzogchen meditation is very easy. The difficulty is not that it is difficult, but because it is too easy."

Garab Dorje summarized Dzogchen for his disciple Manjusrimitra (translated by Tulku Thondup Rinpoche).

> The nature of the mind is Buddha, enlightened from the
>   beginning.
> Mind has no birth or cessation. It is like space.
> All phenomenal existents are peaceful and pure.
> Rest in this realization, as it is, without seeking. That is the
>   meditation.

The two greatest teachers of Dzogchen characterized the meditation practice in the following verses, also translated by Tulku Thondup Rinpoche, in *The Practice of Dzogchen*.

(Dzogpa Chenpo) is the path of the luminous absorption,
   the essence of the ultimate definitive meaning,
And the summit of the teachings of sutras and tantras:
This is the meaning of the instructions on the direct
Approach
To the ultimate nature, the Buddha-essence as it is.
      —Longchen Rabjam

The essence of the discourses on the Three Doors of
   Liberation
Given by the Victorious One in the second Turning of the
   Dharma Wheel is the very Discriminative Self-awareness
Which is present naturally in the nature of beings as the
   Buddha-essence,
And that is known as the Dzogpa Chenpo.
The entire meaning of the vast, excellent paths (of
   Buddhism)
Is only for cleansing of the mind.
So the three precepts, six perfections, development and
   perfection stages, etc.
Are the steps to the path of Dzogpa Chenpo.
      —Jigme Lingpa

The appearances are free from objective (entity), the intrinsic
   awareness is the liberation from primordial (time),
The view and meditation are action-free and the six
   consciousnesses are self-free;
There is no need of apprehending with recollections (for) or
   antidotes (against):
The action-free Dzogpa Chenpo is the cessation of
   phenomena.
      —Jigme Lingpa

Tulku Thondup's Books in English

edited by Harold Talbott

Organized Alphabetically by Title

Boundless Healing: Meditation Exercises to Enlighten the Mind and Heal the Body (Boulder, CO: Shambhala, 2001).

Enlightened Living: Teachings of Tibetan Buddhist Masters (Kathmandu, Nepal: Rangjung Yeshe, 1997).

The Healing Power of Loving-Kindness: A Guided Buddhist Meditation (Boulder, CO: Shambhala, 1995).

The Healing Power of Mind: Simple Meditation Exercises for Health, Well-Being, and Enlightenment (Boulder, CO: Shambhala, 1996).

The Heart of Unconditional Love: A Powerful New Approach to Loving-Kindness Meditation (Boulder, CO: Shambhala, 2015).

Hidden Teachings of Tibet: An Explanation of the Terma Tradition of Tibetan Buddhism (Somerville, MA: Wisdom, 1986).

Incarnation: The History and Mysticism of the Tulku Tradition of Tibet (Boulder, CO: Shambhala, 2011).

Masters of Meditation and Miracles: Lives of the Great Buddhist Masters of India and Tibet (Boulder, CO: Shambhala, 1999).

Peaceful Death, Joyful Rebirth: A Tibetan Buddhist Guidebook (Boulder, CO: Shambhala, 2006).

Zangdok Palri: The Lotus Light Palace of Guru Rinpoche (Bangkok, Thailand: Gatshel, 2012).

Translations

Rabjam, Longchen. *The Practice of Dzogchen: Longchen Rabjam's Writings on the Great Perfection.* Translated by Tulku Thondup. Edited by Harold Talbott. (Boston: Snow Lion, 1989).

Tulku Thondup's Definition of Tendrel

Tendrel is the short form of *rten ching 'brel bar 'byung ba* in Tibetan, and in Sanskrit it is *pratityasamutpada*. Its philosophical meaning is interdependent causation. However, in popular Tibetan, the word is also used as *tendrel yagpo* or just *tendrel* as an auspicious sign, good luck, a good omen, and all auspicious coincidence. It could also be used sometimes as *tendrel ngenpa*, a bad omen or bad sign. So the philosophical meaning is interdependent causation, as all things happen with interdependence on causes and conditions, and in popular culture it is omens, signs, and indications. Having good omens is very important for Tibetan culture as the Tibetans believe many events are indications of what will happen in the future.

The Sanskrit word *samaya* (*damtshig* in Tibetan) means an unbroken sacred bond or vow between two esoteric sources or persons or esoteric relations between two beings or any esoteric sources, lama and disciple, lamas and lamas, disciples and disciples, Buddhas and devotees, and material and material. However, in its popular expression, having samaya also means having a good relationship between two people, especially two dharma friends or lama and disciple.

Mainly, according to the teachings, and especially tantric teachings, through good or bad karma or tendrel or esoteric samaya (the esoteric relation, connection or causations), good or bad results will take place. So the qualities of all that is happening now are dependent on the qualities of the previous causes or deeds.

The Jesus Lama:
Thomas Merton in the Himalayas

an interview with Harold Talbott by Helen Tworkov

In his best-selling biography *The Seven Storey Mountain* (published in 1948), Thomas Merton tells of his conversion to Catholicism and subsequent entry into Our Lady of Gethsemani, a Cistercian abbey in Kentucky. To a world savaged by war, Merton's embrace of a Christian life was made all the more authentic by his Cambridge-educated intellect, stunning candor, and the New York street humor he acquired while attending Columbia University. Single-handedly, he restored credibility to the very possibility of contemplative virtue, which had been long denigrated by liberal intellectuals and traditional Christians alike. His was a voice of sanity, filled with sacred wonder, and replete with inquiry and contradiction.

Merton appreciated perspectives refined by their distance from society and considered them essential to maintaining the health of the community. In fact, he spoke of the marginal view as an obligation for both monastics and artists. From his cloistered outpost, Father Louis (as he was designated by the Church) kept a vigilant eye on the Civil Rights movement and anti-nuclear efforts, and in the last years of his life, he watched with undisguised frustration as the United States lost its footing altogether in Vietnam.

Political concern was one of Father Louis's many departures from monastic tradition. A voracious reader and legendary correspondent, Merton's interests extended beyond Church conventions and, under the influence of Zen scholar D. T. Suzuki, came to include Buddhism. In 1968, after a quarter of a century of life in the monastery, and after repeated requests for permission to travel, the Order finally granted its most renowned and respected monk leave for an Asian journey for the purpose of delivering a paper (on Marxism and Monasticism) to Asian monastic leaders in Bangkok. But before and after the conference, he would have ample opportunity to meet Buddhist masters.

Merton's letters, made public in recent years, confirm that while he submitted to the rigors of monastic life, he was also a man of wild and sometimes whimsical enthusiasms: "a man of accomplished self-discipline," as one visitor described him, "who sometimes acted like a ten-year-old in a candy store." This is the Tom Merton who arrived in India—a monk out of habit, a spiritual traveler hungry for new ground. After nearly twenty years of reading and writing about Zen, he set out for Asia eager to meet Zen roshis, but Merton's first direct encounter with the living traditions of Buddhism was with the Tibetan lamas; three weeks after meeting them, he was already planning to cut short his stay in Japan in favor of returning to Bhutan to begin Tibetan practice. But he never reached Japan. After addressing the conference in Bangkok on December 10, 1968, Merton returned to his cottage, showered, apparently fell, and was electrocuted by a whirling floor fan. He was fifty-three years old.

Would he really have "settled down"—as he claimed—with a Tibetan guru? Or would he have ended up in the Alaskan hermitage or the California redwoods that had inspired similar claims? His sudden death spurred endless speculation about his future that continues to this day.

When Father Louis arrived in New Dehli, by the prearrange-ment of Benedictine Prior Dom Aelred Graham, he was met by Harold Talbott. At the time, Talbott, a skinny, twenty-seven-year-old convert to Catholicism, was studying Buddhism with the Dalai Lama. Today, under the aegis of the Buddhayana Foundation, Talbott works with Tulku Thondup Rinpoche on translations of Nyingmapa scriptures, which include *Buddha-Mind* (Snow Lion, 1989) and *Enlightened Living* (Shambhala Publications, 1991). This interview was conducted for *Tricycle* by editor Helen Tworkov. Recent photographs of Talbott were taken in his office in Marion, Massachusetts, by Anne Converse.

Tricycle: *How much did Thomas Merton influence your decision to convert to Catholicism?*

Talbott: When people ask why I became a Catholic, I often answer, I'm ashamed to say, that it wasn't *The Confessions of St. Augustine*, it was *The Seven Storey Mountain*.

Tricycle: *Why ashamed?*

Talbott: Because *The Seven Storey Mountain* is a terrific book, but it's a paperback.

Tricycle: *When did you first meet Merton?*

Talbott: In 1957, I was working on a newspaper in Memphis, Tennessee, during my summer vacation from Harvard and reading *The Sign of Jonas*, the journal Merton kept on his way to becoming a priest. And I went to Gethsemani to meet him but the world was beating a path to his door, and the abbot wouldn't let me in. The next Thanksgiving I returned after being baptized. I had decided to take my first communion not with the Jesuits but with the Cistercians at Gethsemani.

Tricycle: *And you saw him then?*

Talbott: This time the abbot said yes. Merton took me into a room and said, "I'm always very glad to meet someone who has just come into the church because they are full of grace and the grace overflows from the person who has just been received. And I have only one thing to say to you: the Church is a very big place. Always remember to go your own way in it." Ten years later in India I reminded Merton about that remark and he said, "Did I say that? That's pretty good. And look at where we both are."

Tricycle: *What was the effect of that first encounter?*

Talbott: It was the first time I had met a great man—which always clarifies your path. They raise you to their level. Shantideva (a celebrated eighth-century Mahayana master of India) says that if an ordinary tree grows up in a sandalwood forest, the nearness to the sandalwood makes it smell like a sandalwood tree. And if you encounter a true spiritual master and you recognize it, the recognition disposes your mind to a state which hints every now and then at what good practice will do for you.

Tricycle: *How did you get from Catholicism to Buddhism?*

Talbott: I had gone to Asia as secretary to Dom Aelred Graham, who had just retired after sixteen years as Prior in Portsmouth Priory in Rhode Island. He had already written *Zen Catholicism* and had gotten permission from the Benedictine Order to spend a year in Asia and the Middle East. The Vatican Council then asked him to be *peritus*—or expert—on Buddhism for the Council that was writing a decree on the relationship of the Church to Buddhism. Aelred had said that the encounter between Buddhism and Catholicism cannot take place at the level of the Magisterium, it can only take place at the level of two contemplatives talking together in private. For that reason Dom Aelred refused to be the *peritus* for the Vatican Council.

Tricycle: Peritus *is a Vatican term?*

Talbott: Yes. The *Periti* were the experts, for example, on Hinduism, Islam, Judaism, etc. Dom Aelred Graham had been tremendously influenced by Ramakrishna's writings; he had studied Buddhism, and was deeply moved by the Vedanta tradition. When the Vatican learned that he was going to Asia, Pope Paul VI asked him to be his personal envoy to heads of non-Christian religions in Asia and in the Middle East. He was practicing yoga and zazen and he wanted to meet the roshis of Japan and the lamas of Tibet and sufi teachers and rabbis and Orthodox leaders of the Christian East. He needed a secretary to pack his bags, deal with the tape recorder, write the letters, and get him to appointments on time. So when Merton wrote to Aelred and asked how he could meet the lamas in India, Aelred explained that I was there studying with the Dalai Lama and that I could introduce him to the lamas.

Tricycle: *Did Merton give the impression that he came with a specific sense of what he was looking for?*

Talbott: The fifties were the first time you could buy Buddhist studies. He had spent years reading drugstore paperbacks on Buddhism. You didn't have to be Alexandra David-Neel and go in disguise to Tibet. Merton had studied Buddhism in translations. Finally, he managed to finagle a trip.

Tricycle: *When Merton arrived in Dharamsala (the seat of the Tibetan government in exile), did he ask you to arrange an audience with the Dalai Lama?*

Talbott: No. I said, "An audience is scheduled for you with His Holiness the Dalai Lama," and he said, "I'm not going." And I said, "Why not?" He said, "I've seen enough pontiffs." And I said, "Well I think, Tom—as you want me to call you—if you come to India to study with lamas, I think you'd be making a mistake not to meet the Dalai Lama. And furthermore, Tom, the Dalai Lama has heard all about you from the Canadian High Commissioner, James George, and he's taken the trouble of having a film shown to him of Cistercian monks and abbeys in France. He's done his homework and I think you should go up there and meet him." So he said, "Okay, we'll see."

Tricycle: *What was this attitude based on?*

Talbott: He didn't trust organized religion and he didn't trust the big banana. He did not come to India to hang around the power-elite of an exiled central Asian Vatican. But despite his misgivings, he went.

Tricycle: *Merton stayed with you?*

Talbott: I was living in a bungalow and I gave my room and study to Merton and I bedded down on sort of a wooden sofa. There was no furniture at all, and we were freezing and Merton had the most colossal cold and was sick. He was sick a lot during his later life. He had been maintaining a crushing schedule as a contemplative Trappist working monk, and had also written shelves of books. He burned the candle at both ends to a frightening degree. I would see him at two o'clock in the morning because I was so cold I couldn't sleep and so fascinated that behind that wall was Merton. The light would go on at two o'clock and he would do his prayers and then I would see the light go on in the study at four in the morning.

Tricycle: *Was his meeting with the Dalai Lama the high point of his visit to Dharamsala?*

Talbott: Two or three very significant things happened there. He was taken to meet Rato Rinpoche, who was the head of the Ministry of Religious Affairs. This was his first official appointment with the exiled government, a momentous event for all of Dharamsala. They knew perfectly well who he was and that Merton would be a great advantage for them, spiritually and politically. They knew that Merton would write about them with an absolute outpouring of love and appreciation and it would advance their cause enormously.

Tricycle: *But the significance of this meeting was not political, was it?*

Talbott: No. In their meeting, Rato Rinpoche told Merton that one way to get into meditation is to recognize that there is always an aspect of the mind that is watching the watcher—that is watching the meditative mind. There are two basic practices common to all Buddhist meditation: first you learn to calm the mind, and when the mind is sufficiently calm, you use it as an instrument for insight. This is how I was being trained at the time. Merton came back from his first meeting with a lama and said, "This guy says that there's a meditative mind and then there's a part of the mind watching you meditate. We know that already, and we don't want the watcher to watch it, so that's of no use to us. So let's see what *is* useful around here."

Tricycle: *From his Gethsemani experience, he's dismissing the fundamentals of Buddhist meditation?*

Talbott: Yes. I was very shocked because I considered all Westerners infants spiritually. I thought the Rennaisance had destroyed all of the good work of the contemplative Middle Ages; and that we were hopelessly deficient and that we should go hat in hand to masters in Asia. And here is Merton saying, "We know that already and we don't need it."

Tricycle: *And even having converted to Catholicism, this surprised you?*

Talbott: I was not aware that within the contemplative methodology of the West that survived the onslaught of the Renaissance that this knowledge of a watcher watching the mind existed. *And also* the knowledge that we don't need that.

Tricycle: *How did Merton go about finding what was useful?*

Talbott: He went out to take photographs and met Sonam Kazi. I knew this from his eyes before he told me. And that was the birth of the blues, the beginning of the *dzogchen* teachings for Thomas Merton. Dzogchen is the philosophical standpoint, meditation, and ethic of the Nyingmapa, the Old School of Tibetan Buddhism, founded by Padmasambhava in the ninth century CE. The teachings start with the assertion that our true nature is already enlightened. Sonam Kazi was the official interpreter assigned to the Dalai Lama by the government of India, the interpreter, for example, in the talks between Nehru, Chou En Lai, and the Dalai Lama. Sonam ran into Merton on the road, invited him to a teahouse, and zapped him.

Tricycle: *How did you know from looking into Merton's eyes that he had encountered Sonam Kazi?*

Talbott: Because Merton was in a state of utmost amusement, joy, and conviction that the best was yet to come: "We've got it; we've had this non-event so far and now we're going to get it. I knew there was something among these Tibetans." Sonam Kazi had zapped me a year before and I had gone out carefully holding on to the furniture. I hate to use these words but I'm too lazy not to: Sonam can put a person in an "altered state of consciousness" and believe me, I was not used to altered states of consciousness. But Merton was a ripened and ready object of a visit from Sonam Kazi and he got it. He said to me occasionally after that, "I came to Asia to study Zen in Japan and now I have changed my itinerary and I'm going to study dzogchen in India with the Tibetans."

Tricycle: *Did he know the difference between Zen in Japan and dzogchen in India?*

Talbott: He hadn't been to Japan and I don't even know if he'd been in zendos in America, but he knew something through his own past lives about Buddhist meditation. It's outrageous to say that but that's what I believe. He was sensitive to Zen and his sensitivity had been confirmed by Dr. D. T. Suzuki. When he encountered the flavor of dzogchen through a conversation with Sonam Kazi, he said, "What you're calling *dzogchen*—that's what I want."

Tricycle: *Did your encounter with Sona Kazi lead to your your own dzogchen studies?*

Talbott: I had wanted to remain faithful to the commitment that I had made to the Dalai Lama to study in the tradition of training and scholarship and meditation of Tsongkhapa, who founded the Gelugpa School. (The newest of four surviving schools of Tibetan Buddhism, founded in the fourteenth century. It emphasizes study of the sutras and tantras, as well as the development of logical rigor and dialectical skills to aid the attainment of enlightenment. The Dalai Lama belongs to this lineage.) The change was precipitated by the personality and spiritual impact of Sonam Kazi and followed by the insistence of Merton that if he was my age he would be here studying Tibetan Buddhism. "That's what I would be doing with my life. But you've got to get it straight kid: what the Tibetan tradition has to offer us is *dzogchen* and that's where it's at and the sooner you get out of the Himalayan Vatican the better. If you want to spend the rest of your life being trained to be a curial diplomat and reading sutras and tantras for the next forty years before you even get to start really practicing *shamata* (calming-the-mind meditation), go right ahead and stay in Dharamsala. But if you want to know where it's at, find a *dzogchen* yogi."

Tricycle: *Were there other significant encounters independent of the Dalai Lama?*

Talbott: Yes. His visit with Chogling Rinpoche—a way-out yogi, a very wild man who was an incredible kick-over-the-traces, irresponsible-type person, a tremendous troublemaker, and extremely rollicking in an unpredictable way, a top-flight, wonderful Nyingmapa yogi. He said to Merton, "When Sonam Kazi brings someone, I know I'll be able to talk to them and that it'll be okay." He asked Merton, "Do you believe in karma and rebirth?" Merton said, "Well, I think it's a very, very fascinating, persuasive proposition, but I wouldn't say I believe it, no." So Chogling said, "Okay, well then I can't teach you because the whole thing is predicated on you having faith in karma and rebirth. So let's *say* that you have faith in karma and rebirth, and this is what

I have to tell you. A human being has a *srog*—a life force. He has a consciousness and when he dies, in order to ensure the proper destination of the consciousness, it's very useful to be able to practice *phowa*.

Tricycle: *Is* phowa *a yogic practice?*

Talbott: There's a fontanel on the top of your head. At birth, it's a soft, big space between the head bones, and as babies grow, it closes. Through yogic training you can reopen it and then when you die, you can shoot the consciousness out the fontanel and then it goes straight to the paradise of Amitabha Buddha.

Tricycle: *What is the view expressed in Amitabha's paradise?*

Talbott: At an enlightened level the universe is viewable as a boundless number of Buddha fields—areas of enlightened consciousness. The field around a Buddha and his enlightened bodhisattvas resonates as what we might call, figuratively, a paradise. And the teachings of the *phowa*—yogic teachings about how to direct the consciousness at death and to go to rebirth include the capacity to send the consciousness straight to the buddha realm of Amitabha. The reason Chogling Rinpoche taught Merton *phowa* practice—say I—is that he saw that Merton was going to be dead in a couple of weeks. He needed the teachings on death. He did not need teachings of karma and suffering, calming the mind, insight meditation. He needed to be taught how to dispose his consciousness at the time of death because this was the time of death for him. And Merton scribbled in his journal: "I'm not sure about all this consciousness and shooting it out the top of the head. I'm not sure this is going to be very useful for us."

Tricycle: *All these encounters took place prior to Merton's visit with the Dalai Lama?*

Talbott: Yes. The days were going by with Sonam Kazi taking us to see Nyingmapa lamas, drinking scotch in taverns, and talking, talking. Merton is now saying, "*Dzogchen* is where it's at and that's what I'm going to do." I became very officious. We were about to go up the hill to meet the Dalai Lama. It seemed to me that it would be impolitic for Merton to refer to the *dzogchen* school because it's a different school from that of His Holiness. In the Jeep, as we are going up the hill to

McLeod Ganj—the Dalai Lama's residence—I explained all this to Merton. He was wearing his white robe with black scapular to meet His Holiness. We arrived and after a flurry of exchanged courtesies, the Dalai Lama looked at Merton and said, "What do you want?" And Merton said, "I want to study *dzogchen*." And the Dalai Lama said, "It's true that *dzogchen* is the highest yana (vehicle for Buddhist study), but if you want to study *dzogchen*, I propose a series of meetings in which I will teach you the preliminary practices at the end of which I should hope that you will be ready to go on to *dzogchen*."

Tricycle: *How many times did they meet?*

Talbott: Three times. The first meeting was used to get to know each other. They devoted much of the third meeting to conversations about Catholicism, the Western tradition, and the situation in the world. But the second time, to my astonishment, the Dalai Lama—who of course had sat on an extraordinary elevated throne in Tibet—now, with us still sitting on the sofas, got down on the floor and showed Merton the lotus meditation posture and the hand position and the posture of the back, and taught him meditation. He remained on a level lower than ourselves—for practical purposes—for the rest of the teaching. And he gave us very, very clear, sound meditation instructions that would be completely familiar to vipassana practitioners. He was leading up to teachings on emptiness and compassion and then went on to a gentle explanation of tantra as a field of Mahayana Buddhism that is a very very strong practice throughout history. And then at some point he gave a summation of the schema of Nyingmapa Buddhism starting with some Theravada teachings.

Tricycle: *How did the meditation instruction that Merton received from the Dalai Lama differ from that given to him by Rato Rinpoche, which, as you describe it, did not interest him?*

Talbott: The Dalai Lama didn't get into technical, methodological questions. He showed us posture and how to dispose the mind and how to get yourself into basic meditation practice by calming the mind and there was nothing technical. Of course, it was masterfully taught and there is an inexpressible gravity about the person of the

Dalai Lama. He was—and still is—the supreme man holding the tradition together, the man who has been giving the Tibetan nation an identity and engaging in endless maneuvers for his people amidst the destruction and the torment. And here he was showing us posture and breathing!

Tricycle: *Was the atmosphere very formal?*

Talbott: The Dalai Lama's robe and Thomas Merton's white Cistercian habit with the black scapular looked Giottoesque. It was an image of two figures encountering each other who deserved to wear those robes, who were part and parcel of the world represented by those very robes. So that one really had a surfeit of visual inspiration. Both men were very solid. Unornamental, compact, strong, hard beings. Now the Dalai Lama has an external joviality and graciousness which is appropriate to a sovereign. To put you at your ease, to make it possible for beings to be in relation to him, he plays down the radiance, the dignity, the charisma, the persona that the West has developed a romantic myth about, but who in himself has his own distinct presence and radiance. There is no presumption about him. He's a person who draws a heart-breaking reverence from the people who are devoted to him, and to see him in this room with a man to whom we don't need to apply adjectives, but if we were, it would be things like mensch, authentic . . .

Tricycle: *Merton?*

Talbott: Yes. Mensch—manly, authentic. No gestures. No artifice. No manner. No program, no come-on—just, "Here I am folks"—and folks happened to be the Dalai Lama. And they encountered each other and, appropriately enough, there was utter silence. And then the Dalai Lama challenged him or greeted him by saying, "What do you want?" and he said, "I want to study *dzogchen.*" I was about to clobber Merton. I couldn't take it. But I was very glad to be aboard. It was the generosity of Merton that made it possible for me to attend those meetings. He said, "You're here studying with the Dalai Lama. I want you present." Whereas it might have been delightful to be alone with just the Dalai Lama and the interpreter. It's my good karma that I was there. There was so much good humor and so much laughter and so much camaraderie and so much confidence of understanding and so much no need for explanation and buildup and equipping themselves on their parts, you see. They had done their homework.

Tricycle: *What did the Dalai Lama ask Merton about Christianity?*

Talbott: If I'm not mistaken, it was about how you live the contemplative life in the West and what you do to make it possible in this modern world to live the life of a monk in the West. How do you stave off spiritual annihilation? These conversations were very much Merton equipping himself with the transmission of Buddhism from the Dalai Lama and very much the Dalai Lama equipping himself with the lowdown from a reliable guide. This was not a papal legate. This was not someone setting up a conference for the Pope. This was not a front man. This was an embodiment of something which another embodiment—a tulku—who needs to function in the world, was drawing upon as a resource.

Tricycle: *Did Merton have a daily meditation practice?*

Talbott: I have no idea, but I asked him once, like a very fresh kid, "What is your meditation practice? And what do you think of this stuff?" He said, "My meditation practice is largely walking in the woods in a state of meditative absorption."

Tricycle: *It sounds like the Dalai Lama was providing a transmission to be carried forth to all of Christendom.*

Talbott: The Dalai Lama is saying to him, "I want with my own eyes and ears and speech to assure myself that you have the faith firmly grounded" and—let's be daring—let's think that there are certain beings who do not have to come every day and attend Zen or vipassana retreat. This could be a romantic projection but I have to say what I think: Merton had thirty years behind him and when he walked into a room or the cell of a meditator, monk or lama, he was greeted with a recognition. I've never seen a Western person received by a lama the way that he was received.

Tricycle: *Did the Dalai Lama feel personally responsible that Merton get it right?*

Talbott: That's how I see it. *dzogchen* is the primordial state of mind, it's the enlightened mind, that has never been anything but enlightened. We are living in a world, it is said, which is a product of our own unenlightened experience, our *ma rigpa*, our ignorance of the true nature of reality, absolute and relative. *dzogchen* is the practice of the primordial enlightenment but it is also a view or standpoint towards reality. Its meditation is to sustain and deepen this. That's a contradiction because *dzogchen* is the presence of fulfillment, not a process. We already are in primordial—or original—enlightenment in *dzogchen*. That's the starting place.

Tricycle: *In* Asian Journal, *Merton refers to the* dzogchen Nyingma *lama Chatral Rinpoche as the person he would choose as his teacher.*

Talbott: He was Merton's man. Chatral Rinpoche really gives the flavor of the Tibetans. I wouldn't dream of studying with him, or anybody remotely like him, because he is totally and completely unpredictable. He is savage about the ego and he will put you on the spot and I am not prepared to up the ante to that degree.

Tricycle: *Why did you choose to introduce Merton to him?*

Talbott: I wanted to make sure that Merton met all the outstanding lamas that I could dig up. In Dharamsala he met Avelokiteshvara— the Bodhisattva of Compassion—in the person of the Dalai Lama. And I think okay, I'm doing my job, I'm getting him the whole spectrum of the force field. But of course he must meet Chatral Rinpoche, too, and of course that will be an opportunity for me to hide behind Merton's skirts and also meet Chatral Rinpoche who I'm terrified of. He could throw stones at you—as he does do— and so I will use Merton as the front. We caught up with Chatral Rinpoche down the road from Ghoom in Darjeeling. He was painting the nuns' house and he put some planks on some bricks and we sat and talked with the help of an interpreter. Chatral Rinpoche started by saying, "Ah, a Jesus lama; you know I have never been able for the life of me to get a handle on Christianity so I'm real glad you came this morning."

Tricycle: *Did he know who Merton was?*

Talbott: No. But he explained his perplexity about Christianity. He said, "The center of your religion is a man who comes back to life after death and in Tibetan Buddhism when you have one of these people, a *rolog*, or a walking corpse, we call our lama to put him down. So I want to know what kind of a religion is Christianity which has at its center a dead man coming back to life." So Merton explained the Resurrection in tantric terms about the overcoming of fear and the utter and complete power of liberation which is the center of Christianity. And this satisfied Chatral Rinpoche.

Tricycle: *Freedom from fear?*

Talbott: Freedom from all constraints and restraints. A man has died and he has come back in a glorious body and he has freed us from fear of death and fear of life. That's freedom.

Tricycle: *Because it's eternal?*

Talbott: No. If the universe is a place where a man can live again in a glorified body and teach the truth, then the world is a free place. And Chatral Rinpoche says, "At last I understand Christianity. Thank you very much." And then Merton says, "I would like to study with you." And Chatral says, "Right, we can work together. And so you've got to do your *ngon dro* (the preliminary practice of *dzogchen*, which usually takes a Tibetan about a year). We'll get you a hermitage in Bhutan and that is where you should do your retreat. And I challenge you: see, I'm not enlightened yet, so let's work together and see which one of us can get enlightened first." And so Merton said, "It's a deal." And so then we split and Merton says ,"That's the greatest man I ever met. That's my teacher." But they weren't his exact words.

Tricycle: *In* Asian Journal *he says that if he took a teacher, that's who it would be.*

Talbott: Yes, but he would never have left the Church.

Tricycle: *One of the persistent myths among American Buddhists has been that Merton was just about to leave the Church to pursue Buddhist studies. But Merton seemed to have said yes to everyone. He had people around the world expecting him on their doorsteps all on the same day.*

Talbott: He told Ernesto Cardenal and his brother, "I'm coming down to Nicaragua to make revolutions with you." And he planned to retire in Alaska as well as California and do a three-year retreat in Bhutan, and someone had given him land in Santa Fe, where he'd proposed to set up a Catholic-Tibetan meditation center.

Tricycle: *What did you think he might do?*

Talbott: Having encountered Chatral Rinpoche he might have curtailed his trip to Japan but he was certainly going to go there and talk to Zen roshis. My distinct impression was that this was a man who had found what he wanted in India and was going to round out his experience in Asia as he planned but he was going to modify it in order to go back and study with Chatral Rinpoche. How were Nicaragua, Alaska, and Canada, California, and New Mexico going to fit into that, and how could he be an active member of the Civil Rights movement, of the Peace movement, a poet and a writer and all the rest of it? I don't know. To my distinct certainty he was going to study *dzogchen* and do his preliminary practice with Chatral Rinpoche. I'm convinced of it, but he would never have left the Church.

Tricycle: *Why do you say that?*

Talbott: He had reached a point—unrecognizable to me and perhaps to you—where the Judeo-Christian theistic tradition of the Mother Church of Christendom and *dzogchen* of Nyingmapa Tibetan Buddhism were not in contradiction. Furthermore he had grown up in a Catholic village in France that had so deeply affected him that it had planted a seed which had caused him to enter the Church. He was a man who had spent thirty years in a Cistercian abbey. His training came from the Church. He was a generous man and he was a just man and he acknowledged what he owed to the Church. It was his formation. It was not his cocoon. It was not his prison. It was himself and it was a very good self and he needed to uphold it.

Tricycle: *Why do you make so much of the fact that the school of Tibetan Buddhism that most attracted Thomas Merton was* dzogchen?

Talbott: It is significant because, of all of the methods of introducing humans to their primordially enlightened nature, I am betting that the power and effectiveness and depth of all depths lies in *dzogchen*. Merton came home when he found *dzogchen* and that is my assertion.

Tricycle: *But why is it significant that* dzogchen *attracted Merton?*

Talbott: Because Merton stood for the contemplative life the way— to make a vulgar and irrelevant analogy—Picasso stands for art. For contemplatives there are illuminated beings, there are hidden yogis, but as far as how ordinary people come into touch with the great spiritual heritage of the West—including the apophatic tradition, the Via Negativa—it's through the mystical teachings from St. Paul and St. John, St. John's gospel, Dionysius the Areopagite, the great medieval mystics Thomas Aquinas and St. John of the Cross, and St. Teresa of Avila—and that's just about it, folks—that's it for the big league contributions to spirituality at the contemplative level in the West. And every now and then you get somebody who says, "Wait a minute, I know the chips are down and the circumstances are against us, but let's get in there once more and try to stay alive spiritually." And that's Merton for twentieth-century Westerners. Despite all of his manliness, Merton was a man of the old moment before the Second World War, a man of enormous personal and cultural refinement. He belonged in a French salon as well as in a forest in Kentucky. There is no question about it. He had the qualities we're losing. Gaining, gaining other wonderful ones but losing, losing something. Merton had this consummate worldly culture as well as this jewel of spirituality. He was a gift to humanity, with the naivete and the nerve to take the writings of mystics seriously.

Tricycle: *Everybody wants to claim Merton. The Zen Buddhists empha-size the Zen connection, and the Gelugpas want to claim him for their camp, and you want to claim him for* dzogchen. *So it becomes somewhat political.*

Talbott: The fact is that he told the Dalai Lama that he wanted to study *dzogchen* so the Dalai Lama spent hours preparing him to find a *dzogchen* guru. And he found him in Chatral Rinpoche. He went down to Sri Lanka where he convinced himself that he had the experience of the *dharmakaya* (emptiness), seeing the statues of the

Shakyamuni Buddha and Ananda. Then he was electrocuted and died and we are left to sit here and talk about how *dzogchen* was the final bestowal on Merton by a divinely compassionate savior.

Tricycle: *Do you mean the Dalai Lama?*

Talbott: No. The Holy Trinity. If we do not deny the existence and virtue of the Judeo-Christian tradition and yet acknowledge that Merton found his path, we have to say that from the standpoint of his spiritual presence in the West, he was vouchsafed one final gift and was shown the path. And that the very last things that he was enabled to do were to talk to the Dalai Lama in Dharamsala, to see the traditions of the rinpoches in India; and to hear about the conditions of the life of a sacred people in Tibet. Then he went and addressed the heads of contemplative communities in Bangkok. The conclusions he reached were conclusions that the late Trungpa Rinpoche had drawn too: in Merton's words, "It's every monk for himself now." Structures can no longer be relied on to provide protection to foster the spiritual life. Everyone—ordained or not—for himself, through his practice or her practice. And one of the most congenial means for going on your own is *dzogchen*.

Tricycle: *In retrospect what was Merton's effect on your life?*

Talbott: He seduced me into leaving the Gelugpa schools of Tibetan Buddhism and spending the rest of my life studying with *dzogchen* yogis. Also, I told him I was in a lot of confusion at that moment in my life. Merton helped me by telling me that when he was at an English university he had an affair with the girl who made the beds in his dormitory, and she had a baby, and he said to me, "You know my son would be such and such an age right now and I don't know whether he survived the blitz or not." And he carried that with him. That was on his mind. And he let me know that this was the key to his life.

Tricycle: *I thought he had been shuttled out of England by his guardian while the young woman was still pregnant.*

Talbott: He said, "My son," and I don't know why he said it. The impact was like that of St. Augustine who had been a sinner before his conversion. Merton saw himself as a man who had to purify himself of something that was a very heavy load to carry. But by the time he came to India, whether or not finding *dzogchen* was central—that's my organization of significance in his life—it turns out that he had lived his life and this was the Mozart finale and he was in a state of utmost exuberance, engaged, and absorbing, and eating with delectation every moment of every experience and every person that passed. He tipped Sikh taxi drivers like a Proustian millionaire. He was on a roll, on a toot, on a holiday from school. He was a *grand seigneur*, a great lord of the spiritual life. He radiated a sense of "This is an adventure, here I am folks," and he woke people up and illuminated them and enchanted them and gave them a tremendous happiness and a good laugh. But also there was always a communication from him that he was a representative of the religious life whether he was wearing a windbreaker or a habit. The Indian people greeted him as a pilgrim, a seeker, and that was the basis on which he was met by everybody and congratulated valiantly, whether they recognized his public identity or not. People knew his spiritual quality. People in planes knew it. There was no question about it. Merton was not an object of scrutiny, he was an event.

This interview was first published in the summer 1992 issue of *Tricycle*

Salve Regina

From the First Vespers of Trinity Sunday until Advent.
This anthem is attributed to Adhemar de Monteil, Bishop of Le Puy.
The three final invocations were added by St. Bernard.

Salve, Regina, mater misericordiae: Vita, dulcedo, et spes nostra, salve, Ad te clamamus exsules, filii Hevae. Ad te suspiramus, gementes et flentes in hac lacrimarum valle. Eia ergo, advocata nostra, illos tuos misericordes oculos ad nos converte. Et Jesum, benedictum fructum ventris tui, nobis post hoc exsilium ostende. O Clemens, O pia, O dulcis Virgo Maria.

Hail, holy queen, mother of mercy; hail, our life, our sweetness and our hope. To thee do we cry, poor banished children of Eve; to thee do we send up our sighs mourning and weeping in this vale of tears. Turn then, most gracious advocate, thine eyes of mercy toward us; and after this our exile, show unto us the blessed fruit of thy womb, Jesus. O clement, O loving, O sweet Virgin Mary.

Glossary

The following are my definitions for Japanese, Pali, Sanskrit, and Tibetan words used in my memoir. The glossary also includes three of the Nyingma school's most important figures.

Key: J–Japanese; P–Pali; S–Sanskrit; T–Tibetan

arhats [S], **arahants** [P]: highly realized disciples of the Buddha in the Theravada tradition.

bardo [T]: the intermediate state between death and rebirth.

bDag-dzin [T]: attachment.

bhikkus [P]: monks in the Theravada tradition.

chirolpa [T]: an outsider, a non-Buddhist.

chö-ku [T]: the absolute empty nature of reality without modification or conceptualization.

chopon [T]: assistant to a lama who is giving an initiation.

chorten [T]: a monument in the form of a sacred design of the universe and the enlightened mind of the Buddha that holds the relics of enlightened beings.

daknang [T]: pure perception.

dal-jor nyed-ka [T]: fortunate human birth difficult to attain.

damtshig [T]: the unbreakable esoteric bond between disciples of the same lama, between lama and disciple, and between two lamas of the same lineage. *See* samaya.

den-tsik [T]: "a word of truth," a prophecy spoken by a lama, which always comes true.

dewa [T]: bliss.

dharma [S]: the universal teachings of the Buddha in all schools or traditions.

dharmakaya [S]: the absolute unconditioned body of the Buddha.

Dorje Phagmo [T]: the wrathful sow-headed goddess.

dzin-pa [**T**]: grasping.

Dzogchen [T]: the highest view, meditation, and action teachings of the Nyingma school.

dzogrim [T]: pure meditation of emptiness free from form.

gao [T]: a reliquary; the small ones are worn around the neck.

Gelukpa [T]: the most recent school of the Dalai Lamas founded by Je Tsong Ka-pa in the 14th century.

ge-nyen [T]: a lay disciple who has taken the refuges in the Buddha, dharma, and sangha.

guru [S]: a teacher of dharma; a person's lama who teaches meditation and gives practical guidance.

Guru Rinpoche [T], **Padmasambhava** [S]: eighth century Vajrayana Buddhist teacher from India who founded the Nyingma school in Tibet. Venerated by many Tibetans as "the second Buddha," he left many hidden spiritual treasures or termas for the incarnations of his Tibetan disciples to discover in future generations.

ja-lü [T]: the rainbow body; the attainment of a light body by the highest Dzogchen yogis.

je-nang [T]: a permission to follow a meditation teaching; simpler than a wang. *See* wang.

Jigme Lingpa (1730–1798) [T]: the Nyingma lama who discovered Longchen Rabjam's nying thig or "innermost essence" terma in a mind-to-mind transmission during a meditation retreat. The Dzogchen nying thig practices became central to the Nyingma tradition thereafter. One of Jigme Lingpa's two principal disciples was Jigme Thinley Odzer, the First Dodrup Chen.

jig-pa [T]: fear.

kalpa [S]: eon in both Hinduism and Buddhism.

kama [T]: the lineal transmission of scriptural teachings in the Nyingma school.

karma [S]: Sanskrit for "action": the process of cause and effect in the universe and human lives.

khatak [T]: a white silk scarf offered to lamas or distinguished persons.

kyedrim [T]: meditation on the form of a deity.

lam'ai thug tang yid yer-med [T]: the inseparability of the lama's mind and your mind.

lha [T]: The deity or being who possesses the shaman.

lhö-lhö [T]: relax.

Longchen Rabjam (1308–1363) [T]: the greatest lama of the Nyingma school and author of multiple Buddhist texts, philosophical, poetic, and practical. He discovered the terma of the nying thig cycle of esoteric practices, which he transmitted to Jigme Lingpa four centuries later. *See* Jigme Lingpa.

lung [T]: ritual reading of a sacred text by a lama for the bestowal or transmission of its meaning.

Madhyamaka [S]: the Mahayana philosophical teachings of Nagarjuna; the philosophy of the Middle Way.

Mahayana [S]: the great school of Buddhism as distinguished from the Theravada; it includes the Vajrayana or Tantra.

mandala [S]: a sacred diagram used in wangs and meditation.

mantra [S]: a set of sacred syllables for recitation in meditation.

min-thrid [T]: ripening the student's understanding of the nature of the mind.

monlam [T]: prayer of aspiration.

namtoks [T]: thoughts.

nang-tong [T]: the inseparability of phenomena and emptiness.

ngagpa [T]: a tantric yogi.

ngön-dro [T]: the outer or inner preliminary practice of the Nyingma school.

ngon-she [T]: clairvoyance.

nirmanakayas [S]: the so-called illusory bodies of the Buddha; these are the tulkus who as bodhisattvas are able to take birth wherever they wish so as to free beings from ignorance and suffering.

nyamlen [T]: your practice.

nyams [T]: bliss, clarity, and absence of thought.

nyingmapa [T]: a member of the Nyingma school, the oldest school of Tibetan Buddhism.

Nyingthig Yabzhi [T]: the four volumes of initiations compiled by Longchen Rabjam. (*See* Longchen Rabjam.)

nyonmong lam-khyer-pa'i thab [T]: the skillful means of taking emotional defilements as the path that is as one's practice.

nyung-nas [T]: a period of a day or days of fasting with prayers and meditations.

Ödpagmed [T], **Amitabha** [S]: the Buddha of Boundless Light.

pecha [T]: a Tibetan Buddhist book or scripture, which consists of rectangular pages printed on woodblock and placed one on top of the other and wrapped in cloth.

powa or **phowa** [T]: the yogic practice of shooting or transferring the consciousness out the head, at death, thereby attaining rebirth in the Pure Land of Amitabha Buddha.

Prasangika Madhyamaka [S]: one of the two forms of the Middle Way philosophy of Nargarjuna.

rang sem yer-med [T]: the inseparability of one's own mind with the Mind of the lama.

rang-tröl [T]: self-liberation.

réwa [T]: hope.

rig-pa'i long [T]: the expanse of awareness.

rig-pa'i rang-rtsal [T]: the natural quality or power of awareness.

rinpoche [T]: a "precious person"; a tulku.

ringsel [T]: small spheres of an unknown material found in the ashes of a yogi's body after cremation, usually white but in the colors of the rainbow in the case of great meditators.

rigpa tongpa-nyid [T]: empty awareness.

ro chig [T]: one taste, that is, all phenomenal existents are peaceful and pure, of uniform taste or essense.

rolang [T]: a corpse who rises and walks around and who must be put to rest by a lama.

roshi [J]: a Zen Buddhist guru or master.

rushan [T]: an esoteric preliminary practice.

sadhana [S]: a Tantric ritual practice of meditation.

samaya [S]: the unbreakable esoteric bond between disciples of the same lama, between lama and disciple, and between two lamas of the same lineage.

sambhogakaya [S]: the bliss body of the Buddha.

samsara [S]: the round of birth and death suffused with suffering liberation from which is enlightenment.

sangha [S & P]: the brotherhood and sisterhood of disciples of the Buddha.

satori [J]: enlightenment in Zen Buddhism.

sesshin [J]: a period of days of zazen meditation performed under a Zen roshi.

shad-thrid [T]: knowledge practice.

siddha [S]: a fully accomplished yogi.

siddi [S]: special powers of a yogi.

sonam [T]: merit.

srog [T]: the life force of each person.

tantra [S]: the teachings and practice of Vajrayana Buddhism.

tantrika [S]: one who practices Vajrayana Buddhism.

tathagatagarbha [S]: the absolute nature of the Buddha: "he who comes thus."

tendrel [T]: interdependent causation; the link between beings and phenomena through the process of cause and effect.

termas [T]: the teachings hidden by Guru Rinpoche in the eighth century C.E. and rediscovered by successive incarnations of his original students to aid beings at particular times.

terton [T]: a lama who discovers termas, or spiritual treasures, hidden by Guru Rinpoche, typically in the form of texts, found in the earth, lakes, and the sky.

tetsom [T]: doubt.

thegchod [T]: one of the two highest meditation practices of Nyingma Buddhism, so-called "cutting through" to encounter natural mind.

theras [P]: the elders; those who are senior by their ordination ages, or those who have have attained high degrees of realization.

thigles [T]: luminous circles moving in the air, which in their fullest development become stable and include the heads of Buddhas or lotuses or other symbols of the dharma.

thodgal [T]: the highest meditation of the Nyingma school, "optical yoga," leading to ja-lü, the rainbow body.

tratshang [T]: a monastic community.

tri [T]: verbal or written instructions by a lama.

trikaya [S]: the three bodies of the Buddha: the formless body of dharmakaya, without modification and free from conceptualization, and the two form bodies, sambhogakaya, the bliss body, and nirmanakaya, the illusory body.

tshé mi-tak-pa [T]: the impermanence of life.

tsawai [T]: root, as in one's root lama.

trak-tong [T]: the inseparability of sound and emptiness.

tsondrü [T]: diligence.

tulkus [T]: the teachers of dharma who as bodhisattvas are capable of incarnating to help suffering sentient beings.

Vajrayana [S]: Tantric scriptures and meditation.

vinaya [P & S]: the final one of "the three baskets" of the Buddha's scriptures. The canonical texts governing the rules of the sangha

vipassana [S]: insight meditation.

wangs [T]: initiations in Tantric Buddhism to enable the practitioner to realize the nature of his own mind.

yanas [S]: vehicles of Buddhism: Theravada, Mahayana, and Vajrayana.

yidam [T]: one's chosen deity or form of the Buddha with whom one has a strong affinity and whom one visualizes in meditation practice.

zazen [J]: the meditation technique of the schools of Zen Buddhism.

Index

Abbey of Gethsemani, 66, 67, 72, 235
Abe, Masao, 143
Abrams, Michal, 187, 200
Adler, Stella, 136
Aitken, Robert, 141
Alain-Fournier, 110
Alfred, William, 70, 73, 90, 95, 96
Allen, Freddy, 48, 51, 52, 59, 61–62
Allen, Julian, 48
Ama-la Dorje, 191, 192
Annenberg, Moses, 10
Apfelberg, Ruth, 76–77
Apologia Pro Vita Sua, 57–58, 234
Aris, Michael, 159–60
Asian Journal of Thomas Merton, The, 169, 239
Aung San Suu Kyi, 160
Ayer, A. J. (Freddy), 45–46
Azzam, Abdul Rahman Hassan, 111
Azzam, Issam, 111, 124, 125

Baker, Anthony, 36
Baker, Edith, 18
Baker, George (Button), 36
Baker, Grenville Kane, 18
Balanchine, George, 129, 134–35
Balanchine, Tanny, 129, 134, 136
Balanchine's School of Ballet, 59, 114, 135
Baldwin, Billy, 60
Baldwin, Ian, 50, 53, 59–60, 62, 82, 83, 237
Baldwin, Michael, 25, 58, 63, 72, 74, 82, 102:
    and Dodrup Chen Rinpoche, 217–18, 224;
    and founding of Marion Institute, 237; friend-
    ship with Father Hilary, 82; Talbott's early
    friendship with, 52, 62; Talbott's later friend-
    ship with, 137, 175, 206–7, 212, 213–14,
    227; at Harvard University, 70, 72, 87, 89, 95,
    97; in Marion, Massachusetts, 206–7, 208,
    213–14, 215; and parties at the Frick, 72, 92,
    97; and Porcellian Club, 90, 91; and Samuel
    Barber, 130; travels with Talbott, 107, 239;
    and Tulku Thondrup, 218, 237
Baldwin, Stephen, 102

Bando, Shojun, 141–42, 144
Barber, Samuel, 118, 127, 12, 748, 130–31
Bartlett, Charlie, 49
Beaumont, Vivian, 78
Bénichou, Monsieur, 110
Bergman, Hugo, 158
Bingham, Harry, 38–39
Blofeld, John, 145–46
Bodh Gaya, 156
Bolton Priory, 51–52
Boum, Yen, 145
Bourbons (family), 132
Bowles, Jane, 129
Bowles, Paul, 129
Brattle Theatre, 89
Brigham's Ice Cream Shop, 89
Brown, Elizabeth (Peggy), 87, 92, 96, 97, 98
Bruce, Ailsa, 38
Buccleuch, Duchess of (Molly), 82
Buddhayana Foundation, 58, 237
Buddha, 144, 146, 154, 155, 156, 239: fields
    of, 172; mantra of, 64, 149; nature of, 180,
    190, 197, 22; as part of Three Refuges, 177,
    178; visualization or image of, 165, 180, 181;
    Shakyamuni, 165, 170, 228; teachings of, 187,
    194, 220
Buddha of Boundless Light. *See* Pure Land of
    Amitabha Buddha
Buddhism, 156, 220: Aelred Graham's interest
    in, 80, 81, 133, 150, 232; and Christianity,
    231, 233, 235; Talbott's early interest in and
    study of, 58, 64–65, 67, 68, 90, 93, 105,
    136, 231; Talbott's later studies of, 167, 192,
    229; Mahayana, 145, 150, 170, 190, 197;
    Nyingmapa, 190, 197, 204, 236; Pure Land,
    145, 221; Theravada, 144–45; and Thomas
    Merton, 173; Tibetan, 147, 148, 152, 154,
    159, 162; Vajrayana (Tantra), 144, 145, 170,
    172, 190; Zen, 136, 145
Busch-Reisinger Museum, 88
Buttenweiser, Benjamin, 101

294

Made in the USA
Las Vegas, NV
28 May 2021

23834822R00204